The Secret Life of Siegfried AND Roy

HOW THE TIGER KINGS TAMED LAS VEGAS

JIMMY LAVERY, JIM MYDLACH,
and LOUIS MYDLACH
As told to HENRIETTA TIEFENTHALER

PHOENIX
BOOKS

ISBN-10: 1-59777-560-6
ISBN-13: 978-1-59777-560-1
Library of Congress Cataloging-In-Publication Data Available

Book Design by: Sonia Fiore

Printed in the United States of America

Phoenix Books, Inc.
9465 Wilshire Boulevard, Suite 315
Beverly Hills, CA 90212

10 9 8 7 6 5 4 3 2 1

TABLE OF
CONTENTS

"And now I introduce Montecore, who will be making his stage debut with us here tonight," Roy Horn announced to the 1,500-odd expectant faces in the MGM Mirage audience, gesturing at the 660-pound white tiger he held casually by a leash. Twice a night, for thirteen years, Roy and his business partner/lover/brother, Siegfried Fischbacher, had performed to sold-out audiences. Tonight—Friday, October 3, 2003—was their 5,750th show.

"Siegfried & Roy"—Roy, the dark-haired Robin to Siegfried's blond Batman—had been household names in Las Vegas and around the world for more than two decades, earning more money than any show ever performed in Sin City. Upwards of one million people a year flocked to the world's entertainment capital, desperate to witness these brilliant German illusionists perform their deadly dance with magnificent jungle cats.

Flamboyant high-rollers who oozed razzmatazz, Siegfried and Roy were the absolute embodiment of Las Vegas. The town loved them; they loved the town—and each other. The two were so close that Siegfried referred to Roy as "my brother," and he meant it. The dashing duo had experienced a turbulent on-and-off love affair, often waging jealous battles over handsome young studs. But when it came to business, they were *all* business and had painstakingly built themselves into one of the world's most profitable and respected acts.

Siegfried and Roy pioneered the transformation of Sin City into a family-friendly entertainment mecca, and their success grew with the city. With a price of $110 per ticket, their show amassed upwards of $44.5 million per year for The Mirage—and generated huge profits for other businesses patronized by their fans: hotels, restaurants, and gambling being the crux of them.

* * *

Tonight was a special night. It was Roy Horn's 59th birthday, and despite being the younger by five years, Roy was feeling the effects of his drunken celebration the night before. Even by Las Vegas standards, Roy Horn threw one hell of a party. Five hundred of the birthday-boy's "closest" friends and fellow entertainers had commandeered The Mirage theater—where he and his partner performed nightly for over a decade—and celebrated in debauched merriment until five in the morning.

Roy had spent the night table-hopping, boogying and guzzling X/O cognac. At midnight, he and Siegfried raised a glass to toast their forty-four years together.

Frank Marino, a fabled female impersonator, remembers that Roy "was in great spirits. All of his friends were kidding around with him, and he was making jokes and being very playful."

When someone teased Roy about his age and asked when he might retire, he shot back, in his thick German accent, "I vill retire only ven I can't do it anymore." At age fifty-nine, Roy could still shame younger men by swinging on ropes thirty feet above the audience and contorting his body to slip in and out of the cramped boxes used in the illusions— not to mention the physical challenge he faced performing tricks involving 600-pound cats. To a man as fit and lithe as Roy, retirement seemed a long way off.

Or did it?

In 2003, Siegfried and Roy were nearing the age at which most Americans begin to consider retirement. Neither wanted to quit and pushed such thoughts back in their minds. But in their hearts, they knew the show could not go on forever. Roy's knees had begun causing him a lot of pain, making it hard to perform. His joints became so inflamed at times he'd need Cortizone injections before going on stage, and in 1994, their show was temporarily canceled altogether while he underwent knee surgery.

But on this night, at precisely 8:15 p.m., forty minutes into the first of two scheduled performances, Roy strode onstage with Montecore, a seven-year-old white tiger, trailing him on a leash. For his first trick, Montecore would rise up on his hind legs, looking for the delicious treat that Roy made sure was invisible to the awestruck audience. As Montecore padded across the stage, the audience was mesmerized, watching as the stage lights illuminated the muscles that rippled under the 600-pound jungle beast's glowing white coat, devoid of the trademark black stripes of his cousins, the yellow tigers. Montecore's breed, the so-called "ghost tiger," was so rare that legend had it only one a *century* was born in the wild.

As Roy reached center stage, he repeated the little white showbiz lie he told audiences every night: "This is Montecore's first performance onstage." It was a harmless falsehood, designed to make the audiences feel they were in on something very special—and possibly dangerous. Magicians and illusionists told such fibs all the time. After all, to paraphrase master conjurer Houdini, "Nobody likes to see another person get killed, but they do like to be nearby."

Actually, Montecore was a seasoned veteran of the stage. Although The Mirage housed upwards of sixty-six cats at any given time, only six were rotated to perform the illusions, and the brunt of the workload often fell on Montecore. He had performed this same routine like clockwork for a handful of years, always flawlessly, making him a favorite of the animal handlers. It was a tribute to the calm confidence generated by Siegfried and Roy that the audience never seemed frightened by the absence of a protective barrier between the stage and the seating area. They never seemed to realize that a tiger is one of the most efficient killing machines on earth, capable of running 100 miles a day in search of prey and able to leap thirty feet in a single bound. The distance between the stage and the front-row seats was just ten feet.

Yet far from worrying about the proximity of the huge wild beasts, who've been known to snatch 100-pound sheep and leap over six-foot fences, the "Siegfried & Roy" audience invariably thought the big cats looked cute and adorable. Tonight was no exception.

"Aw, look, a little kitty," a mother cooed to her daughter.

"I want one. Can we take it home?" begged the child, oblivious to the fact that "kitty" was a predatory carnivore capable of devouring a child her size in a couple of gulps.

What happened that fateful night, we may never know. The sequence of events has been told and retold, but accounts vary widely from person to person.

Although an onsite video camera recorded the tragic and terrifying incident, The Mirage and producers, Feld Entertainment, have refused to release the footage to the public—not even to the federal authorities who issued two subpoenas for it. Immediately after the attack, the United States Department of Agriculture staged an investigation into whether or not the show had violated any sections of the Animal Welfare Act. Feld Entertainment fought back, taking the stance of maintaining Roy Horn's privacy in the wake of the tragic event. If nothing else, the lack of footage (or unavailability of it) perpetuates the mystery of how one of the smoothest acts in showbiz suddenly went haywire. Legend has it that there is a copy of the video footage locked up in a safe in their longtime manager Bernie Yuman's office, although being the protective handler he is, he's never breathed a word.

From the audience's perspective, the show was going as planned until Montecore seemed to balk just as he and Roy reached center stage. Jonathan Cohen, a member of the transfixed audience, told the *New York Post*, "Roy tugged the tiger to get him into the middle of the stage, but the tiger didn't like that so much and came up and bumped him with his head."

Amy Sherman, who'd treated her mother to a trip to Vegas, had spared no expense for the occasion, buying front row seats. She was sitting just ten feet from the stage when she saw Montecore suddenly cock his head to one side and leap up onto Roy. She and the audience gasped as the tiger bit the magician's arm, and Roy—desperately trying to remain cool and in control—tapped his nose with the microphone, attempting to shock the beast into releasing his grip. Like most of the spectators, Amy had no idea what she was witnessing and thought Montecore's attack was simply part of the show.

From a seat further back in the theater, Kirk Baser witnessed Montecore jump up on Roy and bite his arm. Then came the true horror as the enormous tiger pushed Roy to the ground, opened his jaws wide to reveal his fearsome, three-inch-long canine teeth, and stabbed them into the ruff of his master's neck. This is the classic way that tigers kill: knocking their prey down, biting into the neck and—crunching down with the world's most powerful jaws, exerting nearly 2,000 pounds of pressure—snapping the spinal cord. Recoiling from the awful shock of the attack that night, Roy lay helpless in the cat's grip, waiting for that final deadly crunch.

It never came. By this time, two crewmembers and Siegfried had raced onto the stage. They tried to wrestle the cat off Roy, but Montecore's jaws were locked and they were powerless. Roy was still putting up a fight, but his efforts were futile—Montecore wasn't letting up. Suddenly, Roy seemed to sag, becoming as limp as a rag doll. Kirk Baser watched in sheer disbelief as Montecore effortlessly dragged Roy across the stage. The crowd fell silent as they both disappeared behind the curtain.

Despite the evidence before their eyes, many audience members were in denial, believing that the attack on Roy had simply been an eerily lifelike illusion. Kirk Baser held his breath. What had just happened? He looked around the auditorium to see if Roy might appear up on the balcony or come riding a tiger down the aisle. After all, earlier in the show, Kirk had witnessed an Evil Queen being sawn in half and a woman's head turning 360 degrees. Certainly this was just another trick, but....

Harsh reality was about to strike.

*   *   *

Baser heard someone in the audience scream, and the graveness of the situation hit him with a jolt. Faintly, he heard Roy's cries from behind the stage...or were they coming from the audience? Baser craned his neck and saw members of the staff helplessly hovering around the theater. Audience members were on the edge of their seats, waiting. Everyone looked terrified.

While audience members that night experienced very similar versions of the unsettling attack, Steve Wynn—a close friend and protector of the act he'd handpicked for The Mirage—issued an explanation of Montecore's behavior that differs vastly from their accounts. After seeing the videotape recording, Wynn made an astounding claim: the tiger had simply been distracted by a woman with a big hairdo, sitting in the front row.

Skeptics snorted! How big could her hair have been? It must have been one enormous bouffant for Montecore to have noticed it, considering that bright stage lights were focused on him and Roy, and the audience was in the dark.

Steve Wynn's public statement had experts shaking their heads. "For whatever reason, Montecore was fascinated and distracted by the guest sitting ringside. Montecore got down on all fours and put his twenty-six-inch head four inches away from the woman. She thinks this is adorable and part of the show and reaches out to try and rub him under his chin. Roy is talking and sees this move [which is] way wrong all the way around. As usual, the heroic fellow that he is, Roy jumps between the woman and the tiger."

Wynn says Roy then pulled the tiger's leash trying to yank him back, which is when Montecore "gently" bit his right arm. "Roy loudly commanded the cat to release his grip by saying, 'No, no, no, no. Release, release,' several times. He had to whack him with the rubber microphone several times to try and get the tiger to release the grip. This **didn't hurt** the tiger, but it did make a loud noise. Roy continued to pull on Montecore's leash, not realizing that one of the cat's paws was behind his leg."

According to Wynn, Roy tripped over the tiger's paw and fell backwards. Explained Wynn, "Since Roy fell down, he picked up Roy and took him with him, not knowing that you can't pick up a human the way you pick up a cub. He even tried to go into his cage with Roy."

In Steve Wynn's mind, the tiger had simply become confused: by the woman's hair in the front row; by Roy's reaction to the bite; and by the onslaught of crew members to the stage. It seems likely that, Roy and the tiger aside, Steve Wynn was trying to throw up a PR smokescreen for the press. Wynn's story was tantamount to: "Just some lady with big hair, folks. That sweet kitty-cat didn't mean to harm a soul. It was just a hair scare!"

The press didn't bite.

"What was behind the public relations campaign to portray the white tiger as trying to 'protect' Roy," explains Norm Clarke of *Vegas Confidential*, "was a case of protecting the assets. After all, the Secret Garden of Siegfried and Roy attraction generates more than $7 million per year in admissions from 750,000 visitors annually, and millions more in merchandizing."

*   *   *

But on that fateful night of the show, Siegfried Fischbacher had no time to indulge in theories about what might have driven Montecore to bite his life partner—he was far too distraught.

He'd watched it all from backstage. He'd seen Roy begin the routine by leading their trusted tiger onstage, then introduce him to the theater audience. He'd had a moment of apprehension as the huge cat stretched and stood up on his hind legs. Roy looked so pathetically fragile up against the muscular, 600-pound cat.

Suddenly, Siegfried saw the tiger bite Roy's arm. He hesitated for a second before his reflexes kicked in, and he ran for the stage shouting, "No, no, no."

In his peripheral vision, he saw two members of the crew running with him. They all knew that the specter of death had suddenly joined the act. The tiger had to be restrained—and quickly—or the result would be lethal.

Siegfried's mind raced. *No vun realizes vot the tigers are capable of,* he thought.

Siegfried certainly wouldn't go near the cats without handlers standing by. He'd seen what happened when you got too close and it scared him shitless. One of their employees, Chuck Flannery, had ended up in a wheelchair after being attacked by a tiger named Magic.

The lions and tigers were Roy's domain, of course. Siegfried had always marveled at his partner's ability to communicate with them. When it came to animals, Siegfried had never been able to compete with Roy; he could not understand the creatures.

That's why he needed Roy. Even when he had thoughts about breaking away and doing his own act, he knew it would never work with his illusions alone. Roy, the animal genius, and Siegfried, the magician, were yin and yang.

Roy had always said that he didn't train animals; he bonded with them through a technique he called "affection conditioning." He raised tiger cubs from birth, sleeping with them until they were a year old. "When an animal gives you its trust," Roy had said, "you feel like you have been given the most beautiful gift in the world."

What he'd failed to mention is that people must *never* trust wild animals, no matter how strong the bond.

*   *   *

Despite Steve Wynn's efforts to shut down meaningful communication with the press, and even though the only known videotape of Montecore's attack had been quickly supressed forever, it had played twice on the news before it was taken off the air. Gerry Therrien, an exotic animal trainer from Canada, had witnessed Roy's mauling right after it happened when the tape played on a Canadian news channel.

Watching the incident as an experienced professional, Gerry immediately noticed that Montecore showed clear signs of agitation from the moment the tiger padded onstage. When a cat is on high alert, its primal emotions are on edge, and it exhibits signs that are obvious to an expert. Gerry noticed the way Montecore had puffed up his tail, tensed his shoulders, and lifted his head high.

Had he been in the auditorium that day, says Gerry, he would have intervened the instant the tiger came into view. Montecore was undeniably "hot," and it was inevitable that something bad would occur. But who is to say why Montecore was so riled? Had something happened backstage to provoke him? In any case, Gerry says, he watched as the tiger walked onstage as usual, but then, instead of continuing to center stage as he had done for years, Montecore stopped dead in his tracks. Why? Who knows? Barring a special investigation with the cooperation of all parties involved, the attack will always remain shrouded in mystery.

Gerry Therrien may be the best judge of the events that Friday night; he has worked with big cats like Montecore for twenty years and runs a company called Action Animals which hires wild animals out to film motion pictures, television shows and commercials.

Gerry was able to watch the recording and evaluate what took place in precise detail. The audience members, on the other hand, were at The Mirage to be entertained...not to mention how fast it had all happened.

The entire incident took place over just a few seconds. Some people didn't even realize the attack was not an act until they heard screaming offstage. People's memories tend to be distorted by shock, but Gerry Therrien was not in a fear-induced state when he saw the footage. His assessment of Montecore's high state of arousal is the only credible clue to what drove him to attack the master who'd treated him almost like his child for many years. Will we ever know the truth?

*   *   *

Monty Cox, an animal coordinator for Siegfried and Roy, explained that "if a big cat bites a trainer, it will lock on and drag its prey to a secluded place in order to finish it off. The trainer will allow himself to be dragged to this place where he can then prepare to be in a position of battle."

If Roy hadn't immediately reacted by hitting Montecore with his microphone, the tiger simply might have dragged him backstage, where trainers on hand could have dealt with the situation.

Roy was first and foremost a performer, not a by-the-book animal trainer. The minute he stepped onto the stage, his concentration was not on the tiger but on his audience. One moment Roy was playing to his fans; the next, the tiger was on top of him. Roy was startled. He reacted instinctively. You could argue that it nearly cost him his life; yet he survived. So who's to say he did the wrong thing?

After Roy had recovered somewhat from the mauling, he'd said—and believed whole-heartedly—that Montecore had actually been trying to save him. Roy had been taking medication for high blood pressure for years and occasionally suffered from dizzy spells. He said, "I started feeling kind of veek.... I fell over," theorizing he'd had some kind of mini-stroke, perhaps brought on by these spells.

"Montecore saw zat I vos falling down. So he actually took me and brought me to zee uhzer exit vehr everybody could get [to] me and help me. He knew better zen I did vehr to go."

Although Roy's feeling for the tiger is touching, it's highly unlikely Montecore was trying to "protect" Roy when he bit him. Tigers are predators; they are born to kill. When attacking large prey, they prefer to bite the throat, using their muscled forelimbs to hold onto their victim and power them down to the ground. If unsure of the territory, the tiger will take its prey to a secluded, safe place and stay latched onto the prey's neck until it dies. Luckily, this didn't happen with Roy.

As shocking as it seemed to the audience that night, Roy's mauling was not an isolated event. Another tiger attack occurred in the same week, and there were many others shortly before that. According to the *New York Times*, in a study published by Professor Nyhus in the journal *Zoobiology*, "seven people had been killed by tigers in the United States from 1998 to 2001, and 27 had been injured severely enough to require hospitalization."

Anyone with access to the Internet can purchase these big cats for prices ranging from $300 to $7,000. The ease with which the tigers can be obtained, on the World Wide Web or from exotic animal auctions, belies the difficulties inherent in living with animals who are genetically programmed to range more than 100 miles a day, swim rivers, and bring down prey twice their size. Nothing can prepare a human being to deal with a tiger hard-wired to attack and kill.

Wildlife experts estimate there may be as many as 10,000 tigers in captivity—twice as many as those roaming around in their natural habitat—whether they be in stage shows like Siegfried and Roy's, circus acts, zoos, wildlife refuges, or city apartments. Bearing this in mind, the biggest surprise is that more maulings *don't* happen! And even when they do, none are reported on the same scale as Roy's.

"Charlie Stagnaro, a sixty-five-year-old trainer at the Keepers of the Wild sanctuary, was feeding a Bengal tiger when it attacked, and Eric Bloom was killed in 2001 at a private (and illegal) facility on Mount Charleston, west of the city, when another Bengal tiger took him by the neck," William L. Fox revealed in his book, *In the Desert of Desire.*

Las Vegas Sun journalist Ed Koch discovered that, also in 2001, a handler in Florida was killed by a Siberian tiger from a bite to the neck.

In May 2007, Tanya Dumstrey-Soos suffered a far worse fate than Roy when an artery in her leg was slashed by a tiger at her fiancé's Siberian Magic exotic-animal farm in Canada. Despite the efforts of her fourteen-year-old son and the fifteen-year-old son of her boyfriend, they were unable to stem the bleeding and she died. The pet tiger was put down by a veterinarian shortly after the attack.

Three days before Roy's assault, a man named Antoine Yates was attacked by his pet tiger, Ming. He called 911 claiming to have been bitten by a pit bull and then waited in the lobby for the police to arrive.

He was admitted to the Harlem Hospital with injuries to his right arm and right leg, but he discharged himself prematurely. On Saturday the fourth, tipped off by an anonymous caller, the police searched his fifth-floor housing project apartment in Harlem and discovered the 425-pound tiger along with its roommate, Al: a five-foot alligator-like reptile.

In order to remove the tiger, an officer had to lower himself from a seventh-floor apartment, armed with a tranquilizer gun and an M-4 rifle. After the tiger was sedated and taken to a New York animal shelter, he was later moved to a wildlife preserve in Youngstown, Ohio, appropriately named Noah's Lost Ark.

Upon his arrest in Philadelphia later that night, Yates said he'd acquired the tiger cub when the animal was three months old. Yates said that the two had bonded as the animal grew, and they often slept together. "We cuddled.... I really put my trust in that animal because there [were] times I put my trust in people and I got disappointed.... **But I had** 100 percent trust in him."

However close Roy was to his tigers, he knew better than to have blind faith in wild animals.

*   *   *

What happened after Montecore dragged Roy backstage is not a mystery: crew members leaped into action, attempting to save Roy's life. The cat was still refusing to release its jaws from Roy's neck—even after the crew emptied a fire extinguisher on the irritated tiger, pulled his tail, and according to the USDA, even jumped on the animal and grabbed him by the mouth. It was all to no avail.

Eventually, the cat reluctantly relinquished Roy and ran to a safe zone: his cage. A stagehand who'd been in the military immediately staunched the wound on the left side of Roy's neck. Luckily, the bite had torn the jugular vein, just missing the carotid artery. There was still the audience to contend with. A few minutes after Roy was dragged offstage by Montecore, Siegfried came out and faced the agitated crowd of fans. His usual tan had paled and he was shaking. He told the audience the performance was canceled, then said simply, "God bless Roy."

A Southwest ambulance had been dispatched to The Mirage at 8:21 p.m.; paramedics arrived on the scene at 8:25 p.m. By that time, Roy had already lost a lot of blood and was struggling to breathe. Medics would later confirm that he had sustained four deep wounds, including two punctures in the back of his head and two deep cuts on the front of his neck. His windpipe had just been crushed and an artery carrying oxygen to his brain had been damaged, leaving him paralyzed and on the brink of death.

He had to be rushed to University Medical Center immediately.

Amy Fink, a friend of Siegfried and Roy's said that as he was being taken to the ambulance, Roy was stable enough to plead for Montecore's life. Fink told Reuters, "When they wheeled him out, he said, 'Don't kill ze cat.'" Bernie Yuman, Siegfried and Roy's longtime manager, concurs with Amy. On *Larry King Live* he reported that while in the ambulance Roy insisted, "Montecore is a great cat. Make sure no harm comes to Montecore."

Bob Leinbach of the Clark County Fire Department also claimed Roy was able to speak after the accident. "By the time we left the theater for the hospital, he was conscious…talking about how his throat was bothering him. We had stopped the bleeding, but he was having trouble breathing," he said.

Paramedics met resistance when they attempted to insert a tube into Horn's throat to help him breathe. "They were trying to intubate him…he was fighting them, which is a good thing because that means he could breathe on his own," Leinbach said.

As Roy was loaded into the ambulance, Siegfried escaped to his dressing room. In an interview with Larry King, the blond Bavarian explained that he just couldn't face it. "I had to go to my dressing room to take…." He interrupted himself, "I know he voz in ze right place [viz] ze right people, ze right thing. And Bernie took care of all of zis…."

Siegfried had just witnessed his soulmate get bitten by their tiger in front of more than a thousand fans; he needed time to absorb what had happened. It was only once Bernie

Yuman called to inform him of Roy's condition that the reality sank in. "It voz an unbelievable shock to me.... I couldn't get it. But zat's how it voz."

In a matter of minutes, Siegfried's world had crumbled beneath his feet.

*   *   *

Thankfully, by the time the ambulance arrived at the hospital, Roy's neck was no longer oozing blood. Paramedics on the scene had radioed-in Roy's critical condition, and a team of specialists awaited his arrival.

University Medical Center (UMC) is the only hospital in Southern Nevada that houses a Level One trauma center. Upon arrival, Roy was rushed into the surgery room to undergo the first of three operations. The neurosurgeon who performed the surgery, Dr. Derek Duke, said, "There's no question in my mind that had there not been a Trauma Center, Roy would not have survived."

According to BBC News, the illusionist was pronounced clinically dead when his heart stopped in the O.R. for a minute. He remembers having an out-of-body experience, before being resuscitated back to life: "I stepped out of my body and looked over the surgeon's shoulder, and I sat while he was cutting me up. And my mom [who had died three years before] is sitting in a chair, and in front of her is one of my lions I had before, and my Siberian tiger was laying there, and my brother who had passed on years and years ago. And I know everything is going to be fine."

However, Roy says, "I voz not allowed to die just yet, because my vings for being an angel ver not quite ready."

By the time the procedure ended at approximately 11:30 p.m., almost every national TV station had broken the news of Roy's mauling. A crowd of well-wishers and reporters had formed outside the hospital, and at least ten TV news trucks had set up across the street directly in front of the emergency entrance.

But there was also a hotbed of people actually inside the Trauma Center, which was now churning in chaos.

The hospital set up a room on the third floor as a base for Roy's entourage of guests and crew to gather. The Green Room, as it was called, served as a press center and supplied Roy's supporters with food and beverages: coffee, tea, milk, soda and some special desserts. The room was kept well stocked throughout Roy's stay at UMC.

The VP of Public Relations for The Mirage Resorts, Alan Feldman, was there from the beginning, along with Bobby Baldwin, Chairman of Mirage Resorts, his wife Donna, and Bernie Yuman. Steve Wynn, out of town that Friday, called immediately upon hearing about Roy's injuries. He and his wife, Elaine, were at the hospital by Saturday morning, joining the entourage.

Others in attendance, including fans and employees of the show, set up their own vigil and chanted, "We love you Roy!"—raising candles in the direction of his hospital room. Siegfried and Roy's employees were a "tight-knit family" that had been rocked twice: once by the attack, and once upon hearing Alan Feldman's announcement that the show would be indefinitely canceled, forcing the 267 employees to search for new jobs.

Jim Mydlach, who had been Siegfried and Roy's chief of security since 1984, was called to the hospital to take control of the situation. When Jim arrived, Bernie Yuman gave the tall teddy-bear-like man a comforting hug. Despite outward appearances, Jim could tell Bernie was putting on a brave face. Bernie was one of the hardest working managers in the world, reminding Jim of Elvis' manager, Colonel Tom Parker. He ate, slept and breathed Siegfried and Roy, yet because of one incident, the crux of his lifetime's work had been nearly demolished.

Within moments, Bernie switched on his managerial side; it was time to take control. He spoke to Jim Mydlach in trademark Bernie lingo for which he has become famous; a blunt mish-mosh of colloquialisms.

"...Say! I've already made the calls; the boys will be here and at the Jungle Palace [Siegfried and Roy's home in Las Vegas] in no time.... There is press everywhere. Mydlach, don't let them get a picture of Roy!" (A tabloid magazine had allegedly put up a million-dollar bounty for a photograph of Roy, and Bernie was intent on maintaining Roy's privacy, especially in light of his current condition.)

Suddenly, the ring of Bernie's cell phone interrupted their conversation. Dame Elizabeth Taylor was calling to send her best wishes to Roy. Other entertainers reached out to Roy as well; many showed up after their performances on the Strip had finished, giving support to their friend and comrade. Fellow magician Lance Burton was on hand at the hospital. In praise of his friends and competing act "Siegfried & Roy," Burton reflected, "They're the guys who opened the door to magic."

At 12:40 a.m., Roy was moved back to ICU, with Jim using his body to shield the horizontal victim from any cameras. When he had first been taken into surgery, someone had managed to get a shot of Roy from behind the glass window. This slip-up could not be repeated; from then on each person coming in and out of the building had to be I.D.'d and no cell phones or cameras were allowed. Bernie's cell phone was, of course, an exception.

As the evening progressed, Siegfried was naturally very somber, waiting for word from the doctors saying Roy would fully recover. Jim Mydlach escorted him on sporadic walks to the parking garage so that he could have a cigarette and get some much-needed space. Ironically, he told Jim, he and Roy had actually discussed retiring in a year or two. But, retiring was one thing, carrying on alone without his partner of forty years was quite another.

In a written statement released the Saturday after the show, Siegfried publicly voiced his commitment to Roy, saying, "For more than four decades, I have had the great privilege of standing at the side of this remarkable man, and I will continue to do so during this very challenging time."

As the early hours of the morning approached, everyone slowly drifted off home to get some rest. Bernie, being one of the last to leave, told head of security, Mydlach, to "keep it sealed up, like an envelope." Jim assured him that if there was any news he would be the first to know. Then he took Bernie to his car and again assured him things would be fine, knowing full well he would probably get three or four more calls from Roy's caring manager before the night was out.

In the early hours of Saturday morning, after most friends and family had left the hospital, Roy suffered a stroke. At about 9:30 a.m., he underwent another round of surgery to relieve the swelling of his brain.

Although the procedure was a success, there was some controversy involving a doctor at the hospital leaking specific details about Roy's surgery to the press.

Lonnie Hammargren, a neurosurgeon and former lieutenant governor of Nevada, had no reservations when it came to the celebrity's procedure. He went on TV saying that he had spoken to Roy's neurosurgeon, Dr. Duke. Then he proceeded to lay the press' relentless curiosity to rest.

He announced that Roy had had a stroke, which fortunately "didn't hit on the side where he talks, thinks and remembers. He can still comprehend things and do things." However, Hammargren informed the public, Roy needed to have the second surgery in order to relieve severe pressure on his brain.

This was strictly confidential, a violation of Roy's privacy and the hospital policy—and what's more, it was illegal. However, Hammargren skirted around the attack, saying he'd agreed to provide some specifics to correct misinformation reported by other media outlets. He was referring to the *New York Daily Journal* report that Roy underwent a "radical procedure called a hemicraniectomy on October 4."

According to Dr. Hammargren, the procedure was neither radical nor a hemicraniectomy, which involves removing half of the skull. "That means the whole side of his head would have been taken off." Doctors instead performed a large decompressive craniectomy, which involves a quarter of the skull being removed and preserved in a pouch in the abdomen.

Roy's surgeon, Dr. Derek Duke, had also attended a press conference the following Tuesday at which he said it was a miracle Roy was alive, a fact that could be mainly attributed to the fact that he was so physically strong at the time of the mauling. However, rightly wanting to maintain Roy's privacy, he refused to reveal any specifics about the surgery to the public.

*   *   *

As for Montecore, he was quarantined immediately Friday night and kept under observation to make sure he was not rabid or in danger of harming anyone. **He was** eventually returned to The Mirage, safe and sound; but his victim's fate still hung in the balance.

Over the course of the next several days, Roy Horn's condition continued to improve. By Sunday, he was able to give a thumbs-up from his hospital bed—a good sign to friends and family, who rightly wanted to know *if*, not when, Roy might recover. He was also communicating via blinking his eyes, another important landmark on the road to recovery.

While Horn looked as though he might make it, what was unknown was the fate of the "Siegfried & Roy" spectacle. Fans and friends around the world waited with bated breath:

Would the show go on?

Chapter 1
VIVA LAS VEGAS!

"Other years saw other near ventures, but never did Las Vegas see a completed resort hotel until 1940 when hotel man Tom Hull and a friend were driving from Las Vegas down the now-paved Highway 91 towards Los Angeles. On the edge of city limits, Mr. Hull had a flat tire, and while his friend hitchhiked back into town for help, Mr. Hull stood on the highway and counted the cars. An hour of this and he became convinced that the mesquite and sage-stippled fright of a desert behind him was a mighty wholesome spot for a luxury hotel."

—The Las Vegas Travel Guide
Best & Hillyer, 1955

On the day Siegfried Fischbacher was born in a small German town in 1939, Nevada's legendary mega-resort was barely even a dream. But when Roy Horn entered the world five years later, the Las Vegas Strip's first resort hotel had just opened and a second was nearing completion.

The city that never sleeps literally sprang from the earth in a geological Big Bang many centuries ago, exploding into life when a string of artesian wells suddenly erupted and brought the miracle of water to an arid desert valley. The first recorded discoverers of the oasis were prehistoric American Indian tribes, the Anasazi and then the Paiutes.

The tale of the first white man to discover the Las Vegas Valley can be traced back to explorer Raphael Rivera's expedition through the uncharted desert almost two centuries ago. Then, on November 7, 1829, New Mexico trader Antonio Armijo led a sixty-man party along the Great

Spanish Trail from New Mexico to Southern California. According to Armijo's diary, a scout named Rivera was sent off to look for water and got "lost" from December 25 to January 6, 1830. When the scout returned after fourteen days, he reported that he'd discovered a valley carpeted with wild grass fed by springs. Spanish explorers named the valley Las Vegas, meaning "the meadows."

By the mid-1800s, Utah's Mormon missionaries decided to build a fort halfway between Salt Lake City and Los Angeles, settling four miles east of the Springs where the Paiute Indian tribes lived. It was a perfect stop on the treacherous Mormon trail pathway, and a man named Archibald Stewart—and his wife, Helen, who later took over for her husband and earned the title "The First Lady of Las Vegas"—gained ownership of a chunk of land known as the Las Vegas Ranch, which provided shelter for travelers. After many successful years, the aging Mrs. Stewart prepared to sell her property. She hired surveyor J.T. McWilliams, who quickly saw the potential riches in the well-placed lot and bought eighty acres himself located just west of Stewart's ranch. His settlement, called Ragtown, earned its reputation as a boomtown. As the Mormon Trail developed into a railroad line—the route from Salt Lake City to Los Angeles formally opened in 1905—McWilliams' boomtown was ready to blow.

By 1890 railroad developers—including a co-partner in the company, Williams Andrews Clark—were well aware that the water-rich Las Vegas Valley would be a prime location for a stop facility and town. Clark bought his block of land from Helen Stewart, located just across the tracks from McWilliam's Ragtown, for a mere $55,000 and named it after himself. His advisers originally chose the grounds for reasons beyond the fact that it was well supplied with water. The town was located on a more direct (and flatter) route from the West Coast to Salt Lake City. Also, the railroad needed at least one stop along the way, and the tiny town proved to have all the resources necessary to support the railroad workers and their families.

Work on the first railroad grade into Las Vegas began the summer of 1904. The very news of the railroad passing through would bring plenty of jobs and considerable income to all three townships—or that's what their owners hoped.

By October 1904, rails were connected with the eastern segment of the track. The San Pedro-Los Angeles-Salt Lake-Railroad, later absorbed by its parent, the Union Pacific, made its inaugural run eastward from California on January 20, 1905. That May, the San Pedro-Los Angeles-Salt Lake-Railroad auctioned off 1,200 lots in an area which is today's casino-lined Glitter Gulch. The lots sold fast—for a total amount topping $250,000—mainly because of the word-of-mouth publicity stimulated from travelers passing through from the East and the West. For this reason, many historians date the official founding of Las Vegas as May 15, 1905.

When the construction of the Hoover Dam began in 1931, more than 5,000 people were brought in to work on it. The young town of Las Vegas was virtually insulated from economic hardships that wracked most Americans in the 1930s. The Hoover Dam project and the development of the Union Pacific Railroad guaranteed good jobs and money.

By World War II, Las Vegans had begun to realize that the success of their city-in-the-desert would be determined by tourism—and gambling. During the Second World War, visiting soldiers and Californian defense workers created a need for more housing, restaurants, and entertainment. Additionally, the Henderson magnesium plant brought an influx of workers and their families, and nearby Nellis Air Force Base grew into a key military installation.

But the real runaway success of the future high-roller's paradise was triggered by a lucky break in 1938, when California launched a campaign to drive gamblers and prostitutes out of the state. These dregs of society migrated from Los Angeles into the wide-open arms of Las Vegas. The merchants of Southern Nevada, already seeing the shape of the future, were only too happy to welcome the fleeing hordes of seedy hustlers.

Legend has it that the New York City gangster, Benjamin "Bugsy" Siegel, was the sole visionary behind the

Las Vegas Strip. In the Hollywood movie *Bugsy*, Warren Beatty plays up this myth in his portrayal of the notorious hood when he declares, as if experiencing a religious epiphany, "What do people fantasize about? Sex, romance, money, adventure. I'm building a monument to *all of it*.... I'm talking about a hotel...I'm talking about a place where gambling is allowed, where everything is allowed. The whole territory is wide open. I'm talking about a palace, an oasis, a city. I'm talking about Las Vegas, Nevada!" Screenwriter James Toback's script credits Bugsy with building the first Las Vegas hotel, and naming the main drag "The Strip." Toback is dead wrong on both points, but it was one hell of a movie—and successful, too.

The true story behind the myth of the Strip begins in 1938, eight years before Bugsy Siegel's arrival, when Fletcher Brown was elected mayor of Los Angeles and began shutting down illegal gambling joints. The alleged boss of underground gaming, Guy McAfee, a captain in the Los Angeles Police Department's vice unit, fled the city and relocated to Las Vegas, where he bought a rickety joint called the Pair-O-Dice Club several miles south of town. He renovated and reopened it as the 91 Club, the first gambling joint on Las Vegas Boulevard.

In 1946, McAfee opened another club, the Golden Nugget, in downtown Las Vegas, which would later fall into the hands of the legendary hotelier, Steve Wynn. As the story goes, McAfee spent so much time driving on Highway 91 between his downtown club and the 91 Club, and—often filled with pangs of homesickness for his hometown—he decided to nickname the route "The Strip," after L.A.'s busy Sunset Strip. The name stuck.

At around the same time, members of the Las Vegas Chamber of Commerce were carefully reassessing the State's swelling economy. The legalization of gambling had been a success, and with the construction of the Hoover Dam and the opening of Nellis Air Force Base, business flourished and the population quadrupled overnight. Chamber members believed that the way to add clout to somewhat shabby Las Vegas was to establish it as a resort city. These drumbeaters for business believed a chain hotel, equipped with a casino, could potentially pave the way for other grand-scale developers. Their prayers were answered when a prolific West Coast hotelier opened the door to the city's flourishing gambling industry at just the right time.

Thomas E. Hull—who had built and managed eight hotels, among them the Hollywood-Roosevelt, the Los Angeles Mayfair, and the El Rancho hotels in Fresno, Sacramento and Indio—envisioned the complex when his car broke down in front of a vacant lot right next to the Las Vegas city limits. While he was sitting on the side of the road in the scorching sun, watching traffic go by, he told himself, "What I wouldn't give to jump into a pool!"

Shortly thereafter, he turned his musing into reality.

It was a huge shock to the city when Hull did not purchase a thirty-five-acre tract of land they offered him in the existing casino town. Instead he chose to buy thirty-three acres—at $150 an acre—off the new and improved Los Angeles Highway, situated on the southwest corner of what's now Las Vegas Boulevard and Sahara Avenue. By building his property on the city's outskirts, his taxes were less, water rights were accessible, and the land was cheaper. More importantly, Hull avoided the cost and nuisance of applying for a gambling license from the city.

Jessie Hunt, the old lady who owned the land, offered to give it to him for free. She thought it was worthless and had tired of paying taxes. She asked Hull, "Son, what are you going to do with this godforsaken land?"

"I thought maybe I'd build a sort of motel," Hull responded.

"Oh, don't go and do that, son! We got one of them already," she replied.

Fortunately, Hull didn't take the old lady's advice. The hotel opened on April 3, 1941, and, with Hull's address book full of Hollywood's A-list stars and starlets, celebrities flocked to the scene, enticed by Vegas' warm weather and old-fashioned opulence. According to the *Saturday Evening Post*, "The Rancho somehow managed to make the riveter, the carpenter and the truck driver at home in overalls in the same rooms with men and women in smart sports clothes, with an eloping Lana Turner posing for news photographs."

On opening night, guests arrived in formal evening-wear, crisply pressed suits and tuxedos, and lavish gowns. Two hours later, Hull arrived sporting blue jeans, boots, and a classic shirt, walking with a rolling Western gait. "Howdy, podners, come as you are," he told them heartily. It was a clever way of identifying himself with the casually clad ordinary folks who'd become the backbone of his business.

The *Saturday Evening Post* prophesied, "No resort is likely to succeed in Vegas that doesn't accomplish this democracy," a statement that still rings true over half a century later. In the late 70s, the casino mogul Steve Wynn continued to exploit this egalitarian image—for both of his Nugget hotels, and later, mega-palaces The Mirage and the Wynn—with his brilliant TV commercial campaigns co-starring him, the just-plain-folks type, opposite such household names as Frank Sinatra and Dolly Parton.

Hull's dream was to build a luxurious layover resort for drivers commuting between Los Angeles and Salt Lake City. He believed that being able to leave your car at the side of the road, jump into a refreshing pool and sleep in a homey self-equipped "cottage," was the ultimate comfort for those sharing the arduous drive and sweltering heat along Highway 91.

In a board meeting shortly after his car broke down, Hull is said to have declared, "We'll put a swimming pool with cool-looking water right in front of them and it's just got to stop traffic." And if that failed to attract passing drivers, the neon-lit slogan, "Stop at the Sign of the Windmill"— plastered on top of their landmark windmill—would be sure to stop them.

The frontier/Spanish mission-style resort, dubbed El Rancho, borrowed from "Hollywood back-lot" architecture: aesthetic taking precedent over functionality. Its décor emulated the Old West, with archaic firearms and cowboy hats, married to the cozy familiarity of residential suburbs. Although it was intended to be rustic and friendly, the hotel also provided full-fledged luxury, a complete transformation from the dingy motels, riverboats and tiny saloon clubs already dotting the desert town. Adding to the package, Hull introduced hotel guests to what was then called, quaintly but accurately, "refrigerated air," an almost sinful luxury that today's Las Vegas crowds casually take for granted.

But nothing was too good for Hull's customers for one simple reason: He did *not* want them gambling elsewhere, so he made damn sure the thought never entered their minds. His motto was: What could you ask for that El Rancho can't provide? Hull's casino pioneered the concept that "all of a guest's needs could be found on the premises," according to staffer Guy Landis. El Rancho featured a travel agency, retail shops, horseback riding, lounge shows, a swimming pool, a steakhouse, and an oh-my-golly waterfall tumbling and crashing down onto native rock. A sprawling compound of sixty-three hacienda-like cottages and stables were built around a central café, nightclub, and...oh, yes, there was a casino, the tempting sticky center of this sweet layout, tacked on almost as an afterthought.

Each cottage had its own private trimmed lawn, well-shaded porch and fully equipped kitchen. As a special touch, extra-large wool blankets lay folded at the foot of each bed. The hotel maintained its own laundry facilities on the premises; a staff of fifteen worked to wash and iron shirts with a turnaround of six hours or less.

Previously, hotels had been conveniently situated alongside the docks of Lake Mead—the lake created by the Hoover Dam—and railroad stations. But Hull recognized that the burgeoning use of cars, buses and trucks meant that highways were becoming more important than railroads for delivering goods and guests. To accommodate passing traffic, El Rancho proudly boasted its own gasoline station, a massive parking lot for 400 cars, and paved and lighted streets that guided drivers right to the doors of their motel-style rooms.

As the Chamber of Commerce had hoped, Hull revolutionized Las Vegas in one fell swoop, igniting the boom in luxury hotel-resorts. Other pioneering hoteliers and players would come in his wake, but Hull laid the foundation for the mecca of hedonism. Luxury hotels built on his model, featuring high-roller gambling and world-class entertainment, continue to erupt from the desert like a perpetual fireworks display.

With the Second World War going full blast in 1942, R. E. Griffith, a movie theater magnate from Texas, decided to compete with Hull and buy land less than a mile south of El Rancho on Highway 91. But sadly, the parcel of his desires was already occupied by the aforementioned McAfee's 91 Club. After much determined haggling, however, Griffith finally managed to buy the thirty-five-acre piece, including the 91 Club, from the ex-Los Angeles cop for $1,000 an acre. Legend has it that after the sale, McAfee told Griffith: "If you'd bargained harder, I would have sold for less!" Griffith allegedly replied, "If you'd bargained harder, I would have paid more!"

Today, that land is worth *billions*!

Griffith immediately hired his nephew, the architect William J. Moore, to build a Western-style resort—The Last Frontier—which they designed with a swimming pool, riding stables, tennis court, sundeck, showroom, casino, and 170 air-conditioned rooms. In an attempt to outdo Hull, Griffith added a Western Frontier Village to the north end of the property, as well as a wedding chapel called the Little Church of the West, where many celebrities would tie the knot in decades to come.

By the time it opened on October 30, 1942, the Village resembled a self-sufficient Western movie set that was the antithesis of "false fronts." To the movie-going public, it looked real and familiar, as if John Wayne himself might suddenly come galloping through in pursuit of the bad guys.

Meanwhile, tough-as-nails R. E. Griffith had made his fortune in the movie-theater industry and had the clout to draw big-name Hollywood stars to the desert, both as guests and performers. Actually, it wasn't a very hard sell because TinselTown celebs, even in those bygone days, were starting to feel trapped by the forerunners of today's paparazzi—the aggressive "foe-togs" and reporters from the era's slavering fan magazines, like *Photoplay* and *Modern Screen*. Even though Hollywood's Sunset Strip had emerged as a legendary playground for the rich and famous, harried stars longed for some quiet Shangri-La where they could escape blazing flashbulbs and adoring hordes of sweaty fans—not to mention evil private eyes sent to spy on them by studio heads hoping to ruin a rival mogul's box-office king or queen with a bit of nasty gossip. But in just five hours on the I-5 in the good old Bentley or Rolls, one could drive from the fishbowl of the Sunset Strip to the anonymous luxury of a stunning suite overlooking the Strip in Las Vegas.

And, oh, how these stars were courted by the slick high-roller lords of Sin City, who knew full well how impressed the growing influx of tourists would be to see stars in evening clothes lounging elegantly beside a roulette wheel or having a flutter at blackjack. By associating itself with Hollywood glamour, plus the seduction of sex and gambling, Las Vegas was a veritable Disneyland for adults and became the fastest-growing metropolitan area in the West.

So...Bugsy Siegel did not invent Las Vegas! But it's fair to say he definitely helped put it on the map. This tough, handsome and charming New York hood never achieved his burning ambition to become a star of the Silver Screen himself, but he became the Ultimate Gangster in real life, mixing easily with the glitterati of Hollywood and gaining more fame than most celebrities of his time. And even after Bugsy got bumped, when a barrage of bullets wizzed through his carefully coiffed head, the legend of his real and imagined life become inextricably entwined in the image of Las Vegas—especially after organized crime engineered a long-term takeover of the town. The irresistible combination of Bugsy's Mob connections, his infamous temper and the stronghold he established in Hollywood is a dramatic saga that will be told and re-told for generations to come. And even though gangland's glamour boy never became a movie star, he scored even bigger in a funny kind of way that he would have loved: Bugsy became a movie.

In 1988, Eugene Moehring, an historian at the University of Nevada, succinctly described Siegel's impact on the transition of Vegas: "While elegant in a western sense, the El Rancho and Last Frontier were little more than opulent dude ranches. The crucial event, which transformed Las Vegas from a recreational to a full-fledged resort city, was Bugsy Siegel's Flamingo Hotel. In a sense, the Flamingo was the turning point because it combined the sophisticated ambiance of a Monte Carlo casino with the exotic luxury of a Miami Beach-Caribbean resort. The Flamingo liberated Las Vegas from the confines of its western heritage and established a pattern for a 'diversity of images' embodied in future resorts like the Desert Inn, Thunderbird, Dunes, Tropicana, and Stardust."

Here's another debunking of the Bugsy Siegel myth: he was *not,* as is widely believed, the original owner of the Flamingo. By the time the New York hood first arrived on the West Coast, Billy Wilkerson, publisher of the *Hollywood Reporter* and a professional gambler, had already begun construction on the hotel. With his expertise, Billy knew exactly what would make customers tick and how to nurture their addictions. He intended to make the casino the centerpiece of the resort. According to his son, W. R. Wilkerson III, "No guest would be able to move around the hotel without passing through the casino. There would be no windows. 'Never let them see daylight,'" his father had commanded.

Wilkerson soon ran out of funds to complete the project. Bugsy seized the moment, and with the help of childhood friend and fellow Jew, Meyer Lanksy, the brilliant Mob financier, he pushed Billy out of the picture. And, with Meyer's blessing, he quickly got financial backing from his organized crime associates across the country—but his venture rolled snake eyes. To the dismay of his partners in crime, the $1.5 million budget he'd projected soon quadrupled, and so did his debt.

Bugsy's grave in the desert was already being dug.

The Flamingo threw its grand opening the day after Christmas, 1946, making international headlines. Bugsy Siegel pulled out all the stops, chartering flights filled with

Hollywood celebrities who came to watch comedian Jimmy Durante perform. Although the hoi polloi celebrated in style for three days, the casino—initially, at least—flopped and was forced to close down.

The joint eventually reopened and started to show a steady profit, but it was too late for Bugsy. On June 20, 1947, he was shot nine times in the head while reading a newspaper in his girlfriend's Hollywood mansion. He died instantly, and his assassination marked the beginning of four decades of Mob control in Las Vegas. Bugsy had ushered in an era of Gangster Glamour and, ironically, ended up making his Goodfellas a pile of dough.

Las Vegas historian Frank Wright wrote, "His death was a great advertisement for the city of Las Vegas in a sense. It certainly brought attention to Las Vegas and created a sort of sense of illicit excitement about Las Vegas."

Glamour, sex, dough...and *danger*.

The Las Vegas formula for success was complete. And no one would understand or exploit it better than two larger-than-life German boys who were just little tykes around the time Bugsy Siegel was getting whacked. Decades later, these Teutonic lads would dazzle Sin City and usher in the opulent era that spawned the new Las Vegas; the impossibly over-the-top gambling and entertainment center of the planet, the place where anything was possible; where huge jungle beasts could be paraded uncaged before awe-struck crowds in a spectacle no Roman emperor ever matched.

Their names were Siegfried and Roy. And decades after Bugsy Siegel proved that the sharp, heady scent of danger brought people flocking to Las Vegas by plane, train and automobile, these flamboyantly brave magicians proved it all over again—with 600-pound jungle beasts instead of gun-toting Mob gorillas.

They were The Tiger Kings. And they tamed Sin City like no one ever had, transforming it into the gambling and entertainment mecca of planet Earth.

"A magician is often born from insecurity, lack of attention, and the need to be loved."
—*Siegfried Fischbacher*

At first glance, Siegfried and Roy's story seems like a traditional rags-to-riches fairytale in which the prince and princess fall in love, become King and Queen of the Fairy Kingdom and live happily ever. In this case, however, the tale takes many unconventional twists as it follows the lives of two golden boys who meet on a ship, fall in love, and transform themselves into the most famous magic act of the century.

The official story of Siegfried and Roy's upbringing and rise to fame has been repeated so often it has become folklore. All the elements are there: talking to animals, magic, fairytale romance, archetypal personalities, and the palace they designed and built themselves. Each polished facet of their glittering tale serves to strengthen a carefully calculated image of two mythical supermen living a magically harmonious coexistence. They have told us what they want us to know—but not necessarily what *we* want to know.

Herein lies the real story: The secret life of Siegfried and Roy....

Once upon a time, in an area in Southeast Germany called Bavaria, Maria Fischbacher, a housewife, and her husband Martin, a professional painter, lived in a modest house on the outskirts of Rosenheim, a town located near the Alps on the ancient trading route to Italy. On June 12, 1939, Maria gave birth to her second baby: an angelic, blond boy she named Siegfried.

Siegfried Fischbacher was almost certainly named after the legendary dragon-slayer in the Middle High German epic poem, *Niebelungenlied*; the hero's name is often referenced in the German arts, comparative to the fictional English character, King Arthur. It is ironic that "Sieg" means victory and the translation of "Fried" is peace, because a scant three months after Siegfried Fischbacher was born, in September 1939, Hitler invaded Poland and World War II ensued. In June 1941, Germany invaded the Soviet Union, and two-year-old Siegfried's soldier father was shipped to the Russian front, leaving Maria to bring up her children alone.

Martin became a prisoner of war, and although it is uncertain exactly where he ended up during the war, it is known that the Soviet Union had not signed the Geneva Convention back in 1929 and consequently did not have to treat their POWs in accordance with it. Instead, Soviet and German prisoners of war were subjected to horrific conditions that resulted in the deaths of hundreds of thousands of troops on both sides. According to historians of that period, after the battle of Stalingrad, starving and malnourished German POWs were forced to trek to war camps in Siberia in bitter cold temperatures. For many, it was a death march.

Although the conditions Martin Fischbacher endured have not been recorded, the horror of war certainly took its toll. After four years away, he returned home traumatized. Like many veteran soldiers, he found temporary escape in the excessive consumption of alcohol.

At home, Martin barely communicated with his family as he struggled to readjust to the life he'd once led. He went back to working sporadically as a house painter, but the business of keeping the family afloat fell to his wife. Maria was a devout Roman Catholic and her three children, Siegfried, Marinus, and Margot, were brought up with strong religious values. As they matured, Siegfried's siblings never strayed far from the conservative morals they'd been taught: his older brother, Marinus, grew up to take over the family business; and his younger sister, Margot, became a nun. She assumed the name Sister Dolores and eventually ran an orphanage in Romania.

The family was starved, financially and emotionally. Siegfried says he never heard his parents say, "*Ich liebe dich,*" [I love you] to each other or their children. Maria and Martin never hugged, never kissed; the house was filled with a sense of pain and hardship. His mother's Catholic beliefs ruled out any thought of divorce, so she resigned herself to an unhappy marriage and a bleak future.

The children were more or less invisible to their father. Martin rarely even acknowledged their existence. For his whole life, naturally enough, Siegfried quested for the affection he'd been deprived of as a child. On the rare occasions Martin addressed his children, he would either beat them or tell them their lives were worthless. Siegfried endured the beatings but refused to accept his father's assessment of his worth as a human being. His father's contempt drove him to seek out success with dogged determination. In his fractured English, Siegfried says his father always made him feel that "I was always the boy he never can be good. He never will be nothing."

In Siegfried and Roy's autobiography, *Mastering the Impossible*, Siegfried never uses his father's name; nor is Martin's name mentioned in Siegfried's interviews, or in his autobiographical movie, *The Magic Box*. He has rarely referred to Martin publicly, except to describe him as an alcoholic and to recall his father's surprisingly impressed reaction to a vanishing coin trick the aspiring young magician had arduously perfected.

As his father watched, Siegfried produced a coin, a glass of water and a handkerchief. Then he dropped the coin into a glass of water and—abracadabra!—made it disappear. His father looked at him in total amazement, and asked, "How did you do that?" His son's magic had momentarily broken the spell of his World War II trauma. His face registering the wonderment of a child, Martin felt around for the coin in the empty glass.

According to Siegfried, "It was the first time my father had acknowledged me. Until that moment I didn't really exist for him; I went to school, came home, ate, went out to play, and then it was bedtime. Now not only had my

father spoken to me, but his astonishment suggested I
had done something he couldn't—and that was a remarkable
moment for a boy trained to believe his father knew
everything."

In that very moment, Siegfried knew he would
master the art of illusion and become a magician. His father's
reaction to a simple coin trick proved that magic could capture the attention of even the toughest audience. In his autobiography, Siegfried admits, "Looking at a magic act, you
may think magicians are the most confident of people. To
present the manipulations, it's true, we have to be, but like
entertainers and actors, a magician is often born from
insecurity, lack of attention, and the need to be loved."

Performing magic for people was Siegfried's way of
securing the love he craved. Yet the attention he attracted was
not always positive; it occasionally got him into big trouble.

When Siegfried was eight years old, he passed by a
bookstore and stopped when something very special caught
his eye: a book on magic. It cost five marks (the equivalent of
about two dollars), a fortune for a little boy in post-war
Germany. But Siegfried knew that one way or another, he
had to have that book.

When he got home that day, he behaved like an
angel, performing all his chores without being asked, acting
helpful and charming to his mother. Being the eldest of eight
children herself, Maria instantly suspected her son had an
ulterior motive, and asked him bluntly what he was angling
for. Siegfried began hesitantly, "Well, there's this magic
book...."

"What? A magic book?" His mother closed the subject
on the spot. In Maria's world, there was no place for magic;
for her everything was a grim reality. Even though Siegfried
now knew that a future of performing magic was in his cards,
his parents were unsympathetic. Never could they fathom
what, to them, was a bizarre, unthinkable career choice.
Maria and Martin wanted Siegfried to take over the family
house-painting business or take up a no-nonsense vocation—
carpentry, perhaps. But *magic*? No, magic was for gypsies.

Siegfried had never wanted anything in his life like he wanted that book. But he knew his mother would never give him five marks for a book when they could barely afford the roof over their heads.

And here's where Siegfried's fairytale story begins, although he insists what happened next is "true...and maybe, in a funny way, this was my first real experience with magic. I was across the street from the bookstore, balancing myself on the curb of the sidewalk like a tightrope artist and at the same time trying to figure out what to do next, when I looked down, and... [Ta-da!] There, lying on the pavement, was five marks."

Whether this account is a figment of the fanciful folklore Siegfried and Roy fabricated over the years, or whether it actually happened, is impossible to say. In either case, his mother certainly didn't believe his story about money materializing out of thin air, and she slapped him harder than he had ever been slapped before, for "stealing" the book.

But Siegfried didn't care. Now he had his first scripture of magical knowledge, and he immersed himself in the tricks of his future trade day in, day out, spending every spare minute memorizing and practicing them. For once, he didn't care about playing with other children. In magic, he had discovered "a way to escape the unpleasant atmosphere of [his] home life," and he was transported to a sorcerer's realm, where anything was possible and illusions were dreams come true.

Siegfried diligently performed his magic tricks on the street and for friends at school, slowly building an enthusiastic fan base. He had a natural flair and skill for legerdemain, and once, when he made an old lady's coat button seemingly disappear, she began screaming so hysterically that his teachers came running, and he ended up locked in the school cellar.

Siegfried's skills finally surpassed the lessons in his magic book, and he came to a temporary standstill. Instinctively, he began to add his own improvisations to touch up his old tricks and created new ones using his limited resources and boundless imagination. Recalled Siegfried: "I taught myself how to eat light bulbs and swallow razor blades. Not as those tricks are done in a magic show, but the Siegfried Fischbacher way—which was really to eat them. With a lot of thought and practice, I figured out a way to digest them so I wouldn't do more damage to myself than cut and scar my tongue." Exactly how Siegfried digested light bulbs and razor blades while miraculously staying alive remains a mystery to this day.

Siegfried also recalled one time when he performed magic on his father...with disastrous consequences. Every Friday, local workmen would get their weekly wages, then head to the neighborhood tavern to drink their money down the drain. Martin, of course, never missed a Friday night at the beer hall, and Siegfried and his older brother, Marinus, would often have to collect their brawling, blood-splattered father and drag him back to the house.

On one occasion, Martin failed to return home for three days, and Maria grew frantic with worry. He'd already been in a few minor car crashes while driving intoxicated, and fearing he might be so drunk by now he'd probably kill himself if he drove, Maria asked Siegfried to figure out a way to make his father's car key magically vanish.

The boy went down to the tavern, sat next to his father and then offered to do a magic trick for Martin and his drinking pals. He put a key on a string, placed a handkerchief over it, and when he pulled it off, the key had disappeared. Siegfried then quickly disappeared himself into thin air and fled home with Martin's key in his possession.

Sadly, Siegfried's father wasn't quite drunk enough to be fooled by what his son had just pulled off. When Martin slammed open the front door of their home a while later, Siegfried sensed his father's rage and huddled under the bed sheets. Martin barged into the room and beat him half to death with a rubber hose. Luckily, his brother Marinus intervened before Siegfried was dispatched to the Pearly Gates.

Growing up, the battered boy found a mentor in the village's Catholic priest, Father Johann, and at one point even considered becoming a priest himself. The good Father was a frustrated actor and projected his ambitions on natural performer Siegfried. He recalls the priest encouraging him to act and exploit his flair for drama. "I loved playing different characters, and when I got to be about fifteen, I developed a stand-up comedy act. I performed on weekends at weddings, parties, and town functions. As my routines lampooned the dry humor of my fellow Bavarians and poked fun at some of our local characters, I soon became a minor celebrity in Rosenheim."

In order to play multiple roles, Siegfried learned how to apply makeup to his pretty-boy face. He found that when he wore these different masks, he felt more comfortable than he did in his own skin. Even offstage, he would adopt different personas to entertain his audience.

Father Johann, who evidently had a fondness for the young boy, took the impressionable child to see the German-born illusionist, Kalanag, perform in München. Kalanag, whose real name was Helmut Ewald Schreiber, had been one of Adolf Hitler's favorite magicians before and during World War II. Like many men in Germany at the time, Schreiber joined the Nazi party in 1939, and as an executive of a German film corporation and producer of more than 180 German movies, he was extremely powerful and well connected in the Nazi regime.

After the war ended and the American Third Army captured München, the illusionist masqueraded as an American officer and fled to the British zone. It is then that he changed his name from Helmut Ewald Schreiber to Kalanag, taken from *Kala Naag*, Punjabi for black cobra, and he went on to new success as a conjurer.

Watching Kalanag's revue demonstrated to Siegfried exactly what it would take to entertain his audience with magic. Siegfried wrote in his and Roy's autobiography, "It wasn't just his illusions that thrilled me; it was his personality and the glamour of the elaborate stage sets. I saw for the first time that with charm and style a magician could color the illusions. Magic, I realized is only 50 percent dexterity. You practice, practice, practice until the moves are in your blood and you don't have to think about them anymore; it's like learning a language. When you're at that point, the magic becomes a part of you, and you start all over again, injecting your personality into your act.

"Kalanag merged magic and personality brilliantly. Seeing him, I realized that my desire to perform on stage as an actor and my passion for magic could be put together."

Kalanag's influence on Siegfried was profound. The bespectacled, balding, pudgy, middle-aged man often dressed as a maharaja to perform the Indian Rope Trick and other exotic illusions borrowed from the Far East. He became famous for illusions such as a floating young woman, disappearing car, and burning tree. Although he did not invent many of these illusions, Kalanag always added his signature touch and made them seem new, just as Siegfried and Roy would in years to come. They would use a floating woman in their act and adopt their predecessor's penchant for dramatic costume changes and multi-cultural influences. They would also create a storyline-based stage act, with sets on a grand-scale and a huge production team. Similarly, Kalanag traveled Europe with seventy tons of props and employed eighty people in his revue.

Kalanag incorporated his flair for movies into his performances, acting out scenes in character, as would Siegfried and Roy in the future. The personas they would assume for their magic act would become irreversibly entwined with their offstage identities. They were a perfect example of life imitating art, imitating life.

Kalanag gained recognition as the first illusionist to emerge out of the postwar period, appropriating the title, "Europe's Master of Magic." However, despite his success in Britain and Western Europe, Kalanag's Nazi background had become known and he was ostracized by many, particularly Americans. And rumors were circulating that he'd used political power to steal his illusions from another magician, one Alois Kassner, who mysteriously disappeared from magic some years after WWII.

The British-born author and illusion builder, Eric Lewis, wrote, "It is a surprising thing to me that Kalanag was not successful with his show in America, where he was met with prejudice because he had served during the war as an officer in the German Air Force. Surprising, because England, the country which really suffered the most, accepted him completely, and his show was a hit wherever it went." The Americans resented Kalanag so much that leaflets calling for a boycott of his 1956 U.S. tour popped up all over the country.

Even without the backlash of a possible Nazi past, it's always tough for foreign talent to break into the American market, and Siegfried and Roy were notable exceptions. Both were the offspring of soldiers who'd fought for the hated Nazi regime, which was the first handicap the duo had to overcome, but they triumphed in the end with their staggering success in Las Vegas.

Although Father Johann encouraged Siegfried to dabble in the arts, pursuing acting or even magic beyond the level of a hobby was considered blasphemous. So Siegfried's brother, Marinus, ended up taking over the family business and his sister, who'd wanted to become a nun since the age of eight, joined a convent. Siegfried, in an effort to appease his family and Father Johann, studied carpet weaving in a local factory, but in the back of his mind he always knew neither the workman's life nor the church was for him.

"Quite simply I wanted a new identity," he says. "I wasn't happy with the way I was perceived; I didn't want to go through life as my father's son. When I performed in a theater, I was the happiest person alive; I was someone different. I wanted to be different in life as well."

This revelation can be construed in two ways. Firstly, as Siegfried admits, magic was considered blasphemous in the parochial, Roman Catholic town of Rosenheim. Overwhelmed by conflict between his natural desires and the narrow-minded nature of his friends, family and fellow townsmen, Siegfried felt suffocated; he felt as if: "There was no room for growth—personal or professional."

Secondly, however, there is an implication in his statement that Siegfried was also referring to his sexual identity. As an insecure actor and performer who needed to wear makeup to feel comfortable in his own skin, Siegfried had apparently already begun struggling to come to terms with his homosexuality. If the thought of pursuing a career in magic raised the heartbeats of Bavarian folk, imagine the fibrillations that would have been triggered by an open admission of sexual attraction to other men.

In those times, in that place, homosexuality was taboo. Lists similar to the McCarthy blacklists of the late 1940s were compiled, and people accused were imprisoned or even killed. During Hitler's reign, homosexuals were on the roster of Holocaust victims who were rounded up and sent to concentration camps by the Nazis, along with the Jews, the gypsies, and the other enemies of the state.

Decades later, Larry King interviewed Siegfried on his CNN show and asked what his big break had been. In his thick, Teutonic accent, the magician explained that his break began when he finally "left my family, home...the fuhrzer I vent away from home, the more secure I become myself." Away from home, Siegfried found it easier to accept his emerging sexuality and no longer needed to hide it from the parents he wanted so desperately to impress.

When Siegfried said goodbye to his mother, she told him, "If you leave now, you never have to come back again." Despite the harshness of these words, Siegfried justifies them, saying that Maria was hurt by what she considered abandonment. His sister and brother had already moved out of their home, and so when Siegfried departed, his mother had no one left. He told Larry King, "But that doesn't mean that.... She loved me very much...I know it. But we never could show it."

Much of Siegfried's upbringing was devoid of emotion. His mother had accepted her lot in life, no matter how miserable it was; his father had never recovered from the war, so Siegfried's childhood was spent craving the love he longed to believe his parents were capable of.

Leaving the cold, closed world of his childhood freed Siegfried in many ways, but he was still a prisoner of his painful upbringing—evidenced by his driving obsession to succeed as a master magician, a larger-than-life sorcerer who could control the way the world was viewed with clever, mind-clouding illusions. The German boy who'd dazzled his sadistic father had many struggles yet to overcome, but now he was free to express himself and seek out his destiny.

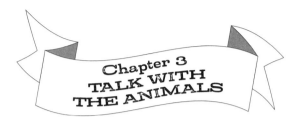

"My animals are the friends who will accept me always for what I am—rich or poor, fat or thin, dumb or intelligent."

—Roy Horn

R oy Horn believes he retains actual memories of the terrifying night in 1944 when his exhausted, frightened mother, Johanna, pushed him from her womb mere minutes after a wild bicycle dash for safety during an air raid by Allied bombers. Thus, Roy became the fourth child Johanna was left alone to care for after her husband was also marched off to the Russian front to fight for the Führer.

On that fateful night, October 3, 1944, Johanna was faced with a life-or-death decision as she and her three little boys cringed in terror while bombs exploded in their little town of Nordenham. The Allies had launched a massive attack on the neighboring port of Bremerhaven. It was the worst timing possible. Johanna knew it was time to deliver her child, and she knew she'd need help. Roy tells friends he's heard his mother tell the story so often that he can vividly remember the awful events that unfolded in the hours just before his birth.

Houses were burning; women and children were screaming. Everyone who wasn't buried under rubble or confident of the family's basement shelter rushed to the Weser, the river where there were small boats and the comparative safety of water.

In her basement in Nordenham, Johanna Horn didn't know what to do. On one hand, there were three small children to protect and comfort. On

the other, there was a life coming. For in the middle
of all this insanity, she was going into labor.

Johanna voted with the future. Telling her
children not to leave the basement, she climbed on
her bicycle and desperately pedaled across the city.
Bombs burst around her, but she reached the safety
of her sister's home unharmed. Fifteen minutes
later she gave birth to the last of four sons. Her
dreams, faith, and destiny—sprinkled with hope—
were placed in a little crib.

And that, family legend has it, is how Roy
Uwe Ludwig Horn was born.

Stop! Rewind!

Roy?

What kind of name was that to give a German child
during World War II? After all, Johanna had christened her
first three sons with typical Teutonic names: Manfred,
Werner and Alfred. Choosing to give her fourth child an
English name derived from the French word "roi," or "king,"
during air raids by the British and Americans would seem a
bizarre, unlikely choice. Actually, the record shows that
Roy's real name is Uwe Ludwig. And as there's no evidence
of a legal name change, the likely explanation is that he
"officially" adopted the name when he and Siegfried became
"Siegfried & Roy" and united to conquer showbiz in 1971. In
that same year, the flamboyant duo toured Europe and,
coincidentally, were invited to perform at Monte Carlo's Gala
des Rois.

When Roy's father finally returned from the Russian
front, he was—much like Siegfried's father and countless
other shell-shocked German soldiers—endlessly tormented
by his battlefield experiences. Before World War II, he'd been
a successful orchestra leader and had bonded with his
children through music, teaching them to play one or another
of the six instruments he'd mastered. The war changed all
that. Upon his return, much like Siegfried's father, the
maestro drowned his mental horrors in alcohol.

The household suffered, of course. But unlike
Siegfried's obedient, long-suffering mother, Johanna chose to

take control of her family's future. She plucked up the courage to divorce her husband—an extremely daring feat for a German woman during those cold, conservative times. And even though Johanna and Siegfried's mother were both small-town girls, Johanna was extremely open-minded and expressive. Her mental and emotional outlook would have a profound influence on Roy as he grew to adulthood.

Incredibly, Johanna quickly found another husband. Roy's new stepfather managed a large construction company and was exceptionally well-off for a man in post-war Germany. Roy was brought up as if he were an only child because his eldest brother, Alfred, had already left home; his brother Werner had chosen to stay with his own father; and Manfred, although old enough to leave home, "stayed with [Johanna and Roy] intermittently," Roy writes in his autobiography, "because of a motorcycle accident that left him riddled with mental problems."

Roy visited his real father occasionally, but their relationship soon disintegrated. Roy's stepfather, meanwhile, was easily able to provide for him and his mother, and for the first time, Johanna felt secure financially and emotionally. Her new husband even hired a nanny to take care of Roy, and Johanna's youngest son became somewhat spoiled in this new family environment. For a while, Roy was the happiest child in town. His stepfather's largesse allowed him to have lavish birthday parties, and Roy developed a taste for grand celebrations every October. After he began making his own money, the birthdays became more and more opulent. Ironically, the most exciting event of his life would occur on a birthday; and decades after that, the most tragic....

Sadly for Roy and his mother, the honeymoon was over all too quickly with her new husband, whose own post-war traumatic stress kept getting worse. And the worse it got, the more he drank. Like Siegfried's father, and Roy's real father, his stepfather descended deeper into alcoholism. A dense, dark cloud floated over the household, refusing to budge. Finally, the man who had rescued Johanna and Roy deteriorated mentally to the point where he had to quit his job. Roy's family went on welfare to survive, and Johanna slaved away at a factory job to buy her son school clothes.

Roy's world had yo-yoed from bad, to good, to worse. Now he was forced to learn how to take care of himself. He woke up on his own, went to school, and fed himself while his mother worked twelve-hour days and the "man of the house" drank himself into oblivion.

Roy played alone, being sure to stay out of his stepfather's way. He would often sneak down to the cellar and escape out a window with his beloved dog, Hexe, which means "witch" in German. Hexe, jet black and half-wolf, was his best friend. Years later, Roy recalled, "As a child, I was not very good in communicating with people. We came from Germany after the war, so we didn't have a whole lot, and I trusted more in my animals than I trusted in people."

When Roy was six years old, he remembers pretending to be a prince, while Hexe was his magical unicorn. Together they'd go off to explore the fields and marshlands. One day, Roy tired himself out and fell asleep under an old willow tree. When he woke up, Hexe was gone.

Roy searched for his dog and encountered a black raven staring him in the eye. When the raven flew away, Roy chased it, hoping to find a nest full of the bright, shiny objects he'd heard the black birds collected. In hot pursuit, he crashed through some tall reeds, thinking the treasures might be hidden in their midst, but he suddenly fell forward and sank into deep muck. He was trapped in the marsh, which kept sucking him down as he held onto the reeds and screamed for help at the top of his lungs.

Hexe reappeared, but there was nothing the dog could do. Instead of helping Roy, it ran away, deserting him. Roy was up to his chest, crying, desperately screaming for Hexe—and then he heard voices coming into earshot. Hexe had brought a farmer to Roy's rescue. As the farmer pulled him out of the swamp with a rope, Roy babbled his thanks, but the man told him, "It's your dog you should be thanking." Hexe had searched out the farmer working in a field, then barked and barked until the man had no choice but to follow the agitated dog.

Roy reminisced, "This was not the first time, nor would it be the last, that I would be thankful to one of my animals for my safety or that the harmony I felt with an animal would be the strongest—and most magical—connection in my life.

"This is, I think, the key to understanding that despite all our apparent differences, Siegfried and I are alike. In magic he found a way to escape the unhappy atmosphere of his homelife and receive attention from other people that he never got from his parents. For me the escape route from a childhood seen through the silent tears to solace and peace was through animals."

As his stepfather's condition worsened, the man turned vicious and violent, often threatening Roy, vowing to kill him with the rat poison in the kitchen cabinet or the ax hidden away in the china closet. "I had discovered the ax one day but never dreamed he would use it," said Roy. "Then, one night, he took it out. My mother and I fled to my room and locked ourselves in, while my stepfather drunkenly cursed us and tried to chop through the thick wooden door."

Now Hexe became Roy's bodyguard and security blanket. Each night, when the day's horrors finally ceased, he'd cry himself to sleep on Hexe's chest. The dog was the only creature he trusted. It was from Hexe that Roy learned animals could sense his thoughts before he had them—a revelation which, in hindsight, is truly ironic.

In order to escape the harsh reality of his life as a child, Roy would delve deeply into his imagination. He recalls becoming a fantasist at an early age. "Despite everything, I believed there was something better beyond my world. And so I made up stories, flew into other dimensions, drowned myself in books, roamed the fields with my animals and played pretend toreador with the bulls that grazed on the meadows of the marsh. Somewhere, I was confident, I would see the true colors of life."

This ability to invent something out of nothing, and block out the bad bits, prepared Roy for his future in show business, where make-believe is real and fantasies can easily materialize into reality. His happy public disposition—regardless of whatever went on around him—was perfect training for a celebrity in the making. He even kept his thoughts from his family, refusing to expose his inner turmoil to a single soul other than his animals.

He admitted, "No one saw me cry; that I reserved for the moments when I was alone with Hexe. With people around, you could beat me and I wouldn't shed a tear; you could never punish me enough to beat me down." Once again, a declaration that we know to be absolutely true, even to this day.

Despite all his travails, there was still a hint of optimism in Roy's life. His mother's best friend, "Aunt Paula," and her husband, "Uncle Emil," had founded the Bremen Zoo, and they arranged for Roy to have access to it whenever he wished. From age ten, Roy all but lived at the zoo whenever he wasn't in school. He gradually befriended the zoo staff and begged to help take care of the animals. At first, he accompanied the veterinarian on his rounds but soon was allowed to help handlers clean the cages of the tame animals, such as the flamingos.

Roy desperately wanted to enter the cage of the zoo's tigress but was told it was too dangerous. Then he fell in love with a cheetah named Chico—a sleek feline who would become the gateway to bigger and better things. Chico was two years old and had been caught in Somalia. The beast was still wild, of course, and before Roy could get too close he had to establish a relationship through the fence.

With no prior expertise in taming a cat, he improvised by instinct, making up techniques as he went along.

Said Roy: "It so happens that a cheetah can be made to purrrrrr like a house cat—if you can just get on its wavelength. As I had befriended many stray cats, I was able to sense Chico's emotions a lot more easily than I might have a tiger's. And so I began. I spent months talking to Chico through the iron bars, slowly building up his trust. Every day before I reached the zoo, I gave a special whistle call. By the time I appeared at the fence, Chico had returned my whistle with a chirping birdlike sound that was so sensitive you would never associate it with a powerful animal."

Roy and Chico soon became inseparable. Roy was given permission to enter Chico's den, and he nurtured the cat every spare moment he had. He scrubbed out Chico's cage and fed and groomed his new best friend. He then got a collar and took the cat out for walks, as if the large animal was Hexe. Chico became so accustomed to Roy that he wouldn't allow anyone else near, so Roy had to go the zoo every day. He recalls, "In the quiet of the cheetah's den, I would tell him little stories and speak from my soul to his."

Roy learned early on that animals, unlike human beings, are not judgmental. "My animals are the friends who will accept me always for what I am—rich or poor, fat or thin, dumb or intelligent."

And straight or gay.

At the tender age of thirteen, Roy made a decision to break away from the restrictions of Nordenham and travel the seas, leaving behind his beloved mother, and even more sadly, his two best friends, Hexe and Chico.

"In magic, anything is possible."
—*Siegfried Fischbacher*

Having had quite enough of carpet weaving, Siegfried, still in his teens and still infatuated with performing, decided to explore the exciting idea of a career in show business. He took a job as a dishwasher at a small hotel resort in Lago di Garda, Italy, worked hard and got promoted to barman. He took a shot at entertaining the guests with his Bavarian comedy routines, but his folksy humor went down like a lead balloon among the sophisticated crowd. After three years, he accepted that he just didn't fit in there and moved on to a resort in Brig, Switzerland. Although the owners liked him as a hotel worker and took him under their wing, he knew this wasn't a path to the future he envisioned. Siegfried had a talent for the service business and by now was quite experienced, but show business was the dream he'd never let go. Even though the hotel owners offered to let him run their establishment as manager, he declined and moved on yet again.

Then a thought struck him. *If I'm going to travel, why not find a job in the travel industry?* Not simply sitting in a boring office selling tickets, but something adventurous, something fun, like....

Suddenly, Siegfried was jolted by a brainstorm that would change his life forever. He applied for a job on a cruise ship and was hired immediately as a steward on the TS *Bremen,* a German luxury liner that sailed from the port of Bremerhaven to New York. This was the perfect setting for

Siegfried, affording him the chance to mingle with the elite and finally show off his talents as a magician.

At first, his only audience was the ship's crew. After hours, off-duty workers would go below decks, order drinks at the bar and watch Siegfried perform his magic tricks. Incredibly, his act clicked, word spread, and before long he was summoned by the ship's captain himself, who said:

"I hear you do magic."

Siegfried nodded.

"Show me some," ordered the captain.

Unfazed, Siegfried put on an impromptu show that flatly dazzled the captain, who told him, "Tonight, you perform for the passengers."

Siegfried's repertoire was limited, of course. All he had were the tricks he'd practiced as a wee boy. But although he used only the usual magic props that night—ordinary objects like cards, coins, cigarettes and razor blades—and really had nothing exceptional to perform, the audience absolutely loved him. His pretty-boy looks and angelic blond hair had all the ladies, and a few gentlemen, sighing as Siegfried made coins and cigarettes disappear and swallowed twenty razor blades, then made them reappear, hooked to a long string. His act went over so incredibly well that the captain ordered him to replace the ship's regularly scheduled talent show with a half-hour solo stint of his own.

Thrilled, Siegfried took his first major step as a professional; he named himself "Delmare the Magician," or "magician from the sea." It was a rather ironic choice, considering that he was perpetually seasick.

Determined to keep his audience entertained non-stop during his thirty-minute time slot, Siegfried introduced rabbits and doves, then began performing two shows a night to accommodate his growing fan base. When he needed assistance with props and synchronizing his stage lighting, he'd ask another steward to help out. One night, when he was running late and still hadn't found an assistant, his eyes fell upon a young boy whose cabin was across the hall from his own.

The lad was skinny and pubescent but had an endearing, vulnerable way about him. With his short, dark brown hair and charming grin, he quickly melted the hearts of nearly every woman aboard. Even the captain was not immune to the boy's charm, promoting him to the post of personal valet.

Siegfried roped Roy into working for him that night, and after the show, as was his custom, he invited his young assistant *du jour* for a beer. As Siegfried sipped his brew, he waited for the compliments that were usually forthcoming, but the boy sat speechless. Siegfried finally broke the silence and asked, "Well, what did you think of the show?"

The boy didn't respond. Siegfried blinked. What on earth was wrong with this imbecile? He was acting very nervous and fidgety. But when the lad finally spoke, he dropped a bombshell.

"Well, the audience really liked you," he said hesitantly, "and it's great that you can do all those tricks, but…quite honestly I didn't really like the show that much. The magic seems so…predictable."

Siegfried couldn't believe his ears. *What? How dare he?* Then he thought, almost charitably, *Clearly, this smug little punk doesn't know any better. The kid's just too young to understand my talents.*

Incredibly, Siegfried just couldn't bring himself to be angry with the strangely appealing lad. At that moment, some deeply felt spark flashed between Siegfried Fischbacher and Roy Horn, igniting a relationship that would endure over four decades. The two youngsters, cruising aboard the TS *Bremen,* had each found his soulmate, and—although they didn't yet know it—were destined to embark on a lifetime of performing tricks; in every sense of the word.

That first night, when Siegfried recovered from his surprise at Roy's critique, he demanded indignantly, "Well, if you're so smart, what would you do to improve my act?"

Roy was ready with an answer. He'd already been plotting.

"If you can make a rabbit and a dove appear and disappear, then could you do the very same thing with a bigger animal...say, a cheetah?"

Siegfried, assuming he was being tested by the pushy kid, had far too much pride to appear anything less than absolutely confident. "In magic," he said at last, "*anything is possible.*"

Those words instantly became the motto by which the two would live the rest of their lives.

Siegfried and Roy had no opportunity to speak again until the ship's next voyage to New York. One night after they'd embarked, Roy knocked on Siegfried's cabin door. The younger boy whispered, "I have a surprise for you." Leading the way to his cabin, he opened the door—and cocky, cool Siegfried froze in abject terror. Crouched on Roy's bunk bed like a demon, back arched, snarling and spitting, was a live cheetah, looking ready to pounce.

Smiling at Siegfried's reaction, Roy quickly told him, "Just be calm, it's okay. This is a cheetah. He's my pet, and his name is Chico. Don't worry, he won't hurt you."

As Siegfried stood quaking, Roy explained how he'd taken Chico from the zoo in Bremen and smuggled him aboard the ship in his laundry bag. No one had laid eyes on Chico until Roy showed him to Siegfried. And given Chico's reaction to the first stranger he'd encountered outside of a cage, that was a truly good thing. Although tame and friendly around Roy, the cheetah had instantly eyeballed Siegfried like prey, flashing his formidable set of predator's teeth. After the initial shock, Siegfried quickly backed out of Roy's cabin and escaped back to his own.

The next day, Roy kept hounding Siegfried, asking him over and over, "Well, what do you think?"

Think about what? That was Siegfried's first thought. *What on earth was he supposed to do with this creature?* Siegfried was stunned by Roy's audacity. Imagine, smuggling a wild animal aboard a cruise ship? He feared for both of their jobs if the captain found out about Chico. Yet Siegfried couldn't help feeling a grudging admiration for this amazing young boy, who'd managed to secretly sneak the cheetah aboard, and—even more impressive—knew how to handle a wild animal that Siegfried was almost too terrified to even look at.

"Roy, what are you going to do when the captain finds out?" he demanded.

"Look, we just won't tell him yet," Roy replied coolly. "But when he sees you do your magic act with a live cheetah, he'll love it. And he'll understand, I promise you."

Siegfried was skeptical. But he had to admit that the thought of incorporating a cheetah into his magic act excited him. It would add a unique element to his performance; bring him stature as a magician and performer. He decided he would take the chance.

On his next trip ashore, Siegfried purchased a stuffed leopard he'd spotted in a souvenir shop; it wasn't a cheetah, but it was close enough. He cut the toy's legs and tail off and sewed each part up so the stuffing wouldn't fall out. Then he put the fake kitty back together again. In due course, the ship's carpenter delivered a box he'd been asked to construct. Now Siegfried was ready. He was about to debut the embryonic act that would launch his glittering career.

On the night of the performance, Siegfried did his usual sequence of magic tricks and then asked Roy to bring out the box and a basket containing the chopped-up toy leopard. Siegfried began his illusion by dramatically pulling out the faux cat, tearing off its limbs one by one and tossing each part across the stage and into the box. He then closed the box's lid as the ship's band played a suspense-building crescendo, the drummer rolling his timpani as the spotlight narrowed on the box.

Suddenly, the lid banged open, and there stood Chico the Cheetah—restrained by a chain Roy was secretly holding—snarling and flashing his teeth as the audience gasped. Amazingly, a toy kitty had become...a live jungle beast! It was sheer magic—until Chico added a very scary, unrehearsed flourish. Confused by the crowd, the loud music and applause, he began hissing and snarling loudly, then sprang off the box and stalked straight through the audience to the end of the dance floor. Roy, in utter shock, dropped the restraining chain. As he ran to catch up with his cat, the metal clanked loudly on the parquet floor.

Chico bounded up the grand staircase of the ship's ballroom with Roy following behind. When the cat reached the top of the stairs, he stopped, turned, and dramatically faced the audience below as if to say, "Behold the King of the Jungle!" The audience leapt to its feet, wildly applauding the three of them: Siegfried, Roy and Chico. Only one person didn't join the standing ovation: the furious captain, who fired Siegfried and Roy that very night. They were ordered to leave the ship, along with their damn cat, the moment the ship docked.

"Nothing succeeds like success," as one old saying goes; another is, "Some people have all the luck." The very next day, Siegfried and Roy had a new job. The American president of another shipping company, North German Lloyd, happened to be aboard, and liked the jungle illusion so much that he offered the magical duo, and their wild cat, a job on one of his company's Caribbean cruise liners.

Chico, of course, was now as much a part of the act as Siegfried's magic. And since Roy was the only person who could control the cheetah, Siegfried had no option but to partner up with him. The two performed together on Caribbean cruise liners for three years. They were no longer stewards but full-time entertainers.

It turned out that working the cruise ships helped the duo develop their act. Having to perform for the same audiences on board day after day was a challenge. Siegfried was forced to invent new illusions to keep his repertoire fresh. He would spend hours on end in solitude, imagining and testing new tricks, and studying magic books. In the evenings, he'd experiment, each audience reaction unerringly telling him whether a new trick worked or not.

During these three years, Siegfried and Roy developed a bond, based predominantly upon Siegfried leading the way toward the future and Roy following along. On his own, it's unlikely Roy would have foreseen a career in show business or magic, but once again, an animal, namely Chico, had guided him into this new world. For Roy, animals were magic beings he could trust, and they'd always drive his ambition.

Having found a partner for the first time in his life, Roy was finally able to trust a human being the way he trusted his animals. He grew to depend on Siegfried for a sense of purpose, and he recalls that at this point in his life, "my focus was all on Siegfried and what he had to offer. Siegfried was, very simply, the key to a different world. He had the power to put my cheetah in the show. He also had the power to bring me into a wholesome world."

Roy was still lost in his fantastical world of escapism at age sixteen and totally influenced by the motivated Siegfried, five years his senior. As Roy once put it, Siegfried represented "the world I wanted to escape to, to live in, to enjoy. It was an extension of the make-believe world I had lived in for so long."

He'd never forget hearing Siegfried say that in magic, anything is possible. That was magic to Roy's ears; an endorsement of the dream he longed one day to live.

But even though blind faith in Siegfried gave Roy confidence, it also put a heavy responsibility on his shoulders. He was determined to make sure Siegfried achieved his goal of becoming the greatest living magician. In turn, Siegfried felt he had to live up to Roy's expectations. The two had found the perfect partnership. Their personalities clashed *and* complemented each other. Roy, always the fantasist; Siegfried, ever practical, encouraging Roy's far-out ideas, but always bringing him back to reality. Together, they would achieve far more than either one had ever hoped for on his own.

As they honed their act together, Siegfried taught Roy everything he knew about magic: how to execute tricks and perform them dramatically, always building toward the illustrious climax. Most important of all, Siegfried taught Roy how to manipulate the minds of audience members, allowing them to see exactly what you want them to—and nothing more.

The undisputed crown jewel of their act, of course, was Chico. No performers had a wild animal like their cheetah. It made them unique, and that, says Siegfried, "is the true secret of magic."

However unique they were in those early days, however, Siegfried realized that the novelty of the cheetah would eventually wear off, so he began incorporating more illusions into their act, involving Roy even more.

Roy's first illusion was a levitation, which he performed flawlessly, despite the handicap of being aboard a rocking ship. Next, Siegfried adapted Houdini's famous "Metamorphosis"—an illusion they worked into their act and constantly refined throughout their career, always on a progressively larger scale.

Their Houdini illusion begins with a trunk—which, in magical terms, is called a "substitution trunk." After it's rolled onstage, Roy handcuffs himself, then gets tied in a sack and locked inside. The trunk is closed and padlocked. Once the audience is made to believe the trunk is fastened, and there's no way for Roy to escape, Siegfried throws a big hoop—covered in cloth to form an opaque cylinder—over him. But by the time it flutters back down, Roy is seen standing atop the trunk, and Siegfried is discovered inside, handcuffed and tied in the sack. This trick was always followed by their debut illusion, in which Siegfried tears apart the stuffed toy, throws the pieces in the trunk, and Chico pops out snarling.

Siegfried then added a third exchange that involved Chico. Instead of throwing the stuffed toy pieces inside the trunk, Roy would jump inside it, and magically transform himself into a cheetah!

Siegfried wrote, "It was this illusion that really started the organic growth of our act. All illusions are derived from five basic ideas: appearance, disappearance, transformation, levitation, and sawing. The challenge for a magician is to put these principles into his own wrapping or adapt them to his given situation. Because I had to make it work for our situation—Roy's, Chico's, and mine—it was natural that the Metamorphosis would evolve into a triple effect.

"And out of that came our trademark of effortlessly rolling three illusions into one."

During these three years, Siegfried and Roy clung to each other—they had no one else. But who else did they need? During his days on the *Bremen*, Siegfried had gone back to see his mother just once, despite the fact that Maria had told him to never return. When he'd arrived at his childhood home, his parents looked so fragile and aged since he'd seen them last, and his father was so ill, that he knew neither of them would live much longer. After Siegfried arrived, Maria wanted to visit her daughter, Margot, so she asked Siegfried to take her to the train station. As he saw his mother off, she said, "You know I have only one worry now in my life. I'm not worried about your brother; he has a family and a business. Margot has found her calling and has chosen a life for herself. My only worry is you, Siegfried."

It was a heavy moment. "Ma, you don't have to worry. The time will come when you'll be very proud of me, I promise," he reassured her.

Their eyes welled with tears as she boarded the train, and as Siegfried waved goodbye, he suddenly knew that this was the last time he would see his mother. She died shortly after, and his father passed away one year later. Neither of his parents ever witnessed the success he would achieve.

Roy, who could never spend too much time away from his mother until the day she died and beyond, would invite Johanna and Aunt Paula to visit him on special occasions; Johanna would later move to Las Vegas and adopt Siegfried as one of her own.

However, on the water, they only had each other. Roy described his relationship with Siegfried at that time as a fraternal one, but it was already much more than that.

"America! Show business! Here we come!"
—Roy Horn

Performing on cruise ships challenged young Siegfried and Roy to constantly sharpen their act and bring the audience screaming to its feet night after night. But inevitably, the excitement wore off as they became more confident and professional. The seafaring show-boaters were experienced hands now and eager to sail on to new adventures.

Working onboard had an advantage they'd begun to exploit. Cruise ships attracted an endless stream of showbiz professionals, who were aboard either as performers or paying guests. Siegfried and Roy chatted them all up, figuring that one of these pros might help them jump ship and find safe harbor with a great gig on dry land. Then they met Elmarie Wendel, who seemed like an answer to their prayers. Elmarie, a German-American comedienne who performed on the ship, loved Siegfried and Roy's act and set up a meeting for the starry-eyed boys with her New York agent, Mark Leddy.

The meeting was a disaster. Leddy took an instant dislike to Siegfried, whom he marked as an Aryan Nazi, and ranted about his own family who had experienced great pain at the hands of Germany during World War II.

Siegfried and Roy were aghast at Leddy's vicious, unfounded attack. At that point in their young lives, the Germans boys could barely string together an English sentence between them—much less fight back in the language effectively—but they tried. And that just made the meeting worse. Leddy's unprincipled verbal assault stunned them. They'd both just been little boys during the war, and here was an American who passionately hated them just for being German. Used to being praised night after night by audiences, many of them Americans, they were suddenly being reviled as mass murderers.

Just to make it worse, Leddy announced nastily that he wasn't impressed by their act. He called it "ordinary"—an insult that staggered the young magicians, who'd worked so hard to be creative and different.

Siegfried, angered by Leddy's unwarranted put-down of both their heritage and talent, exploded. In the best English he could muster, the young German drew himself up and snapped: "Mr. Leddy, I zink you vant to tell me that vee are not good enough for you. Vell, I vill tell you something. I'm gonna leave here now. And you gonna hear from us."

In actuality, Leddy never heard from Siegfried or Roy ever again. Nor did any other agent. Remaining true to themselves, and to the memory of that ugly day in New York, the lads made a vow: they would stay united forever, no matter what prejudices they were forced to endure. Leddy's overbearing arrogance had outraged them, but it had also stiffened their spines. From that day forward, Siegfried and Roy refused to sign with any agent.

Their meeting with Leddy aside, Siegfried and Roy gradually began to realize that overcoming the "Nazi" image that tainted Germany after the Second World War would be incredibly difficult. Considering the barriers of prejudice the duo faced, breaking into the American entertainment industry in the second half of the century was an uphill battle that made their subsequent stardom in America a phenomenal achievement.

Even years later in 1989, after their success in Las Vegas, Siegfried and Roy would have to fight to overcome their critics' unsubstantiated first impressions. When they were booked to play Radio City Music Hall, show business insiders and critics sneered at first that it had to be a joke; New York was where "true" artists escaped the neon and glitz of tacky venues like Vegas. Everyone thought Bernie

Yuman, the tough hustler who'd signed on as the German duo's lifetime manager, was crazy for booking a Las Vegas magic act in Manhattan, the center of serious theater in America—no matter how popular they might be on the Strip.

Buoyed by Yuman's unflagging confidence and a belief in their own talent, Siegfried and Roy not only played Radio City, they sold out three-and-a-half weeks of performances, breaking a fifty-seven-year box-office record. Commenting on the engagement, Roy said simply, "We haven't done too badly for a couple of immigrants.... When two guys come from Germany with absolutely nothing, it's a great thing to have your name in lights." Two stubborn "krauts" had proved agent Leddy, and every other skeptic, dead wrong. German heads held high, nostrils flaring, Siegfried and Roy breathed in the sweet smell of success.

The break that had finally catapulted them from the high seas to heady heights on dry land occurred just as they'd guessed it might: via another passenger on their cruise ship, named Frau Fritz. She owned the Astoria Theatre in Bremen, loved the act and offered the boys a month-long gig, performing two fifteen-minute sets a day. They accepted, of course, but were immediately beset by the normal fears of facing a completely new setting and new expectations. They had different music, lighting cues, and costume changes to contend with, and their show needed to be re-staged for the larger scaled theater.

Although they pulled it all together, their first performance at the Astoria almost didn't happen. Siegfried collapsed in a horrible bout of stage fright just before their debut. A bright future suddenly looked dark, but Roy brought Siegfried back to life with a hotdog and Coca-Cola from a street vendor. Roy had learned how to calm the nerves of the man who'd become his life partner. And it didn't hurt that Frau Fritz dropped by to gush about how great they'd looked in rehearsals the night before. So calories and encouragement saved the day. Super-confident, Siegfried strode onstage that night and performed the first in a string of stellar shows at the Astoria.

Roy's intuition in helping Siegfried recover from his funk was an important marker in their developing relationship. Roy observed, "I could never allow us both to feel the same thing at the same time because it would stifle us, and we both would be vulnerable." He knew the balance that was necessary for the team to work and, as he puts it, the little tricks that would keep their "relationship sane."

During those tough years in Europe, the boys learned much more than how to survive as a team; they learned how to survive, period!

Although working the European nightclub circuit was an upgrade from the cruise ship, performing on smaller, strip club-type stages took some getting used to. The audiences were different; often full of strange, seedy nightlife characters. Siegfried observed: "If they wanted to see a magician at all, it was one who had a generously endowed, scantily-dressed female assistant." To say the boys were working out of their element was a gross understatement.

Even more difficult than altering their act to fit club venues was transporting—and being forced to conceal—their pet cheetah, Chico. Siegfried remembers having to sneak the beast, which was impossible to disguise as a house cat, into bed and breakfasts on a leash. Under tight financial restrictions, their main concern at dinnertime was being able to afford lean cuts of meat for Chico. So while the cat ate like a king, Siegfried and Roy often made do with burnt potatoes. They willingly sacrificed luxuries in their struggle to achieve the ultimate dream: a booking at the Lido or Folies-Bergère in Paris.

To Siegfried more so than Roy, Paris was the end-all of the world's artistic cities. It was every performer's fantasyville, and Siegfried knew he'd feel right at home among its sophisticated, cultured natives.

From the Astoria, Siegfried and Roy and their half-hour magic act journeyed to Hamburg, then on to Switzerland, an important stop on the road to the bigtime, with lots of surprises along the way. The country boys from Germany were nothing if not naïve and still quite inexperienced when it came to show business. On one occasion, they were offered a show at the Eden-Saloon in Berlin, owned by Rolf Eden, a playboy of the time, which was supposedly the "it" place to perform. However, they arrived to find a club that was not only incredibly small, but it also featured transvestite strippers.

Worse, they were stunned to see themselves head-lined as a wild animal act: "COME SEE THE FEROCIOUS CHICO! HE WILL DAZZLE YOU!" The lads were insulted to discover they'd gotten second billing to their cheetah.

While the club was packed every night, the audiences were mostly there for the drag-queen strippers. It was hardly the venue for a magic act, but Siegfried and Roy worked laboriously to win over the crowds at the Eden-Saloon, and they finally succeeded. The duo had developed what would become a key factor in their success: unashamed sincerity onstage. What made Siegfried and Roy unique wherever they appeared—in post-war Europe or decades later in Las Vegas—was unfaltering commitment to their show and their obvious passion for performing. They learned how to transmit positive energy—their own special brand of karma—to live audiences, breaking down whatever initial resistance they encountered. Even in Berlin, one of the darkest and most corrupt cities in all of Europe at the time, they prevailed with the power of their magic and their mysticism.

An even more amazing example of Siegfried and Roy's belief in their own show came when Kalanag, the greatest magician of his time, suddenly died and his widow offered the up-and-coming German lads the opportunity to take over his act and follow in his footsteps. They would be given all of Kalanag's resources: his secrets, his home, and his huge throng of fans. Siegfried was humbled by the offer. He'd admired the great magician as a child and still remembered the thrilling day Father Johann took him to see the show.

Still, he could not fathom the idea of simply taking another magician's place. He was ready to make his own mark in the magic world, with the help of the one person he truly admired; the man he would one day openly admit was his lover, Roy Horn. Forty years after their first European adventure, Siegfried and Roy would finally announce their homosexuality to the world in a *National Enquirer* exclusive.

However important Roy was to Siegfried's success—or vice versa—it's quite clear in hindsight that the two couldn't have climbed the heights without each other. In the beginning, Roy was unquestionably sidelined. His main duties were to look after the animals and follow Siegfried's orders. He had little opportunity to shine under the shadow cast by his incandescent partner. But finally, the time came for him to join Siegfried onstage, and when it happened, it felt like a natural, inevitable evolution.

In Switzerland, Siegfried and Roy were afforded another fantastic opportunity: Freddy Knie, owner of the famed Circus Knie, had agreed to watch their act. For Roy, who dreamed of working with wild animals like elephants and lions, the prospect of Circus Knie was especially thrilling. Unfortunately, the night that Mr. Knie chose to join the audience, Chico turned in a bizarre performance. Toward the end of the show, when he was supposed to jump out of the trunk, the cheetah—spooked by the smell of wild animals exuding from the nearby Circus Knie—burst out of the trunk and took off running straight out of the theater.

That's showbiz, as they say. The Circus Knie was not to be.

Nearing their big breakthrough, although they didn't know it yet, Siegfried and Roy continued working and dreaming, aiming for a booking at one of the Parisian Folies. They groaned over what looked like another obstacle in the road when they took a meeting at Cabaret Tabaris, owned by Madame Pashe, a testy French-Swiss woman infamous for the near-impossible standards she imposed on performers at her club. The boys were reassured—to say the least!—when Madame not only loved their performance but recommended that they perform nightly at the nearby casino of Monte Carlo after finishing at her club.

From Monte Carlo they were offered the opportunity to perform at the Sporting Club for the annual Red Cross Gala: La Gala des Rois. Siegfried loves reminiscing about this momentous occasion: "To think that in less than nine months we had gone from walking off the street into striptease joints, to actually performing for Grace Kelly—from hookers to royalty!"

The Prince and Princess of Monaco were not the only celebrities in attendance that first night Siegfried and Roy performed for them; they were joined by glittering stars Sophia Loren, Cary Grant, Maria Callas, Elizabeth Taylor, and more.

For two German boys still dreaming of making it big, this event was overwhelming. It took them out of their element. "It wasn't really stage fright," Siegfried said about that evening, "but more the thought of performing in so elegant an atmosphere before people whom I admired. I felt so out of place. How could Siegfried of Rosenheim live up to this evening?"

Live up to it he did, but it seemed nothing could alleviate Siegfried's creeping feelings of inadequacy—the sad, hard-to-shed baggage of a poor and lonely childhood.

The duo's task didn't end with their invitation to the Gala, however. They still had a big performance ahead of them; not just for the huge audience, but for a host of celebrities that Siegfried and Roy had idolized as children and who were now their peers.

Everything went as planned until the moment of the Metamorphosis, the grand finale of their act. Chico jumped out of the trunk, and this time—spooked by fireworks that were exploding outside the picture windows—he streaked up the center aisle through the audience. Roy, trying to hide his surprise at Chico's ad-lib, followed him up the aisle as if it were all just part of his act, waving to the cheering crowd, and winning a standing ovation. Later, he admitted he'd faked his composure that night, a skill he cultivated over the years. Never would he allow an audience to witness his inner fears.

Both performers worried that the show had been ruined by Chico's unexpected move, but they garnered rave reviews. "Gala Des Rois, Siegfried and Roy, The New Kings," headlined newspapers the next day.

That settled it: no longer was it "Siegfried & Partner" performing to sold-out crowds. From now on, it would be "Siegfried & Roy" (from the French "Rois" for King), the name by which millions would grow to know them. Uwe Ludwig Horn would never again be known as *Uwe*, not to his fans at least. And it's quite likely Roy adopted his name from the French headline praising their Gala performance. For a boy who felt as if he'd been in the shadows his whole life, the English name for King, "Roy," had a nice ring.

Beyond inspiring their new title of "Siegfried & Roy," the response to their performance that night gave the duo a confidence boost like no other; they were a "special act" indeed. What's more, their new press notices would open the door to bigger and better arenas. Next stop: Las Vegas, by way of Paris, and the Folies-Bergère.

Their offer for Folies-Bergère came about in an unexpected way. By this time, they'd gone from their grand performance at the Gala in Monte Carlo to the city of Nice, and now they were in Madrid at the Passaboga. Although the club was smaller (most were after Monte Carlo), Roy "loved the Latin temperament, the colorful personalities, the constant eye-rolling that made every situation seem like high drama, and the passion the Spaniards put into everyday life." Without a doubt, this passion triggered Siegfried and Roy's burgeoning sexuality; it felt good to loosen up after keeping everything so tightly under wraps in Switzerland and Germany.

While touring Europe, Siegfried and Roy had always aspired to perform at the renowned Lido in Paris. When the Lido's booker, René Fraday, sent a telegram informing them he'd heard about their act and was planning to catch them at the Passaboga, they were overjoyed.

Every night thereafter, the two young men anticipated Monsieur Fraday sitting in the audience, which made them even more nervous about their delivery. One night in 1967, after finishing an especially amazing performance—both men could feel the electricity onstage—they received a telegram. Thinking it was Monsieur Fraday, whose visit they had been expecting, they'd already devised a plan: Siegfried would meet with him first and negotiate, calling upon Roy only if he had any questions or concerns about the contract.

Upon meeting the representative at the restaurant that night, Siegfried was shocked to discover Tony Azzie, the charming and incredibly handsome Lebanese booker from the Folies in Paris. Tony, it turned out, desperately needed a last-minute revue act for the Folies show in Las Vegas.

This was music to Roy's ears, and had it been up to him alone, he would have snapped up the offer. The chance to voyage across the Atlantic and start anew in Las Vegas was enticing to the duo's younger member. Better yet, Azzie was offering a huge sum of money, not to mention a shower of compliments in his effort to seduce them away from Europe.

Despite the excitement of being offered a dream show in Las Vegas, then Paris, the boys held out for a meeting with Monsieur René Fraday, the tall, nervous Artistic Director of the prestigious Lido. The Lido had racked up many kudos for its reputation of discovering acts with style. The Folies, by contrast, was more of a Can Can parlor; too similar, perhaps, to the bawdy cabaret nightclubs they'd frequented in Europe.

However, when Monsieur Fraday visited them the following night, he left Siegfried and Roy with a bitter taste in their mouths. The French booker came on with an air of Parisian aloofness and cut straight to the punch with a blow to Siegfried's fragile ego. Fraday told him, "Well, I reely zought you would be talleur. You shood poot leefts in your shoos." He continued to nag Siegfried about the color of his beautifully coiffed hair as being "a leetle too blond."

And doves in their act? "Others have done it," sniffed Fraday. Even transporting Chico's trunk would be "très difficile." The boys were wise to Fraday's tactic—degrading them so they'd accept less money. But this was going too far!

Fraday's negative comments aside, their performance that night was not quite as spectacular as it had been on the night Azzie attended. To young artists strongly swayed by energy and karma, this was an important factor; perhaps it was an ominous sign when their show didn't sizzle for Fraday that night.

To confuse matters for the naïve performers even further, they ran into a group of little, old American ladies outside of the theater in Spain that night—eerily similar to the fans that reporter Steve Freiss would describe after Roy's tragic mauling forty years later. On the day the "Siegfried & Roy" show was permanently canceled in 2003, "an 80-year-old lady from rural Illinois with a 'WHAT WOULD JESUS DO?' pin on her lapel, and an ornate cross around her neck" stood outside The Mirage in mourning.

While they were touring Spain in 1967, the American women outside the Passaboga did their best to convince Siegfried and Roy to cross the Atlantic; their comment to the boys would prove to be prophetic: "Oh, you and your partner are terrific," the ladies in Spain told Siegfried and Roy. "Have you ever performed in America? You should! You're absolutely tailor-made for Las Vegas.... You would be fantastic there. We love the animals."

If that didn't set Siegfried's mind spinning, what would?

Still, Siegfried and Roy were not quite ready to make their decision. Azzie had asked them to perform once for the owners of the Folies, and they figured it was a good opportunity to also visit the Lido in Paris and see if it lived up to its buzz.

At the Folies, they performed beautifully, getting three curtain calls and a standing ovation—not only from the audience but from stagehands and dancers in the wings. The owner finalized his offer to them that night: one year in Las Vegas, then a year in Paris.

Upon visiting the Lido, Roy felt some initial disappointment about the theater's look, but knew its prestige surpassed any venue in Paris—and possibly the world. This particular evening they were meeting with Monsieur Louis-Guerin, the general director of the Lido, who was the epitome of a Parisian show-runner: well-dressed, fastidious, and handsomely charismatic. He was not thrilled by Siegfried and Roy's request to go to Las Vegas before setting up their act in Paris. In Louis-Guerin's world, an act debuted at the original Lido, then went on to the Lido in Vegas. Never the other way around...not in a million years.

"Well," he prophesied, "eef you do go with the Folies in Vegas, you weel neveur work again in Parie. Neveur. Don't even botheur coming to zee Lido when you reteurn."

Needless to say, the boys took their chances with Azzie and his high-rolling offer. Little did they know how important that one decision would play out in their future as performers.

*   *   *

Although it's said that, "What happens in Vegas, stays in Vegas," Siegfried and Roy looked to defy that statement in the 1960s—at least in the beginning. Their first show at the Tropicana, as part of the French Folies production, did not go as well as they'd hoped. Just three months later, after a second offer from Fraday and the Lido in Paris, they accepted joyfully and it was back to Europe for the young performers.

The story of that first gig in Las Vegas is perhaps the duo's favorite. Booked at the Tropicana hotel as part of the Folies' American show, the hotel owner, Mr. Houssels, did nothing to disguise his cynicism. Houssels groaned, "Boys, I have to tell you, magic don't work in this town."

Today, the world knows just how wrong Mr. Houssels was, but at the time, Siegfried could not help but take his put-down personally. He considered it a bad omen of what was to come in that dusty desert town. "When we arrived," he recalls, "entertainment had not yet evolved from, uh, how do you say it...?"

"T&A."

However right Mr. Houssels might have been at the time, what he could not have anticipated was the astounding effect Siegfried and Roy would have—not only on magic but on the future of Las Vegas!

Today, magic is intrinsic to the town. But before Siegfried and Roy, magic acts were simply vaudevillian teasers before the headline show. In those days, Las Vegas was very much "Tits & Ass." Siegfried described it perfectly: "It was a gambler's town, pure and simple, and the Rat Pack was in charge.... Entertainment was no more than just a rest period between gambling sessions—you know, bring on the scantily clad showgirls, strike up the band, tell some jokes and...ba-ba-boom, you've got a show."

Siegfried and Roy would be the first magicians to have an entire extravaganza built around their act, thereby carving out a niche that would inspire others to follow in their footsteps: Las Vegas suddenly found itself brimming with Siegfried and Roy impersonators. The duo would pave the way for such world-famous performers as David Copperfield, Lance Burton, and Penn & Teller, irreversibly increasing the value of magic acts and their popularity with audiences around the world.

Their manager, Bernie Yuman, recalled their effect on the town: "After them, every show had a magician. I mean, there are Elvis impersonators everywhere, and there are Siegfried and Roy impersonators everywhere."

Siegfried and Roy, beyond starting a craze for magic in a town where gambling was god, were a major part of Las Vegas' transformation into a family vacation mecca. The German boys, "never understanding the fascination with topless women in shows" anyway, covered up their showgirls and made their act a child-friendly phenomenon in "the town that never sleeps. Siegfried and Roy started the non-nude show," says Yuman—making the duo a "first" in what would become a major Las Vegas trend later popularized by Steve Wynn and his family-targeted resorts.

Houssels couldn't have known it at the time—nor did our naïve German duo—but very soon Siegfried and Roy would share top billing on the Strip's largest marquee!

Back in Las Vegas in 1967, though, the two were living examples of the phrase: "If anything can go wrong, it will!"

Their opening night at the Tropicana followed in this cursed tradition. In yet another memorable finale by Chico, the cat jumped up out of the trunk, and then leaped into the orchestra pit, distracted by a light reflecting off Ray Sinatra, the orchestra leader. Chico managed to snatch Mr. Sinatra's toupee and spring into mid-air with the hairpiece in his jaws, before landing atop the piano as the stunned audience strained to keep up with the hilarious action.

The only positive outcome of that debacle was Roy's tighter integration into the show. From that night on, Siegfried's partner would walk their unpredictable cheetah from the trunk to the front of the stage, giving Roy a showcase role in their partnership.

From that refinement, the finale grew even more exciting, and eventually Siegfried got the idea that Roy should be in the cage with the tiger so that they'd both appear at the same time. For this trick, they would use the troupe's newest addition: a loving cheetah named Simba. For the new Metamorphosis sequence, they'd build a giant cage, which would be dropped from the ceiling. Then, for a surprise ending, Roy and one cat would end up inside the cage; the other would pop out of the trunk.

This new exposure to the audience gave Roy a sense of value to the relationship that he'd rarely experienced. "Once I got to share the applause at the Tropicana, I realized my second-class status had been bothering me, but I hadn't been able to verbalize it. I had begun to feel a little bit like a cat handler.... When Siegfried conceived the new illusion, I was determined to find a way for me to be a presenter of the magic with him. The only way that could happen was if we brought yet another person into the illusion.... Enter Virginia."

Virginia, a gorgeous showgirl type, seductive and coquettish onstage, was the sexy assistant audiences were accustomed to seeing with magic acts. Offstage, Virginia became the duo's romantic pawn; both men would go on to describe her as a "girlfriend." But Virginia's alleged "intimate" relationship with Siegfried and Roy was as much a part of the show as the tigers or costumes, even though they would talk about how fiercely they'd fought over her. "Finally, she wanted one of us to marry her," Roy says, "and either one of us would do. So, as you can see, things got a bit tricky."

Tricky indeed.

During these early years, Siegfried and Roy were still feeling out their sexuality. When a voluptuous young lady named Lynette replaced Virginia as the lead female in the show, she confided to a friend that she'd slept with Roy while vacationing in Acapulco. Yet it appears that at the time of Lynette's claim, Siegfried and Roy were very likely in the throes of their own passionate affair.

One thing Virginia had always delighted in doing was pushing Roy to share the limelight with his domineering partner. This new situation intrigued everyone, even Siegfried, who admitted, "Underneath the surface there was something more emotional happening—like the competition between two men who had been working together for seven years."

As for the work itself, everything was going well enough—but every night that Siegfried was forced to endure the Tropicana's version of the Folies-Bergère, he regretted their decision to leave Paris. Little did he know that help was on the way. Monsieur René Fraday of the Paris Lido flew in to see Siegfried and Roy's show and decided to re-offer them a contract. Although Siegfried couldn't wait to perform again at the *crème de la crème* of Paris venues, he wasn't desperate enough to give the Lido a Las Vegas-caliber show for the lowball money they were offering. In the contract the duo finally signed, they agreed to do the act they'd performed in Madrid, without Simba and the new finale.

But once back in Paris, the boys felt like they might have outsmarted themselves. They were bored with the stripped-down act, and fretted that "Siegfried & Roy" were even *more* of a bore to their public. It seemed silly to be performing at a level less than their very best. They were not simply losing money…they were losing face; or so they thought.

So Siegfried came up a new way to present the big finale. Instead of lowering Chico's box from the ceiling—a physical impossibility in their new theater at the Lido—it would be dramatically wheeled onstage as he marched beside it. And Roy, with his newfound confidence, came up with a few tips for ringmaster Siegfried that would become the act's new signature.

"Siegfried," Roy told him, "I've noticed how you let the cheetah present himself. You have to present the cheetah, not the other way around. You are the representative, you are the star. And another thing: You have to be different. You're now going to be mysterious...!"

He went on to describe an interesting twist on the traditional big bow that stage performers take at the end of a routine. Instead, said Roy, Siegfried should simply nod his head at the audience as the lights slowly dim until they finally show just the upper half of his body, and then...darkness.

Audiences loved the new staging, and the duo renegotiated their contract for bigger money. Roy, who was no longer a part of the finale, devised another way to tweak the act and insert himself into the performance. He came up with his own signature style of dress: gold chains, open shirts, tight pants, and boots meant to reflect his self-proclaimed "untamed, animalistic personality." Siegfried didn't fail to notice the attention Roy was getting. Having a naturally jealous personality, he grumbled a bit, but Roy's new look stayed.

Three years more in Paris—theirs was the longest contract the Lido had ever signed—flew by. Siegfried and Roy used the time wisely to change their act: new staging, a new rhythm that Siegfried labeled "fast-paced illusion," his new "mysterious" stage presence...and the boys even changed a few things at the Lido itself. For example, they insisted that waiters wear red jackets instead of blinding white because it upset their animals, so the staff wears red to this day.

One night, the duo was approached by the Lido's general director, Monsieur Louis-Guerin, who asked them to go back to Las Vegas and open the Lido show at the Stardust

Hotel. Siegfried—again, to no one's surprise—didn't want to leave Paris for Las Vegas. In his eyes, they'd just made a home for themselves, and he didn't feel that their last trip to the Strip had been a tremendous success.

Roy, on the other hand, loved the idea.

"This is the greatest thing that could happen. America! I love it. It's the greatest country in the world. We'll be conquering it all the way. Please, Siegfried, we've got to go."

It was understandable why Siegfried felt uneasy about moving to Las Vegas: He was very much a son of Rosenheim, his provincial hometown in Bavaria, populated mainly by conservative peasants who rarely ventured out into the world. He was certainly not acclimated to razzmatazz cities like Las Vegas. The self-proclaimed "mountain boy" had traveled extensively since leaving Bavaria, but he still felt unsettled by the idea of living in the Mojave Desert Disneyland for adults.

Roy was also from a small town in Germany, but his heritage was notably different. He was born in Nordenham, in northwestern Germany, which was linked to the major port of Bremerhaven and the North Sea by the Weser River. Bremen, a member of the Hanseatic League set up in the Middle Ages to protect merchant associations bordering the Baltic Sea, the North Sea and most of Northern Europe, was a far more sophisticated, progressive area. Roy adjusted to Las Vegas with the ease and enthusiasm of a hyperactive chameleon, the result of his more open-minded upbringing. He hit the town accompanied by a flock of pink flamingos from his uncle's zoo and two cheetahs. He bought himself a silver Thunderbird station wagon with a flame red interior, and rented the house of late movie legend Errol Flynn.

But Siegfried felt like a German fish out of water. Although he had no intention to return to Germany in the immediate future, he pined for his homeland. He missed the grassy, leafy forests of its countryside, which he'd longingly describe as if it were a movie poster with Heidi yodeling and cavorting in the Alps, her braids swinging in the crisp air as she shepherded a herd of goats.

As Siegfried freely admits in their autobiography, it was Roy, with his unconstrained sense of adventure, who insisted on making the big leap to Vegas. Siegfried begrudgingly followed suit—but then, to his own great surprise, never looked back. Over the years, he and his partner not only became dyed-in-the-wool citizens, they evolved into veritable symbols of Sin City. But when they were first offered the Stardust contract, Roy was forced to alternately beg and scold to influence the stubborn-minded Siegfried. After ten years together, Roy was perfectly aware of his role in their relationship:

"I would have to plead, coax, manipulate, and threaten, and finally he would come around. In fact, by the time he made up his mind, he would think it was his idea in the first place."

Sexual sparks were no doubt struck by this constant conflict, but it's still a wonder that the two have stood by each other almost ceaselessly.

Finally, after convincing Siegfried that the challenge of America would fire up their stage show, Roy sealed the deal with his ace in the hole—a three-month vacation between their last show at the Lido and their first at the Stardust...in sun-filled, sexy Puerto Rico.

*   *   *

"Boy, this is paradise," Roy noted as he and Roy stepped off the plane in San Juan. Paradise turned into hell moments later. When the duo went through customs, Siegfried showed an official the four trained doves he'd carried with him in a basket on the plane. "No problem," shrugged the official. After he was passed through, magician Siegfried "materialized" back into the basket an additional fifteen doves he'd "disappeared," figuring rightly that the fewer the birds, the lesser the problem.

But just minutes later, another customs official heard the flock of nineteen birds billing and cooing and instantly disagreed with the decision to let them into the country. "Send the doves back to France, or we'll have to dispose of them," the distraught duo was told.

Siegfried, not wanting his birds killed or deported to Paris, ran to get Roy, but before they got back, the creeps at customs had brutally gassed the entire flock. For Siegfried and Roy, dedicated animal lovers, this mass murder was devastating, a potentially dark precursor that, in their own words, left them "heartbroken, helpless, and angry."

In Puerto Rico, Siegfried and Roy endured several outrageous incidents concerning their animals—more than in any other country they'd ever visited. Even as they left the airport in San Juan with Roy at the wheel of their rented car, they were stopped by a police officer for speeding. While Roy worried about a possible arrest, the cop was worried about whether the gigantic, live tiger in the backseat would eat him alive! Forced to choose between dismemberment and law enforcement, the policeman suddenly sped away without even giving him a ticket.

One of Siegfried and Roy's most bizarre encounters in Puerto Rico was with a woman named Bettina Saade, an American woman with platinum blonde hair, shiny pink lipstick, and tight-fitting clothes. Bettina was a famed animal lover who rescued strays and injured creatures of all species, caring for them in her home. After making her acquaintance, the boys were shocked to find she harbored scary-looking giant toads she fed dog food to every evening and a wild-eyed baboon named Cheetah, who'd sit on Siegfried's lap while he nervously hummed religious arias to keep the ape calm. Roy enjoyed the fact that his partner was unnerved by Cheetah, although Siegfried was rightly scared, because baboons are aggressive, dangerous creatures, not to be monkeyed with.

Bettina Saade became a good friend to the German lads and actually saved Roy's life on one occasion. Roy, always looking for ways to enhance the "Siegfried & Roy" franchise, had found a beautiful black jaguar for sale in South Florida. He'd wanted something "larger than life" for the upcoming Vegas show, and thought he'd found it in this gorgeous cat whose owner had raised him from birth. Roy was slightly nervous about his purchase, knowing jaguars are notoriously difficult to train, but the seller had convinced him that "Jahmal" was a good cat; perfect for their act.

After making the buy, Roy became increasingly distressed as he gazed into the jaguar's cold, green eyes. His instinct for animals was telling him that he'd made a hasty decision; that this animal was no tame, family-raised pussycat. Unfortunately, by this point, Roy and the cat had arrived at Bettina's home in San Juan. Within moments of releasing the cat into her backyard, Roy was scrambling for his life as the cat suddenly charged. It was a close call, but Bettina saved the day. Luckily for Roy, a pal of hers owned a jaguar, so she knew just what to do: spray the snarling feline with a stream of cold water from her garden hose, buying Roy just enough time to escape into the house unscathed. Needless to say, Jahmal was quickly shipped back to Florida.

Siegfried and Roy's Puerto Rico vacation was more than just animal adventures: there was fun-in-the-sun galore as they spent lots of free time befriending the young local studs who pranced along the beaches, sun-tanned, shirtless and irresistible to the German men. They made many "friendships" that were enduring enough for repeated sojourns to the islands.

Many years later, Siegfried would disguise his secret trips, using the excuse that he'd gone to help starving children in Romania with his sister, a nun doing missionary work for the Catholic Church. Siegfried returned from one trip boasting about how the impoverished children had recognized him, eyes popping out of their sockets in disbelief. But the visa stamps in Siegfried's passport told another story; although they showed he'd indeed been to Romania, they also proved he hadn't "*just* been there," as he claimed. Had he been visiting friends made on one of his exotic excursions so many years before? Why all the cloak-and-dagger deception? Perhaps Siegfried was simply playing the role Roy had conceived for him so many years before...man of mystery!

In the mid-80s, Siegfried and Roy bought a condo in Puerto Rico, where they supposedly housed one of their lovers. Years later, the young man would be flown to Las Vegas to visit, see their show and stay at the Frontier. In the late 90s, they sold the condo—reportedly to Henry Kissinger's mother—and began frequenting Santo Domingo, an island in the Dominican Republic that's a notorious haven for wide open prostitution. Rumors of Siegfried and Roy's sexual encounters with handsome Puerto Rican and Dominican native lads bubbled up constantly, fueled by talk of their homosexuality. Curiosity about their sexual proclivities, of course, meant that they were now major stars.

After that first vacation in Puerto Rico, minds and bodies revived by the warm weather and laidback atmosphere, Siegfried and Roy traveled on to Las Vegas and the Stardust Hotel. Siegfried, cranky about missing the luxuries of his European lifestyle, had a predictably difficult period of adjustment to the sleepy town he remembered all too well. Roy was content, happily familiarizing himself with their new tiger, Sahra. She'd been bought to replace Simba, who was sick and unable to perform any longer.

The boys weren't terribly familiar with their new home, the Stardust, or its wild history, which is perfectly in tune with other Las Vegas mega-hotels. According to the *World Encyclopedia of Organized Crime*, "Allen Glick purchased the Stardust Hotel and Casino in August 1974 with the help of a $62.7 million loan from the Teamsters Union Pension Fund. He obtained the casino with the help of Frank Peter Balistrieri, head of organized crime in Milwaukee."

Glick technically owned the hotel, but in actuality he was just a front man for organized crime operations in Kansas City, Chicago, and Milwaukee. After five years, his services were no longer needed, and the Mob forced him to sell out—and get out.

The Stardust's CEO, Frank "Lefty" Rosenthal, had close ties to Chicago Mobster Anthony "Tony the Ant" Spilotro. In 1976, the Nevada Gaming Control Board discovered CEO Rosenthal was operating a profit-skimming scam, raking in up to $40,000 per week in coins and $40,000 in $100 notes by altering the "hard count" scale that weighed coins from the slot machines.

All through the 1960s and 1970s, the Stardust was the poster casino for Mob activity. "Management" consisted of career criminals and crooked gamblers. Skimming, shakedowns, and murder lurked beneath the resort's shining façade. Hollywood—always just a hop, skip, and jump away from Vegas—would later make movie magic with the Stardust's story in the 1995 film *Casino*, starring Robert DeNiro as Ace Rothstein (the character based on Frank Rosenthal), with Sharon Stone as his wife, and Joe Pesci as ill-fated Tony Spilotro.

During their first of two runs at the Stardust, both Siegfried and Roy became inspired artistically. Siegfried discovered a way to "vanish" a tiger before their Metamorphosis finale. Although it would add another two minutes to their show, which in Vegas is tantamount to thousands of dollars of "casino time"—the precious moments when customers could be gambling away their savings—the hotel's general manager agreed to grant their request. Consequently, their three years at the Stardust became one of their best runs ever in terms of improvements to their performance. Twice during their run they were named "Show Act of the Year."

By 1973, "Siegfried & Roy" were being offered deals that would move them up the ladder of American fame and fortune. After their contract expired that year, they had several new venues and offers to choose from, but instead they decided to re-visit old friends and accept a limited engagement in Puerto Rico, where they would perform at the Americana Hotel. New additions to the act this time around were Sabu, a black panther; Sasha, a leopard; and Sahra and Radscha, Sumatran tigers.

During their Americana run, they received an offer from producer Donn Arden to join the MGM Grand's new show. They accepted the gig, and Roy thought it was a perfect cue to add a lion to their act, as a tribute to MGM. The king of the jungle was, after all, the studio's trademark mascot. The duo's trusted veterinarian, Marty Dinnes, found the perfect African lion, and Roy ended up buying the big cat from a company called Africa USA, which rented out animals such as lions and tigers for motion pictures.

To introduce Siegfried and Roy to their new lion, and to help the wild animal get acclimated, trainer Monty Cox and his girlfriend, Suzie, flew with the beast to the duo's house in Puerto Rico. Leo, as Siegfried and Roy named him, had an unusually laid-back temperament; his low energy level perfectly matched Siegfried and Roy's casual attitudes.

Monty, however, had difficulty understanding Siegfried and Roy's secrecy when it came to magic tricks. When he arrived with the lion, he asked them to explain exactly how they planned to use Leo in the show. Siegfried replied that he'd been working on a new illusion, but when Monty pushed to find out more, Siegfried insisted, "We can't tell you. If we tell you how to do the illusion, it's not an illusion."

Monty was stunned. "How can I possibly teach you how to train this cat without knowing what it's supposed to do?" Obviously, he'd never worked with German prima donnas before.

Despite the fact that Leo was a much larger wild animal than they'd ever worked with, the lion was ready to perform by the time Siegfried and Roy made it back to Las Vegas to star in "Hallelujah Hollywood" at the MGM Grand.

*   *   *

Hallelujah Hollywood was right! Siegfried and Roy had good reason to praise the gods of Hollywood—they'd just made their biggest deal yet. Thanks to Donn Arden, the vodka-guzzling, chain-smoking tyrant who produced the MGM hotel's entertainment, Siegfried and Roy would now be the closing act at the biggest show venue in Las Vegas. The MGM Grand, opened by mogul Kirk Kerkorian in 1973, had cost $106 million to build. Literally the biggest casino on the Strip—and the tallest at twenty-six stories high—the hotel had 2,100 guest rooms and five gourmet restaurants. By this time, Las Vegas had become the entertainment capital of the world, so it was only natural that one of the largest studios in Hollywood would want in on the profits.

With the instant success of Siegfried and Roy's show came new publicity. Since they had originated the magic-with-animals spectacle, hotels and casinos all over Las Vegas were beating the bushes to find similar acts. Suddenly, it became standard for magicians to bring animals to auditions. Siegfried and Roy—with their wild cats and daring magic tricks—were the talk of the town, and no hotel on the Strip wanted to miss out on having a hit like theirs.

Imitation, not always the sincerest form of flattery, was something Siegfried and Roy had grown to expect. Roy describes the wannabes arriving with "dyed blond and dark brown hair. Some started affecting...the look [of] shirts open to the waist, jewels, and three heavy sacred crosses on gold chains around their necks." The only act that stood in the way of their being something too unique to copy was Günther Gebel-Williams, another Aryan-blond, handsome German animal trainer/performer who found success in Irvin Feld's Ringling Bros. & Barnum and Bailey's Circus.

Springing onto the American scene in the late 1960s, Gebel-Williams was touted as the greatest wild animal trainer of all time and posed a threat to Roy's stature. With training techniques similar to Roy's, Williams maintained that, "Respect is the foundation.... I worked with tigers never as a tamer.... I taught them to listen.... I never tried to break their spirits and so I did not use brutality. I built a world around the animals with whom I worked, and in it I was their father and they were my children." Roy, undaunted, always considered himself the superior trainer.

Born in Germany in 1934, Günther Gebel began working in a circus at the age of twelve alongside his mother, who was in charge of costumes.

The owner of the circus, Mr. Williams, took a liking to young Günther and helped him develop an act in which the novice performed tricks while riding horses. Günther would stay until 1968, when the circus was bought out by Ringling's Irvin Feld. Eventually, Günther took on more responsibility, adding "Williams" to his surname in honor of the circus, and began working with horses, elephants, and other exotic animals. He especially loved the tigers, praising their beauty, wildness and intelligence.

Growing up during the same post-war period as Siegfried and Roy, Günther went through childhood without a father—who'd become another alcoholic veteran of World War II—so it's no wonder that he, like Roy, clung to animals as a source of love and comfort. And like Siegfried and his surrogate Father Johann, Günther also had a sort of father figure in circus owner Harry Williams.

Gebel-Williams' rapport with wild animals, along with his outlandish style, caught the attention of American proprietor Irvin Feld, who kept him on and made him a star after acquiring the Circus Williams. That turned out to be a shrewd move. Despite the jealousy of Siegfried and Roy, Günther Gebel-Williams, while flashy and an apparent egomaniac, was not just all show and no substance. He was a hard-driving perfectionist, epitomizing the phrase "the show must go on." In 12,000 shows, he never missed a day because of illness or injury, despite numerous scratches and scars inflicted by his tigers' sporadic paw swipes.

Creative differences—or similarities—aside, Gebel-Williams and rivals Siegfried and Roy shot a television special together during the duo's last year at the MGM. The event was set up by Feld, who not only discovered Gebel-Williams but was also a great fan of Siegfried and Roy's. In 1979, the duo was asked to shoot two more television specials with Gebel-Williams, under the aegis of Feld and his son Kenneth.

Despite the abundance of "Siegfried & Roy"-style acts springing up around Las Vegas in the 1960s and 70s, the German boys were destined to be the biggest of them all. "Hallelujah Hollywood" transformed them into real-life celebrities—full equals to the stars who frequented their joint on a regular basis. They developed friendships with the likes of Cary Grant, Shirley MacLaine, Zsa Zsa Gabor, and even Michael Jackson, the effeminate man-child they'd first met when he was the adolescent lead singer of the Jackson

Five. In fact, when they first met Jackson, he was underage and, while allowed to perform onstage at the MGM, was legally prohibited from watching shows in the audience.

The lads grew quite close to the adult Jackson, visiting him often at his home in Florida. Siegfried has said: "If I had to describe an angel, I would be describing Michael. His purity, his sincerity, his boyish sense of wonder—I know no adult like him.... For us, Michael is quite simply magic." Jackson even wrote a song for their *Secret Gallery* album, which they released in 2001 as a salute to their show. The accompanying lyrics were:

"'Cause when it's Siegfried & Roy/ It's the mind of a magic in true/ Your own thoughts play the game/ In the magical wonders they do/ The mind in the magic is you."

Jackson loved animals. His private zoo at infamous Neverland Ranch was legendary—and he'd actually planned a tiger habitat to emulate Siegfried and Roy's at the Jungle Palace and The Mirage. The habitat's preliminary models were to be made by Thomas Maple, one of Roy's animal trainers, but the deal took so long to finalize that Jackson lost interest and his habitat never materialized.

Jackson hired Siegfried and Roy's veterinarian, Dr. Dinnes, who had found Leo, their African lion. Dinnes acted as veterinarian of the Neverland Zoo and supplied Jackson with many of his animals, including some that had grown too large for Siegfried and Roy to use in their show. Years later, with what he claimed was "great reluctance," Dinnes filed suit against Jackson for $91,602 he was supposedly owed for veterinary services, plus orangutans, giraffes, flamingos, and elephants he'd provided for the self-styled King of Pop. The lawsuit was filed by Dinnes in January of 2006 after Jackson had left Neverland Ranch following his criminal trial on child molestation charges. Characteristically, even while persuing his case against Jackson, the doctor continued to care for the animals' medical needs and find them homes elsewhere.

Siegfried, Roy and Michael Jackson had been just boys when they first met, but they became more intertwined as time went by. The three men shared a close friendship with movie legend Elizabeth Taylor. Siegfried and Roy had known Elizabeth since their big showbiz breakthrough at the Gala des Rois in Monte Carlo.

It's no surprise that when Siegfried and Roy signed on for the gig at the MGM Grand, they "continued to operate on the belief that [they] had made the right career move." And even though their new stage had given them several new obstacles to overcome—the entire space was just sixteen square feet—they succeeded in making a little "disappearing" go a long, long way: five years, to be exact.

Their show became so outrageously popular that the duo found themselves performing two shows nightly and three on the weekends, with no days off except for one short vacation per year. While they won several awards during their stay at the MGM, including the Magicians of the Year award in 1976 and five Production of the Year awards, stress was wearing them down, physically and mentally. In order to cope with their pain, they turned to medicinal relief, mainly in the form of highly addictive Valium.

Siegfried, especially, sunk into deep depression, fueled by the monotony of performing the same show night after night and feeling artistically stunted. As Roy would describe it, "We had dug our own grave.... More money [is] always great, but in the end it didn't give us the satisfaction we wanted; our creativity was at a standstill." Their contract with MGM—which prohibited involvement in any other project during its term—was drowning them. And both were too stubborn to find a way out.

The fairytale which had started so happily once upon a time now turned sour. Their personal relationship faltered: Siegfried, a self-described walking zombie during this period, moved out of their house. The two never laid eyes on each other except at show time. They seriously considered splitting up the act because the relationship had been poisoned by drug use—and Siegfried's short fuse. Friends and witnesses say his mood swings, combined with his desire for control at any cost, triggered violent outbursts that scared everyone around him.

One member of their staff described him as having a "hair-trigger temper...and when he was mad, it was best to avoid him." Anger issues, Valium-related and otherwise, were like a rabid beast that threatened to devour them; an out-of-control tiger that couldn't be caged away in a zoo— although Siegfried claims he weaned himself off of the Valium on a two-week vacation to Puerto Rico.

If not for the strength and dedication of the man who would later become their manager and confidant, Bernie Yuman, it's unlikely "Siegfried & Roy" would have made it out of "Hallelujah Hollywood" alive...but they did.

Hallelujah.

"It's better to be an ordinary guy having an extraordinary life than the other way around."
—*Siegfried & Roy*

ccording to Roy, while Siegfried and Roy were in their third year at MGM Grand's "Hallelujah Hollywood," "a very animated, energetic man in the audience caught [his] attention." That man, Bernie Yuman, was destined to become their lifetime manager.

At about 5'8" tall (in platform shoes) and 150 pounds, Bernie was an average-sized guy. He was born in Brookline, Massachusetts, in 1949, to parents Sydney, a Russian immigrant, and Doris. His trademark uniform, worn in all weather conditions, consists of a black suit and cowboy boots, which conceal bright aqua-and-orange striped knee-high Dolphins socks. Wearing this outfit has been a ritual since the Dolphins' inaugural game on September 2, 1966; later, Yuman became obsessed with trying to become manager of the team's head coach, Don Shula, whom he'd met at a "Siegfried & Roy" show.

Bernie's outfit is habitually adorned with a huge, gold and diamond ring emblazoned with the words: "ALI, Athlete of the Century." He met the three-time world-champion boxer, Mohammad Ali, on a golf course back in 1962—when Ali was called Cassius Marcellus Clay Jr. and Bernie was thirteen years old—and they've remained close friends ever since. In 1999, Ali asked Bernie to be his manager, and just two years later Bernie secured an unprecedented multi-year deal with Coca-Cola for his new client. Bernie would, however, start making history twenty-two years before Ali's Coke deal by signing two up-and-coming young performers, Siegfried and Roy.

Back in 1977, aged twenty-seven, Bernie Yuman had huge ambitions. In his own words, he wanted to "build the largest entertainment company in the history of the industry," and on his way from Miami to Los Angeles, he made a stop in Vegas to see what the entertainment capital had to offer. While he was there, his mother came to visit, and he took her to see what was supposedly the best show in town. As Bernie watched Siegfried and Roy perform, he realized he'd found what he knew would be his future; he just had to work out how to make it happen.

Bernie spent a lot of time in Vegas representing entertainers who performed there and began to build working relationships. He was close to the owners of the Stardust, and when attendance at Lido de Paris began to decline, they asked him to help save their long-running production. When the "Hallelujah Hollywood" show opened, the Lido's numbers halved, and to boost ticket sales the Stardust invested a seven-figure sum to revamp it into a brand new Lido de Paris revue, no expense spared.

Donn Arden, who pioneered Las Vegas' most durable image—the statuesque showgirl in sequins, feathers and impossibly tall headpieces—was hired on as the Lido's producer, and by the time Siegfried and Roy left the Lido in 1981, Arden had produced their show for a decade. Their Lido show at the Stardust would also star the world-famous European showgirl troupe, Girls of Madame Bluebell, whom Arden had brought to the Lido in Vegas from the Paris Folies in the late 50s.

According to Frank Rosenthal, the CEO of a hotel chain that included the Stardust, the hotel's then-new Lido offered "exotic new costumes, imported ostrich feathers, all tied together with a dynamic state-of-the-art stage and lighting display to complement the finest trained dancers and showgirls ever to set foot on the American stage. Pre-production costs were approaching $10,000,000.00."

The bombastic galactic theme was abandoned, though the Stardust's roadside sign remained and was given a bright new finish with thousands of light bulbs that sparkled in the expanse of the desert.

Despite these efforts, the Lido's seats were barely at one-third capacity. When the Stardust owners asked Bernie Yuman for advice, he immediately thought of the "Siegfried & Roy" show he'd just taken his mother to see. He told the owners that the German duo's magic act was the answer to the hotel's problems. Unfortunately, the Stardust bigshots didn't believe this young Jew could arrange the deal.

Frank Rosenthal claims that bringing Siegfried and Roy aboard was *his* idea. Rosenthal says that it was he who approached Bernie Yuman, whom he describes as "a bearded gofer." Bernie was "living on short street," and Rosenthal offered him five hundred bucks if he could arrange a meeting in his office between him and the two magicians.

Siegfried and Roy were the most sought-after entertainers around; they were unobtainable. But Bernie was adamant, insisting he could get them. He started negotiating with the Stardust on behalf of Siegfried and Roy as if they were already his clients.

There was just one obstacle to overcome: Bernie had yet to meet the famous duo.

Opting for an uncharacteristic variation from his all-black uniform, Bernie changed into an English navy blue velvet coat with a white rabbit fur collar (his "most conservative outfit") and headed back to see the show again. He sat in the audience and made sure he captured Siegfried and Roy's attention, which according to Roy, he certainly did.

After the show, Bernie walked straight through security and into Siegfried and Roy's dressing room. He waited and waited for them to appear, but when Siegfried finally did, Bernie found himself being ejected by a burly guard. As he was forced out the door, he yelled to Siegfried, "I'm gonna change your life!" Despite all the odds, Bernie triumphed. His spontaneous chutzpah got him an invite to drop by Siegfried and Roy's house the next day.

Bernie drove his burgundy Corvette up to their home, introduced himself and declared that he'd like to be their personal manager. Over Cognac and cigars—luxuries Bernie had never cared for much but imbibed with good grace—he outlined the deal he'd already secured on their behalf.

Siegfried and Roy listened attentively and respectfully. Within twenty-four hours, the contract was signed.

The rest is history. Bernie Yuman stayed in Vegas indefinitely and became Siegfried and Roy's "five-star general."

Under his direction—and with a doubled salary and a contract packed with "perks"—the boys turned their backs on the boredom and depression that had plagued them during "Hallelujah Hollywood." They left the MGM revue to prop up the struggling Lido de Paris. There, they'd be the first to perform a complete thirty-three-minute show within a show as the Lido's closing act.

Next, Bernie—a man who could sell ice to an Eskimo—pulled off an astounding coup for his new clients: Star billing! And he made it clear from the start that the issue was either a deal- maker or breaker. What Bernie demanded was marquee billing that read: "LIDO de PARIS STARRING SIEGFRIED and ROY!"

Such billing was unprecedented. Acts on the Strip were never "starred," they were just featured. Siegfried and Roy, aware that they had the upper hand in the deal, hung tight on their demand, even though they knew it posed real problems for all the other players.

Madame Bluebell and her troupe of dancers were opposed to Siegfried and Roy diverting the spotlight from their headgear and tail feathers, but Frank Rosenthal convinced the Madame that the addition of the illusionists would only benefit her beauties by bringing in an audience to appreciate them.

Next obstacle: The Lido de Paris name and production concept were owned by Joseph Clerico, the billionaire Frenchman who also owned The Moulin Rouge. But Frank Rosenthal, seeing dollar bills flashing before his eyes, wasn't about to let them vanish into thin air. He offered Mr. Clerico a personal guarantee, assuring him the new Lido would surpass any show in the world—including the Lido in Paris, Folies-Bergère and even the Moulin Rouge. Intrigued, Mr. Clerico dubiously gave his go-ahead.

The deal was sealed. Siegfried and Roy had become the first stars in the history of Vegas to receive equal billing with the show's title on the tallest marquee in the state—and on all advertising. In addition, the Stardust agreed to build them an elaborate, custom-designed dressing room and apartment, plus high-end accommodations for their lions, tigers and panthers.

Among the other precedents set, Siegfried and Roy were the first act to be given a run of the show contract, as well as a clause calling for a full month off every six months. They were now the highest-paid specialty act in Las Vegas history. According to Vegas newspaper columnist Norm Clarke, they'd get $11,000 per week in their first year, $13,000 in the second, and ultimately $15,000.

Despite these extravagant salaries, Siegfried and Roy earned their keep. The show opened on July 1, 1978, with fifteen performances a week; the audience tripled. The show got so hot that management raised the cost of tickets three times during their three-year run.

Frank Rosenthal recalls the success of his investment:

> Marvelous reviews, the hottest ticket in town, everyone is jubilant, other than the MGM's President, Al Benedict and the Vice President, Bernie Rothkopf. They were asleep at the switch and by the time they woke up, the best show on earth was out of their Casino and down the street.
>
> This was the steal of the decade, probably second only to the Brinks armored car robbery. The only difference was, one was legal, straight up and above board, the other was not. We didn't carry shotguns, nor did we wear masks. The show had everything you might imagine. The entire hand-picked cast was spectacular—and did we ever pack them in. Generally, it was standing room only. The audiences were startled, enthusiastic and completely entertained. I watched the show virtually every night. I fantasized with them as we watched the most beautiful group of women ever assembled under one roof. The Casino no longer had to subsidize Lido de Paris. Siegfried and Roy were thrilled and genuinely euphoric when I presented them with a brand new, sparkling silver Rolls-Royce

Corniche at the entrance to the Stardust Casino on behalf of our corporate jubilation. Our families became united. And we've been friends ever since.

As for the bearded gofer, he moved from Short Street to Wall Street, projecting a confident swagger and positive hysteria. Young Bernie was on his way, laughing all the way to the bank with a mega-jackpot. Some guys never look back, and Mr. Bernie Yuman became a notable power broker throughout the world of entertainment.

It was at this point in their career that Siegfried and Roy had the resources and stage time to finally introduce two more characters into their act: Lynette Chappell and Toney Mitchell, both of whom would stay on for the long haul.

Siegfried and Roy spotted Lynette Chappell—a tall, leggy beauty—while she was performing with Madame Bluebell's troupe of topless showgirls at the Lido in 1967. She was born in Mombasa, Kenya, and Seagram's Liquor sponsored her to move to London to train at the Royal Ballet School.

Recruited by Madame Bluebell, she was contracted to dance in the Lido show in Las Vegas, where Siegfried and Roy first laid eyes on her. All three of them moved on to the MGM Grand to perform in "Hallelujah Hollywood," but they remained in separate acts. It was not until the late 70s that Siegfried and Roy were in a position to snap her up. With their dramatically increased production budget, they offered Lynette a role in their star-billing debut, and she once again returned to the Lido—but this time around, she was part of "Siegfried & Roy."

Fortunately, Lynette loved animals and had grown up surrounded by nature in Africa. When she first started, Siegfried brought a snake into her dressing room and told her, "If you're going to vork for us, you're going to have to learn how to handle zee animahls." Lynette had knee-high snakeskin boots on, and on the spur of the moment, she soothingly told the reptile, "Don't take these boots personally." Luckily, the snake didn't, and she ended up dancing with the reptile around her neck for years to come.

Lynette went on to become the Evil Queen at The Mirage and has been sawn in half so many times that she made it into the *Guinness Book of Records*. She is a workaholic, and over the years, Siegfried and Roy have become her life. When Lynette separated from her husband, the boys gave her a house on their property, which was eventually put in her name. She performed every show they did for twenty years, reluctantly missing just a few days when she became bed-ridden with a broken back.

Lynette had trained under a strict regimen with Russian teachers who taught her extreme discipline. Like most dancers, she was extremely conscious of her figure, ate like a sparrow and often resorted to prescribed weight loss pills—even if it meant getting them from the veterinarian!

She didn't want children of her own, because she thought motherhood would get in the way of her career. When she reached forty and passed child-bearing age, she considered adopting. But although Roy wasn't opposed to having a child in their makeshift family, it is alleged that Siegfried was adamant they shouldn't. Ultimately, Lynette never had her own family, save for the one she'd created with Siegfried, Roy and their animals.

In their autobiography, the other person Siegfried and Roy mention hiring at the Stardust was a well-built, young man named Antonio Mitchell, or Toney for short. In his own words, Toney was a young black boy drawn to "the high-cloistered, serene white walls and mystical gates of the 'Jungle Palace.'" However, the duo's account and Toney's romanticized version don't present the same picture.

Siegfried and Roy didn't purchase their Jungle Palace mansion until 1982, at which point they'd already left the Stardust and launched a new run at the Frontier. If Toney magically appeared at their front door, it was either after the Stardust or at a different door. In any case, they found each other, and Toney was hired to help at the house.

According to Roy, "the boy had no pillow to rest his head on, no father, no mother, no shelter from the stormy winds of life. He came from nowhere to the 'Garden of Eden' I had created for my family. I took him in, gave him responsibility—and hope." Once they moved into the Jungle Palace, Toney started off as a gardener, but he was more like a valet, laying out clothes for his bosses, shining their shoes, doing their shopping.... Along with the job, the duo gave Toney their guesthouse to live in, making him a de facto member of the family.

Toney had a special bond with both Siegfried and Roy, but he was especially close to Siegfried. They would go to the gym at the Las Vegas Athletic Club together and parade around nude. It was *the* place to be seen—and Roy and Tony made sure everyone saw it *all*.

When Siegfried and Roy decided to get permits for their big cats to live at their house, they threw a party to butter up the neighbors and show them how safe their animals were. But when the pompous wife of a local vet went downstairs to use the bathroom, she suddenly reemerged and abruptly left the party. Siegfried and Roy were bewildered by her beeline for the exit until the next day, when they received a letter from the woman. In it, she expressed her disgust that they would treat *any* individual so cruelly—after all, slavery had been outlawed.

It turned out she'd walked in on Toney, who'd been busily polishing the Germans' boots—and jumped to the wrong conclusion. Despite this incident, the boys got their permits for the animals.

Toney clearly suffered from an identity crisis, both socially and sexually, changing his image at the drop of a hat. He would whimsically fabricate any heritage that sprang to mind. One week he'd say he was Afro-American; the next he'd wear a turban and claim Arabic roots, when in reality Toney was born and raised in Illinois. He had a shaved head with a really long ponytail in the back, but one day, while shaving his scalp, he accidentally cut his remaining hair off. Other staff members teased, "What will Ali Baba metamorphose into next...Gandhi?"

In Roy's words, "It didn't take long for this exotic creature, who could very well have been from Zanzibar—or any place along the Ivory Coast—to become an integral part of his surroundings."

Toney's mysterious background fascinated Roy, who also didn't like being limited to only one culture. Roy believed in mysticism and a more general spirituality as opposed to one dogmatic religion. His homes—best described as multi-iconographical—were a reflection of that.

Siegfried, who habitually wears jeans and heeled boots, sticking to fashion classics rather than going through personal phases, is Toney's (and Roy's) complete opposite. Roy told an interviewer, "Siegfried, as long as I know him, hasn't changed his haircut or anything else."

Toney and Roy continuously reworked their identity on every level. Roy changed his style from Indian, to Western, German, and American, only to repeat the cycle full circle—and his ever-increasing costume changes on set did absolutely nothing to cure his vacillation. Roy would go from being fixated on his animals to having a crucifix built in his house; or to practicing Buddhism, meditation or anything else that caught his fancy. He loved to spend money and had creative ways of doing it. Roy had mail order catalogs delivered daily, and he'd spend hours sifting through them. Nearly every page got a yellow sticker to mark what he wanted. If there was a selection to choose from, Roy would be sure to order one of each!

Then Roy started collecting badges—another of the many phases he went through. It was thought that buddy Michael Jackson, who always wore badges, had piqued Roy's interest. Oddly enough, collecting badges wasn't a unique passion for performers. Elvis Presley once approached President Nixon because he wanted a secret undercover DEA badge. The King acquired a large collection of sheriff badges over the years, just as Roy eventually did.

Meanwhile, Toney kept dreaming of performing on the stage, and eventually Siegfried and Roy granted his wish. Roy wrote in his autobiography: "He was a natural in dance and motion, with the illusions and the animals. Over the years, Toney has flourished as a performer and has developed into a great stage character. Today at The Mirage he plays the role of the chief spiritual acolyte. It couldn't be a more fitting part, for he is the good spirit and majordomo of our house. Toney also sees to all our backstage needs, and to be more efficient as our self-appointed bodyguard—his talents are never-ending—he's upgraded his karate skills to perfection. But he is, at all times, a gentle soul with a great and happy, contagious smile, and I am proud to call him family."

Siegfried and Roy had a bizarre notion of what a family was, and much like other successful homosexual men, their family consisted of people they could either control or have sex with, or—more commonly—both. They would calculatedly choose to have an affair with men in their tight circle because it ensured that whatever happened would *stay* in that circle. Sexual encounters with strangers were a potential danger to their public image. This may be why they employed men they were attracted to in the first place. It was crucial to their self-generated, squeaky-clean image not to have spicy, tell-all stories plastered across the media. This was decades before the flamboyant performers would surprise almost no one by finally admitting they were gay!

Toney was one of many men on their team at their disposal for sex. And as their story unfolds, there are many more to come.

Sadly, Toney contracted HIV and had to be put on "the cocktail" medical regimen. As word of the frightening new AIDS epidemic started to spread, it put the fear of death into everyone around the unfortunate young man. No one knew who he'd contracted it from, or if he had passed the disease on.

Toney suffered typical symptoms: weight loss and constant lethargy. Toward the end, he stopped showing up to work and finally passed away. Rumors were spreading even after his death, but the AIDS was hushed up, because Siegfried and Roy's handlers knew that, inevitably, people might speculate about whether they'd been exposed, which was not the case. However, because it was known that AIDS spread more commonly among gay men, it was only natural Siegfried and Roy would want to distance themselves from the tragedy. Even though they worked with several

HIV/AIDS awareness charities over the course of their careers, they did not immediately admit that one of their closest friends, Toney, had succumbed to the disease.

In January 1999, about a month before Toney died, Siegfried and Roy's secretary, Rosemary, called Lynette's boyfriend, Jimmy Lavery, and told him Toney was not at work. It was then 6:10 p.m. and he was supposed to have shown up at 5:00 p.m. Jimmy lived next door to Toney, so he went over to check up on him. He ended up kicking down the door and found Toney lying unconscious in his bed, soaking wet and unresponsive. Jimmy told Rosemary to call 911, but instead she called Bernie Yuman to ask what she should do. Everything went through Bernie, Siegfried or Roy. People were nearly scared to breathe without their permission.

Bernie told Rosemary not to call 911. Instead, he called their doctor, who immediately arrived at the house to treat the sick patient. Toney had always been in amazing shape, which is why—the doctor said—he'd lived so long with HIV, but after the AIDS took hold, he died in about six months. Toney wanted to die in peace at home and tried to avoid going to the hospital. He took his "cocktail" faithfully, but despite the medication, lived just a few weeks longer, staying in his room until he tragically passed away on February 2, 1999.

But the show must go on, and Siegfried and Roy began developing big ideas about adding to their ever-growing onstage family. Because they had more space and better amenities at the Stardust, Roy was finally able to indulge a lifelong dream and add an elephant to the show. Bashful, a twenty-seven-year-old, five-ton elephant, would be used in a new disappearing act. It was an amazing feat just to get a full-grown elephant into a theater, much less make it disappear!

Houdini had made an elephant vanish at the New York Hippodrome in 1918, long before the German illusionists were even born. Houdini rightly trumpeted his illusion as "the biggest vanish the world has ever seen"— quickly stifling any doubt about his abilities. His promotional tactics garnered results: his live show attracted thousands, and the rest of the world read in awe of his astounding accomplishment. No longer would he be known as just another escape artist but as the planet's "Master Magician."

Like Houdini, Siegfried and Roy had learned the value of confidence and self-promotion. By the time they opened at the Stardust on July 1, 1978, their names blazed from the tallest marquee in the world. And in a publicity stunt to stimulate ticket sales, Siegfried and Roy arrived at their press conference on opening day in a limo filled with ferocious tigers. They showed Las Vegas they were a world-renowned act, had already made history, and could vanish an elephant to boot.

For their new thirty-three minute Lido show at the Stardust, Siegfried and Roy incorporated sceneries and backdrops on a scale the stage manager and his crew had never handled. It was a new challenge for all involved, making opening night more exciting—and nerve-wracking. Siegfried's ulcers had already flared in anticipation, and neither performer had ever lost the fear that any failure, no matter how small or seemingly inconsequential, could snatch away their dream-come-true.

They say it's never smart to work with children or animals if you want your show to run smoothly. Now, in addition to their five-ton elephant, Bashful, Siegfried and Roy had accumulated a menagerie of ten young, wild cats to add to the challenge. In the tradition of Siegfried and Roy's earlier shows, opening night at the Stardust's new Lido had its surprises. Everything went magically for the most part, but at one point, Leo—the African lion they had bought for the MGM—took a sudden, unplanned bite out of Siegfried's arm.

As part of the show, Siegfried always staged a pretend-fight with Leo, getting the lion to growl. The boys had developed this trick back at the MGM, after discovering the audience sometimes didn't believe Leo was real. So Siegfried always engaged playfully with the beast to remove any doubts that he was a stuffed animal or robot.

Leo was trained using a reward system, so that when it was time to perform in front of an audience, he roared right on cue. He was an actor, too, and knew his "lines" by heart. On the night of the Stardust premiere, Siegfried, high on adrenaline, came onstage perhaps in too dramatic a mood, emphasizing every move he made and working especially hard to prompt Leo into action. But when he opened the cage, Leo stood immobile; static as a stuffed toy. As the lion stood silent, Siegfried used slightly more force, prodding the cat to play along. Roy later described the prodding as a light "slap" to instigate Leo—all in good fun and all for the benefit of the crowd. But what Siegfried did not realize was that the lion was suffering from a sudden bout of stage fright. Leo was terrified of the huge audience and the unfamiliar setting, and when Siegfried pushed, Leo struck back—taking bits of the magician's arm and hand in the process.

Even a tiny lion bite is a big deal, but Siegfried refused to stop the show. Backstage, a doctor administered shots of novocaine along with thirty-eight stitches to the mauled star. Siegfried managed to perform in their second show that night, ignoring the blood oozing out of bandages the doctor had placed on his arm.

It's hard to be sure why the lion attacked Siegfried; it makes Roy's tiger attack feel like déjà vu. But one likely explanation involves a "Hot Shot," or cattle prod, used in the event the lion fails to perform. The Hot Shot would allow Siegfried to give the animal an electric jolt to shock it into action—or make the lion jump at the right time. It's possible that Siegfried, facing a motionless tiger that night, triggered the Hot Shot—which was fitted into the floor of Leo's, and later, his replacement Raj's cage—and startled him so much that the lion bit the performer.

Luckily for Siegfried, his arm healed; luckily for the act, the audience didn't notice the bite—or, at least, didn't realize that the bite wasn't planned. They gave the duo a standing ovation at the performance's end. Cary Grant was in attendance that evening, and when he went backstage to congratulate them, he told Siegfried he'd noticed tears in his eyes.

When Siegfried showed Grant his bloody arm, the suave star almost fainted—he'd had no idea that Leo had actually taken a bite out of the performer!

With a new budget came innovations that made "Siegfried & Roy" even more spectacular than their many imitators. It was at this point in their career that the duo developed their magical, rising ball illusion. In the illusion, Sahra would jump on the giant-sized disco ball—with Roy by her side—and the two would float up over the audience's heads. Adding the dramatic touch of fire shooting from the ball—and playing on Roy's well-known fear of heights for a little heart-in-your-throat comedy—this marvelous illusion became one of their most popular.

Another notable refinement was Siegfried and Roy's idea to make the Las Vegas stage more like a European theater-in-the-round. They thought, and correctly so, that their act would be even more exhilarating and engaging if the audience was close enough to the action that they could reach out and almost touch the duo's sequin-studded spandex pant legs. At their request, the hotel built Siegfried and Roy a passerella: a walkway that came off of the stage and cut the audience in half. This brought the crowd closer to the animals, so they were that much closer to the magic, making Siegfried and Roy's illusions even more unbelievable.

After constructing the passerella, the two, always scheming, created the "death-defying crystal chamber" as Siegfried calls it. This trick involves a glass cage holding Lynette suspended in the air. In a flash, Lynette is transformed into a tiger: "beauty into beast" is how Siegfried describes this masterpiece. After the glass cage was built and the trick was integrated into the show, it caught the eye of movie director Hal Ashby, well-known in the 1970s for his films *Shampoo* and *Coming Home* and the now-cult classics *Harold and Maude* and *Being There*. In 1982, when Ashby saw the crystal chamber, he was in the process of filming *Lookin' to Get Out*, starring Ann-Margaret and Jon Voight. Siegfried and Roy, eager to make their film debut, agreed to let Hashby film a scene from their show, but they made one very important request: no additional lighting could be used. If the film crew brought hundreds of watts of outside light for the shoot, the tigers could get spooked and run amok.

And that's exactly what happened.... Magic, the cat Roy was accompanying down the passerella, jumped backwards when the extra light flooded the stage. He flew into the pit, where hundreds of extras were seated in the audience, then fell on a table, which broke under his weight. Roy held tight to Magic throughout the chaos and landed on top of him and the table. The scene must have been incredibly dramatic to witness firsthand, but the scary thought both Siegfried and Roy immediately had was: *What would Magic do next, in a crowd of unsuspecting observers?*

Siegfried said, "The incident frightened me completely, my entire body was shaking, but I had to calm the crowd down before anything else happened, and it took a great deal of strength to appear composed and in control." If anything, his years of stage performing had taught him to always look cool and unsurprised.

Roy couldn't have been happier that no other mishaps occurred, and the scene went very smoothly on the second take. "Any number of unfortunate things could have happened," he admitted, "But it didn't, and it never has. It's in situations like this that I truly believe I have a guardian angel." Little did Roy know that, years later, another wild tiger would put his life in the balance.

In their final year at the Stardust, the TV specials made by their great friends and legendary producers Irvin and Kenneth Feld, finally aired. Siegfried and Roy, a stage act from the beginning of their career, enjoyed the shoots because they were able to stage more elaborate stunts and play new and different roles; not just performing magic and working with animals, but singing and dancing with new props and effects, like motorcycles, jeeps, cannons, and laser lights. Their TV specials had everything the stage would not allow.

For the shoots, Irvin Feld costarred as promoter, producer, and impresario with his son, Kenneth Feld. Siegfried and Roy's relationship with the Felds grew, as did Bernie Yuman's. And this group was about to make history at another legendary Las Vegas hotel: that wild, Wild West landmark, the Frontier.

Chapter 7
A NEW FRONTIER

"We never understood the fascination anyway with topless women in the shows...."
—Siegfried Fischbacher

Irvin and Kenneth Feld would prove to be much more to Siegfried and Roy than simply promoters and producers: they would become integral to the burgeoning Fischbacher-Horn heritage.

"The big top was in [Irvin Feld's] blood" from an early age, Roy reveals in their autobiography. Feld, who had an innate talent for salesmanship, grew up working for his father, who owned a store in Maryland. From high school, he was hired to run a pharmacy in the black section of Washington, DC. When the National Association for the Advancement of Colored People (NAACP) offered to finance his pharmacy, he couldn't have been happier. He accepted their offer and expanded the store to sell black music. His sales experience drove his store's success in the local neighborhood, and soon he and his brother owned several record shops around town.

But Irvin was too intelligent to stop there. Realizing he had a knack for recognizing talent, he started his own record label and worked with such artists as Fabian, Chubby Checker, Fats Domino, Buddy Holly, and the Everly Brothers. During his years in the music industry, Feld was not only credited with discovering pop singer Paul Anka but also for bringing the Beatles to America for their first tour. In addition, Feld made the first independently produced record ever to sell a million copies: a song by Arthur Smith and the Crackerjacks. Feld made a habit of setting records and making history—much like his friends and business associates, Siegfried and Roy.

Feld continued working in the music industry, but he'd always nurtured a desire to work for a circus. He finally found his big top: the legendary Ringling Brothers and Barnum & Bailey Circus. Siegfried described Feld's circus fixation as "an old itch, and in 1956 he scratched it." That fateful year, Irvin Feld contacted John Ringling North, the owner of the iconic American circus, which—after decades of delighting "children of all ages"—was slowly failing. Feld told North that to return the circus to its former glory, he'd have to quit all the other industries he dabbled in, namely restaurants, hotels, and construction. Instead, North would need to focus totally on the circus to make it bigger, better, and more profitable.

Impressed, North hired Feld as a booker for the circus. But the shrewd young operator, a genius at contract negotiation, actually ended up owning Ringling Brothers and Barnum & Bailey Circus—lock, stock and barrel—in just two years. Feld's business savvy was legendary. He finally sold the circus to Mattel in 1971 for an unprecedented $50 million. In 1992, when Mattel decided they didn't want the troublesome big top anymore, they sold it back to Feld for only $23 million. To call Feld "brilliant" doesn't even begin to describe him.

Irvin Feld and his son, Kenneth, along with Siegfried and Roy's manager, Bernie Yuman, made a deal with the Frontier hotel, drafting the richest contract in the history of Las Vegas—not the first time Siegfried and Roy had set that record! The boys had known Irvin for years, of course, from his producing the 1970s television specials that co-starred animal trainer rival Günther Gebel-Williams.

Although Feld claims to have instantly recognized Siegfried and Roy's talent, and their money-making potential, he didn't actually offer them the deal until *after* their second TV special together. Before his Frontier contract with Siegfried and Roy, this sharp operator hadn't been able to break into the Las Vegas scene. "At the same time that Irvin Feld was our key to a new dimension, we also held the key to one of his aspirations," Roy explains. In other words, they were Feld's ticket to Las Vegas fame, just as he was their ticket to the big time.

Still, Roy insists, "The moment that really cemented our relationship with Irvin wasn't financial. It was a piece of showmanship, pure and simple." For Feld's press conference on the day of their opening, he arranged for a police escort to bring the boys to the hotel, a red carpet for them when they arrived, a marching band and a swarming crowd of photographers and journalists...the usual over-the-top Siegfried-and-Roy-sized spectacle. But the lads actually managed to upstage Feld by having a helicopter drop them in front of the hotel just before their opening. Feld, mightily impressed, called it "the most spectacular arrival in show business."

Although Irvin Feld had money and success enough to play the typical elusive, condescending producer, he truly supported his acts, especially Siegfried and Roy. Even after their show opened, he flew to Las Vegas twice monthly to see them perform, staying for both shows every night. He was a fan from the moment he booked them for his TV specials, to the day he died in 1984. Without Feld's help, it's doubtful that Siegfried and Roy would have climbed as high on the heights of popularity.

Despite their tremendous grief when Irvin Feld finally passed away, Siegfried and Roy were fortunate to have his son, Kenneth, to guide them through their next several years at the Frontier hotel, plus a Japan tour, and their eventual booking at The Mirage.

Kenneth Feld had grown up learning the tricks of his father's trade and was equally ambitious, but being from a younger generation, he had the cutting-edge perception necessary to take Siegfried and Roy's career to the next level. Kenneth's commitment to the German stars stemmed from a deep admiration for the boys themselves and the magnitude of their work. Their relationship was of such importance, because Kenneth was now in charge of fine-tuning their act. Siegfried and Roy, although naturally nervous about the eventual outcome with young Kenneth, had a feeling all would be well, just as it had been with Feld Senior.

Recalling those early days, Kenneth described the first time he and his father worked with Siegfried and Roy:

"The day after the show, they sent us a telegram: 'This is the greatest thing we've ever seen, you did a wonderful job, thank you.' That's unheard of. Performers just don't do that. This gesture was important for them—it was the first time someone had delivered exactly what had been promised. And what came out of that was trust."

Siegfried and Roy's show at the Frontier, "Beyond Belief," marked the first time they'd ever had total creative control over their one-hour-and-forty-minute show.

Once again, the duo was able to utilize an elephant in their act, provided by Irvin Feld. He had bought Gildah the elephant for the Barnum & Bailey Circus before Siegfried and Roy became part of the scene. When they started their act at the Frontier, Gildah—like a big puppy dog who would just stand there and wobble back and forth—was easily integrated into their show.

At the Frontier, Gildah's handler, a young smart aleck named Chris, lived out back of the hotel in a trailer, while the elephant and a show horse lived in the barn next door. Chris spent almost every minute of the day by Gildah's side. When he wanted to go to a bar, he took her for a stroll across the street from the hotel. They would stand in the parking lot outside while a waiter brought each of them an Amstel beer to quench their thirsts; Chris drank his out the bottle and poured Gildah's into her mouth. When Siegfried and Roy and their entourage moved to The Mirage many years later, an apartment was custom built for Chris and Gildah to share. Their rooms were separated by a glass window, which Gildah could look through and watch TV with her buddy (and master).

Chris was a character who figured in many of the hilarious stories from that period, often being cast as the troublemaker. He was covered in tattoos and looked like a biker. With his charming smile, he had the demeanor of a mischievous boy, and he behaved like one. When you start off with taking elephants to bars, there's not a lot crazier you can get, but Chris managed. His hijinks actually got him fired a couple of times, but Siegfried and Roy always rehired him.

At The Mirage in the 90s, wacky Chris photocopied his man-unit on a Xerox machine, then handed out copies to all the girl dancers—and men who might be inclined to show an interest. Bets were placed among the staff over who swung the lowest: Siegfried, who was rumored to be quite well endowed, or Chris. Siegfried and Roy found out about the photocopies, and fearing a sexual harassment suit, they asked employee Jimmy Lavery to investigate. Jimmy knew the photocopies had to be attributable to Chris. Confronting him, he asked, "What have you done this time?" Chris innocently denied that he was at fault: "Well, the girls bet me...." he began. Jimmy just gave up. Luckily, the ladies were more bemused than offended—at least not offended enough to file a lawsuit.

For one of the segments between their performances at the Frontier, Siegfried and Roy used the King Charles Troupe, a.k.a the KCs, a black basketball team that played on unicycles—described by many as "the Harlem Globetrotters on wheels"—who'd been brought over from Feld's circus. It was a unique act in its use of dance, athletics, and singing/rapping, but it also featured the black ballplayers bopping with white showgirls. The integration of races onstage was still somewhat scandalous even in 1981, but Siegfried and Roy had faith in the King Charles Troupe, and kept them in their always-sold-out shows.

And this wasn't just any old sold-out show—their act was the single most successful box-office attraction in Las Vegas history. Seven years, three million people, two sold-out shows every night, all due to what Irvin Feld called "the most incredible word-of-mouth praise I've ever heard in fifty years in show business." Siegfried and Roy's show, which was supposed to last three years, went on for seven; no one else on the Strip had ever even come close to topping their numbers.

Adding to the hotel's popularity, the Frontier had a special star showroom where celebrity performers from Elvis to Wayne Newton to Kenny Rogers strutted their stuff. Everyone who was anyone played the Frontier showroom, known to employees as "The Theater." It was expanded in 1984 to include 400 additional seats. These were sectioned off by curtains, however, so that if they didn't sell, the hotel would simply keep the curtains closed and still claim they had a "sold out" show.

During their Frontier years, Siegfried and Roy would make a drastic change in their own show's policy, further paving the way for Las Vegas to metamorphose into a bona fide family vacation destination. In 1981, Roy described their show "Beyond Belief" as being "halfway between the old days—a series of illusions separated by unrelated production numbers that featured bare-breasted show girls in sequins and feathers—and what we do today."

Stunned by the number of children clamoring to see the show, the duo pushed the Frontier's owners to make the atmosphere even more wholesome, with no topless women. The first family show sold out on a regular basis, so the duo added another, making it two family shows per week. Siegfried and Roy eventually added a free "cabbie" show to their schedule—a Bernie Yuman idea—to encourage cab drivers to talk the show up to their captive fares.

Years later, Siegfried and Roy's show at The Mirage would include no topless women. Every production was appropriate for all ages. Lynette Chappell was topless at the Stardust before she joined Siegfried and Roy, but she's been covered ever since. Soon enough, all Las Vegas would follow Siegfried and Roy's example and reform the raunchiness.

Laura Deni, who runs the website broadwaytovegas.com, said the city went from "ladies in long gowns, men in tuxedos, Champagne, male crooners and sophisticated sex" to a land where you had to "watch out where you swing your arms in the casino or you'll hit a toddler in a stroller."

The family-friendly shows of these two German lads turned Las Vegas upside down: from a place where solo entertainers like Frank Sinatra and Elvis Presley came to be reborn, to the capital of eye-popping, brain-numbing spectacle that it's become today. Directly or indirectly, their example inspired a cavalcade of spectacular revues that have defined Las Vegas for twenty years—from knock-off shows like EFX, to magic acts like Lance Burton, to the more futuristic spectacles like Cirque du Soleil.

Show policy aside, Roy would make a drastic change of his own during the Frontier years. In addition to the chameleon-like changes he made to his homes and collections, Roy would continually fluctuate between hair and wardrobe styles. While Siegfried consistently kept the faith with his platinum-dyed hair, wrinkle-free face and unnaturally tanned skin tone over the course of their careers, Roy changed his appearance endlessly, remaining loyal only to his tanning bed and plastic surgeons.

He began 1981 with long, black, professionally dyed hair and a moustache. When he decided to chop off his facial hair partway through their run at the Frontier, the hotel's management became concerned; customers were buying tickets to the show anticipating a mustachioed Roy Horn. His whim required changing all "Siegfried & Roy" advertising, at a considerable cost, and the Frontier marquee and show programs had to be replaced with the "new" Roy.

In the late 80s, Roy grew his hair out long again, this time going for a lighter brown color on top, set off in the back by tiny braids and beading. This Caribbean-inspired look was probably influenced by the duo's visits to Puerto Rico and Santo Domingo, although with Roy's fancies changing by the second, it's impossible to pinpoint where or when he discovered the look. Toward the latter part of his career, he would go on to frost the tips of his short black hair and even grow a "soul patch" (a tuft of hair between his bottom lip and chin) in an apparent effort to look younger and hip.

Siegfried and Roy lived a drama-filled life in Las Vegas, and their Frontier sojourn was no exception. One day, staffer Jimmy Lavery discovered that lovely Lynette was sporting a black eye, apparently the result of one of Siegfried's violent outbursts, still prevalent, supposedly, along with his continued Valium abuse.

After work, Lynette would usually get home between two and three o'clock in the morning, sleep from 6 a.m. to noon and then get ready for work again the next night. One particular evening, Jimmy—who was dating Lynette at the time—noticed she hadn't arrived home on time. When Roy showed up on their doorstep at 2 a.m., looking worried and asking for Lynette, Jimmy knew something must be wrong, but Roy quickly made his excuses and scuttled off.

Jimmy was about to call the police when Lynette suddenly showed up. Jimmy noticed her left eye was particularly red, but she told him it was nothing and went to bed.

By the next morning, her eye had turned an ugly black and blue. When Jimmy confronted her and insisted on answers, she said she'd banged herself in an onstage stumble, still not explaining exactly how she had gotten the black eye. Lynette begged Jimmy not to say anything to anyone, but he couldn't let it drop. He went to her secretary, Shirley, to find out what had really happened. Shirley confided that Siegfried had hit Lynette. Jimmy, angry and frustrated, was forced not to open his mouth because Lynette didn't want him to. She would have protected Siegfried and Roy to the grave.

At this point in her life, Lynette was entirely dependent on Siegfried and Roy. She lived in their house, cashed their paychecks, and adapted her life to their every need. Although she was the most prominent female performer in the act, she was not the only woman to find herself in this vulnerable position. Siegfried and Roy were the source of their staff's livelihood, giving them total control over their employees. The showgirls, in particular, were mostly underpaid and trapped. They wouldn't think of leaving their jobs, no matter how badly they were treated.

On at least four other occasions Siegfried's abuse of women was swept under the carpet. It had gone on since their early Vegas days. In 2007, Jimmy Lavery actually spoke to a police officer named John Hannon who had arrested Siegfried in 1978, while he and Roy were performing at the MGM. The officer told Jimmy, "I arrested him in 1978 and I can remember it like it was yesterday." John Hannon is retired today, but in the late 70s his patrol district included the MGM.

One day, Hannon was called to the MGM hotel because a camera girl for Cashman Photos (the company contracted by the showrooms to take souvenir pictures of guests) had gotten into an argument with Siegfried. The girl had been taking pictures as usual, but on this occasion, for some reason, Siegfried had grown annoyed by her.

When Officer Hannon arrived on the scene, the girl told him that Siegfried had violently shoved her, knocking her down. Since the incident did not occur in the officer's presence—and because Siegfried hadn't murdered anyone—the cop couldn't make an arrest...but the camera girl could *and did*. She made a citizen's arrest, and Hannon hauled Siegfried down to the Metro Clark County jail.

Siegfried threw a nasty fuss, actually kicking the back of the officer's seat in frustration. Apparently he argued that this was all a waste of everyone's time because the girl had made the whole story up. But nothing he or his team could do would get him released. MGM management was furious when Siegfried missed the second show of the evening and spent the night in jail.

The camera girl made a witness statement that night, but that was the last anyone heard of the incident. Whether it was resolved in court or privately between Siegfried and the girl, no one knows, but when Hannon looked through police files years later, he found no record of the girl's complaint or the hearing.

By 1987, Siegfried and Roy were ready to move on. As Roy put it, "we knew we were the single hottest attraction in Las Vegas, and we knew we now had the power to have a show that would be a total break from the Las Vegas mold of entertainment." The Frontier was bursting at the seams accommodating Siegfried and Roy's fans, and the stars once again felt overwhelmed and stifled by their surroundings. "Siegfried & Roy," the act and the egos, had outgrown the Frontier.

The Frontier Hotel has weathered ups-and-downs over the course of its history on the Strip. When the hotel-casino opened, it hosted Elvis' Vegas debut—and it was the first themed resort in town. With its western motif, which later morphed into a "space age" theme much like the Stardust's, the resort would eventually become known for "bull riding, cheap hotel rooms and $5 craps," as *Las Vegas Now* described it. Even those glory days came to an end on November 13, 2007, when the Frontier went out with a bang—literally.

Land in Las Vegas, like everything else there, changes value at the speed of light, so it was only a matter of time before big money would snap up the coveted ground. The Frontier's spot on the Strip was bought by Yitzhak Tshuva, an Israeli billionaire, who partnered to build an $8 billion mega-resort—living spaces, retail businesses, and a luxury hotel and casino—set to open in 2011. Tshuva's company, The Elad group, owns The Plaza hotel in New York and has similar plans for the Frontier property.

The Stardust was also imploded, making way for Boyd Gaming Corp.'s Echelon, a casino complex costing a colossal $4.4 billion dollars, set to open in 2010.

Considering that Howard Hughes had paid a then-whopping $14 million for the land in 1967, it's unbelievable how the Frontier's value—or, rather, the *land*'s value—has increased in just four decades. Some forty-odd years before that, the land was all but given away, thought to be worthless! Although "it's another budget option on the Strip that's gone," according to David Schwartz—director of the Center for Gaming Research at the University of Nevada, Las Vegas—not everyone was sad to see the two old 70s standbys bite the dust. Steve Wynn famously said that there were fewer twenty-five-cent slot machine players wandering into his deluxe hotel across the Strip..."because the Frontier and Stardust are closed." Despite the popularity of both of those hotels during the 1970s, Wynn's observation wasn't just a clever aside, it was fact. As all things inevitably do, the Frontier's time had passed.

Chapter 8
LITTLE BAVARIA

"There was no green, no grass, no birds singing.
So we had to create our own world."
—Siegfried Fischbacher

When Siegfried and Roy came into money, Siegfried wanted to save it and Roy wanted to spend it. Siegfried's motto was: always have a million dollars in the bank. Roy's attitude: if you've got it, spend it, and you might earn even more.

Knowing how much Howard Hughes' property had escalated in value, Roy realized the potential of investing money in "dirt," as the flats of desert were then called, and he went on a rampage to snatch up as much of it as he could without rattling Siegfried's cage. After purchasing the estate which became the Jungle Palace, they purchased a trailer park and some apartments behind the MGM hotel, where they now have a street named after them.

In 1979, Roy, who was always concocting grandiose schemes, spotted a plot of land that was perfect for an idea he'd long had in mind: bringing a little piece of Bavaria to Las Vegas. Knowing Siegfried would probably oppose spending the money, Roy convinced him to buy the plot and construct a virtual replica of their native land.

His ploy worked like a charm. Siegfried, who tended to get homesick, had suffered minor culture shock when they'd first arrived in Las Vegas in 1967. He and Roy had been raised in completely different environments. Roy came from an open-minded, seafaring community. Siegfried's upbringing was far more provincial. In his little town, the locals considered their archaic customs sacrosanct. The

Bavarians' reverence for local beer (München's annual Oktoberfest is the largest public festival in the world) is equaled only by their devotion to the Roman Catholic Church.

Siegfried had a traditional Catholic upbringing in a town where the greeting *"Grüß Gott"* (God bless you) was more common than "good morning," "good day," and later, "hello"—one of the few English words Siegfried could spit out when he landed in America. His pronunciation was incomprehensible, and Siegfried grew frustrated by his inability to communicate in his new environment. Four decades later, he speaks English fluently—with a full-fledged Teutonic accent intact—but when Siegfried first arrived, the language barrier felt as impenetrable as the Berlin wall, and he had no desire to claw his way up it. Matters were not helped by the fact that Siegfried did not have a car or a driver's license, a major handicap in Vegas' vast terrain.

To make his partner feel settled, Roy decided there was only one thing to do: bring Bavaria to Siegfried! He would reunite Siegfried with his roots by designing a luscious, green environment for their rustic home—an oasis in the desert. Ironically, Siegfried rarely visited the little piece of his homeland that Roy created, but Roy loved the place and it actually became *his* retreat more than Siegfried's.

Roy Horn purchased the first land parcel, around ten acres, in November 1979, for $8,999. "The Land," as the ever-expanding property is often called, is located fifteen miles from the center of Vegas, off Rancho Drive. When it was first acquired, The Land consisted of a few acres adorned with a shack, a few modest trees and a solitary neighbor living in a trailer. It has since expanded into a seventy-five-acre estate, equipped for a full-scale farm.

Roy immediately started buying trees for The Land and today the foliage surrounds the estate like a fortress. Roy's next venture was to build a pond, which started off small and doubled at least five or six times to become the lake it is now. Walking bridges were built from both sides to a tree- and shrub-saturated island in the middle, with a serene weeping willow draped over the clear blue water. It is an image reminiscent of one of Monet's Arcadian paintings, with ducks, black swans, and King Ludwigs—plus a pair of plastic alligators—swimming around it. The only interruptions in this tranquil setting were the ducks' quacking and peacocks' honking—extremely irritating for the neighbors when the birds escaped and roamed the streets and rooftops in the early morning hours.

Once they'd planted trees and built a pond, there was still nowhere for Siegfried and Roy to live. As the story goes, Roy was driving in Utah when he spotted log cabin home kits for sale along the side of the road. They looked like the real McCoy and were exactly what he had in mind for his Bavarian microcosm. He bought one, shipped it back to Vegas, and formed the foundation for the home, now famously known as Little Bavaria.

By the mid-1980s, Roy had his mind set on taking over his neighbor's trailer and five acres of land. He sent employee Jimmy Lavery to negotiate with the old man who lived in the trailer with a swamp cooler. The old fellow was quite well-off because he owned a lot of "dirt," but he clung stubbornly to his modest existence and had no intention of moving forward with the accelerating expansion of the desert city. He firmly declined Jimmy's offer.

Roy persisted. Jimmy was sent back again and again to talk to the old man. And he ended up spending so much time with him that they became friends. The old guy, who lived by himself, didn't talk much. He didn't even have a phone at home. But one day, he spoke up out of the blue and announced he'd changed his mind, saying, "You know, I'm gonna sell you some land." The old man told Jimmy he would hand over the property for around $1,000 in cash, and it was further agreed that he could live in the trailer until he died.

In his excitement, Jimmy agreed to the terms and said he'd bring his attorney over right away to sign the deal. Immediately, the old man retracted his offer and abruptly announced, "Attorneys, no deal!" It was either a handshake and cash, or nothing. Jimmy quickly assured him he'd get the cash and lawyers wouldn't be necessary. They shook hands and the deal was made right there on the porch of the trailer.

Roy enlisted the help of his brother, Werner, to act as caretaker of The Land. When the old neighbor died less than two months after he'd sold his property to Roy, Werner was given his trailer—thereby keeping him onsite twenty-four hours a day to supervise Little Bavaria. But instead of working all day, Werner would drink, often starting on his first bottle of alcohol at eight o'clock in the morning and encouraging the gardeners to drink with him.

With Werner in charge, Little Bavaria was out of control. The animals were often not fed. And on the odd occasions they were, wild ducks would fly in and eat all their food, scattering scraps across the property. It was a vicious cycle. There was no end to the mess because no one was sober enough to take responsibility for the property. Making matters worse, the same wild ducks and geese that robbed the domestic birds' food would leave droppings all over the pristine lakes and ponds. Not surprisingly, no one was cleaning them either.

Roy was always looking for new ways to entice Siegfried to visit his Bavarian oasis. Every year, he'd find new animals for Little Bavaria, whether it was his cats, farm animals, horses, llamas, white peacocks, roe deer, chickens, dogs, or any other living creature he could get his hands on. Even though there was a mutual understanding that Roy loved the animals, and Siegfried was a magician who liked to keep a distance from them, Roy maintained that each addition to their animal kingdom was intended to complete *Siegfried's* Little Bavaria.

One year while at The Mirage, Roy wanted to buy something special for Siegfried's birthday. At the time, a breed of swine now commonly known as Vietnamese Potbellied Pigs was being imported from Vietnam and bred in the States. As a result, there was a huge craze to buy miniature pigs, and instead of the normal cat or dog, people would spend a fortune to have a pig—Roy included. He'd heard these cute pigs made loving pets and thought one would be perfect for Siegfried to dote on at Little Bavaria.

After their show one night at The Mirage, Siegfried, Roy and their staff stayed on to celebrate Siegfried's birthday. Lynette discreetly lifted the surprise out of its transport box, and the entire room was shocked into silence by an unbearable caterwauling. Potbelly pigs don't like to be picked up, and the second the porker's little hoofs left the ground, it emitted a deafening, high-pitched squeal. The delicate ribbon tied in a bow around its thick neck looked ridiculous in contrast with its coarse, black-haired potbelly and stubby legs, which manically spasmed as the beast struggled. The cute little animal was transformed into a monster possessed. However, Lynette had little choice but to walk over to Siegfried and hand him his squirming birthday gift.

Siegfried looked anything but pleased as the little swine continued to wriggle, squeal and grunt at the top of its lungs, showing no inclination to pause for breath. By the next day, the potbelly pig had vanished faster than their elephant did onstage.

As the years went by, Little Bavaria became a charming hodgepodge of almost everything imaginable: an Arcadian garden with a huge pond; a quaint log cabin over-crowded with an amalgamation of international artifacts; and a farm teeming with animals. With its long rows of tall trees and the endless driveway adorned with stately gates—arbitrarily erected a quarter of a mile past the front entrance—it looked like a setting straight out of medieval times. There was also a unique, wayside shrine with two wooden angels imported from a Spanish monastery. This ecclectic theme illustrated how Roy was influenced by Buddhism, Catholicism, and nearly every religion known to man. Roy wasn't as concerned with religious belief as he was with the *aesthetic* of the iconography. He had a tendency to invent a back-story about every square inch of his house, all in support of the duo's self-promoted image of spirituality and oneness with their home environment.

To the south of the house, there are pastures where all of the animals—even Gildah the elephant—have roamed freely on The Land.

One Christmas at Little Bavaria, Roy decided he wanted reindeer "like the ones from the North Pole" that pull Santa's sleigh. As long as they had antlers, it didn't matter where they were from, so Dr. Dinnes found a handful of standard reindeer from a farm near the Grand Canyon in Arizona. After Christmas was over, Roy wanted to send them back—a huge challenge in itself. Roy and his entourage of helpers quickly learned that these deer weren't tame like the ones you pet and feed at the zoo. Getting them to do anything they didn't want to do was nearly impossible—unless they were knocked out first.

As Jimmy Lavery tried to capture the biggest deer in the group, it charged him. Instinctively, he grabbed onto its antlers to protect himself. Then, too scared to let go, he hung on grimly for the ride of his life. At one point, Jimmy managed to steer the deer into the fence line, but it ripped the fence posts right out of the ground—with Jimmy still clinging on for dear life!

Now the fight was on. Dr. Simon, the local vet, had stopped by to help load the animals, but when he tried reining in the deer, the animal gored straight through his jeans and ripped a gash on his thigh, barely missing his *cojones*! It soon became apparent that the men would have to lasso each reindeer to get the herd into the truck. While Dr. Simon managed to lasso most of them, Roy's men just weren't strong enough to wrestle them into the truck, and the deer were getting more agitated by the minute.

Dr. Dinnes, Roy's veterinarian, was offering advice by phone as the battle raged, but to no avail. In the end, he worried about the implications of aggravating the deer too much, and so he ordered them to be released until he could get there to load them personally. Two weeks later, the reindeer were finally loaded and driven away.

Today, Little Bavaria is still the oasis that Roy envisioned. Although he spends increasingly less time there, it is now, more than ever, the "happy place" where he finds the strength he needs to endure his ongoing ordeal.

"Siegfried and Roy have always been extremely responsive to charitable affairs. They realized that was part of their assignment in trying to change the face of Vegas, to make it more receptive to families.... They knew that doing good was not only to their advantage but was to the advantage of the city itself."
—*Robert Maheu*

---

iegfried and Roy maintained their clean-cut celebrity image by pitching in and supporting local causes. As pioneers of the new, family-friendly Las Vegas, they threw themselves into projects aimed at cleaning up "their" city. And the high-profile do-gooders were hotly pursued as sponsors for worthy causes. Howard Hughes' alter-ego, Robert Maheu, a local mover and shaker, recalls seeing Siegfried and Roy at almost every charity event he attended over many years.

At first, the duo concentrated on animal-related projects: protecting lions and tigers and supporting local animal shelters. As time went on, they became boosters for the Clark County School District's "Kids Helping Kids for Education," and Opportunity Village, a charity aimed at bringing physically and mentally disabled people closer to the community.

In one highly publicized, feel-good event, Siegfried and Roy opened up their house to blind and deaf children and were photographed with their tiger, Sahra, and a young blind girl who wanted to "feel the tiger's stripes." Even a magician couldn't make that trick possible, but Siegfried, Roy and Lynette took turns holding the child's fingers and running them along Sahra's silky fur, telling her, "Okay, feel that? ...Now you're touching a black stripe...and now you're touching a gold stripe...!" It was a riveting photo op, and a deeply emotional moment for all involved.

Lynette organized most of the duo's charity events, always coming up with new projects that Siegfried and Roy happily sponsored. She collected used clothes from members of the show and donated them to homeless people, initiated a children's book club fund to raise money for the local library, and set up a program for disadvantaged young people to attend the College of Magic in Cape Town, South Africa.

On one occasion, Siegfried and Roy cheered up the children of Child Haven, a charity for children removed from dysfunctional families, by organizing a picnic at Lake Mead, with elephant Gildah as guest of honor. Park rangers needed to issue a special permit for Gildah, which they stamped amid much laughter when the five-ton animal pulled up in her trailer.

There were picnic goodies aplenty for the children to feast on at the Lake Mead park. McDonald's donated hamburgers, Subway sent over six-foot-long sandwiches, and Coca-Cola supplied the drinks. The highlight came when Gildah was led into the lake to swim with the delighted kids. She plodded in as fast as her stumpy legs would carry her, then swam around with giggling tykes hanging off her from all sides. And everyone cracked up when Gildah began sucking water up with her trunk to spray her little play-mates. These were memories the children would never forget.

Manager Bernie Yuman attended the picnic, smoking a cigar and wearing his standard black suit, vest and cowboy boots, despite the 115-degree heat. He refused to loosen up and take a swim, so Roy ordered Jimmy to throw him into Lake Mead, fully clothed. The kids loved that moment. Bernie didn't, of course, but it was all for a good cause.

Siegfried and Roy's charity work included supporting the Las Vegas police force in its ongoing battle to clean up Sin City. The cops' breakthrough in eradicating Mob influence began in the early 70s, when the Las Vegas Police Department merged with the Clark County Sheriff's

Department to become the LVMPD (or Metro), and John Moran Sr. became Sheriff.

Moran Sr. was what they called a cop's cop; he would always stand by his officers. He was tough but fair, and when he walked into a room, his 6'2" presence always commanded respect. He became one of the most powerful law enforcement figures in Nevada's history—and one of the most liked. When he took over as Sheriff, he made a simple promise: he pledged to sweep gangs and prostitutes off the streets. Within ninety days, hoods and hookers knew Moran meant business. Cops were on them like flies on feces. And just to make life really difficult for the harlots who were picked up and arrested, Sheriff Moran's cops took them to a holding area far from the Strip, so that when they were finally released on bail, they'd have a very long walk, or an expensive cab ride.

By taking a stand against sleaze, illicit sex and the old-time Mob guys, Moran garnered huge respect, especially from parents fearing for their children's safety. He won two more elections hands down, serving a twelve-year term. He was often urged to run for Governor, and many of Nevada's most powerful people, Siegfried and Roy included, would have supported him. Moran died in 1998, but family ties to the German duo remained when John Moran, Jr., the Sheriff's son, became their lawyer.

By 1982, Siegfried and Roy had lived in Vegas on a permanent basis for nearly a decade when an LVMPD cop, Officer James MacLaren, was shot in the head during a traffic stop. The officer survived his injuries, but he was forced into medical retirement; his family was left with a particularly heavy burden to carry, because government programs didn't cover all of the costs required for his care. Sheriff Moran and his wife, a colorful lady named Goldie, organized an event to benefit injured police officers in situations similar to Officer MacLaren's. She called it "Steppin' Out With the Stars"—"stars" referring to celebrities who were asked to pitch in and perform, as well as the star-shaped police badges.

The Sheriff reached out to Siegfried and Roy through their manager, Bernie Yuman. The boys from Germany leapt onto the charity bandwagon, became honorary chairmen, and immediately enticed other celebrities to support the cause, which included what evolved into an annual event called The John and Goldie Moran Memorial Golf Classic, first held on October 10, 1982. At the ceremony that year, a memorable moment occurred when Siegfried and Roy appeared onstage with their baby tiger cub, Sitarra, who sat on the podium with a ribbon tied around her neck, from which dangled a check for $10,000.

One hilarious incident marked the second annual show in 1983 when Sitarra—again with a big bow around her neck, and another $10,000 check for John Moran—padded onstage with Roy. No longer a cub, and a few hundred pounds heavier, Sitarra didn't look quite as harmless as she had the year before, and the Sheriff looked just a little bit nervous. A moment later, he nearly jumped out of his skin when the big cat looked down, caught her reflection in the white glass stage being used that year, and emitted a rafter-shaking roar. Moran's cops teased him unmercifully about how scared he'd looked. The Sheriff, who didn't take himself too seriously, just laughed and said, "That fucking cat nearly ate me."

Siegfried and Roy never had too much trouble recruiting big-name celebrities for the glitzy annual event, making it an even bigger success than anyone could have hoped. Stars knew they'd be escorted to and from the show in a limo, surrounded by police cars with flashing lights and sirens. Joan Rivers, who was playing at Caesar's Palace, was escorted by twenty police officers and loved the attention so much she invited them and their families to her show the next night.

Better yet, everyone involved in the extravagant charity event got special police officer badges. Siegfried, Roy and Bernie Yuman—all badge collectors over the years— each had one and supposedly understood that the shields did not endow them with any police powers. But about six months after they'd received the badges, a captain for Metro saw one of the event's organizers, Las Vegas security expert Jim Mydlach, and asked, "You're a friend of Bernie Yuman's, right?"

"Yes."

"Do me a favor, Jim. He drives his black Corvette up and down the Strip, and when he's stopped for speeding, he flashes that fuckin' badge every time. Tell him to slow it down, okay?"

Jim Mydlach, with a few of his cop friends, decided Bernie Yuman needed a lesson in law enforcement. On his birthday a few days later, Bernie was in his office suite at the Hacienda Hotel when someone started pounding on his door. He opened up and was confronted by two big cops, who snapped, "Are you Bernie Yuman?"

"Yes?"

"We have a warrant for you and we're taking you to jail downtown."

Bernie immediately tried flashing his badge again, but the cops were unmoved. "Let's go," they said. They escorted him down the hall, then stopped in front of a room and one cop said, "Wait, I have to talk to my supervisor. We're doing a sting here in the hotel."

Bernie nearly had a heart attack as the door suddenly swung open with a bang...and he saw a roomful of his friends, leering at him over a big birthday cake, shouting, "SURPRISE!"

Siegfried and Roy became big supporters of the Metro K-9 unit after seeing TV footage of a police dog injured in the line of duty. Since 1990, the Friends for Las Vegas Police K-9s group has sponsored the Annual Las Vegas Police K-9 Trials—the most renowned fundraising event of its kind in the country. During the trials, awards are given for the top five finishers in Narcotics, Bombs, Area Search, Building Search, Obedience, Agility and Handler Protection, as well as for Top Dog and Top Agency. Every year, Siegfried and Roy publicize this event for the media, helping to raise money for the unit.

Their unceasing efforts for their community were recognized in July 2001: Siegfried and Roy were named

Honorary Deputy Sheriffs, "in recognition of their civic activities and support of the Metro Police Department K-9 Unit."

As if all this weren't enough, Roy contacted Jim Mydlach and asked him to make a request to Sheriff Moran. "Jim, will you talk to the Sheriff and ask him if I can pay for two police salaries for a year?" Mydlach, who was later hired as the duo's chief of security, never did speak to the Sheriff, because Siegfried thought that offering to pay money to a police department might look improper, to say the least.

Improper as it may look, or be, Siegfried and Roy had already established quite a bond with the Las Vegas Police Department. Although Siegfried and Roy's tireless charity work was consistent with their squeaky-clean image, it certainly wasn't a bad idea to befriend the local police department. The entertainment industry has a history of maintaining close ties with police forces.

From the 1920s on, the Motion Picture Production Association made generous contributions to city officials, and hired police officers to guard sets and see that the studios were well protected. Charity donations are tax deductible, so Siegfried and Roy had nothing to lose by donating a lot of their cash as they could later write it off. Accounting purposes aside, Siegfried and Roy had newfound friends with power and invaluable connections; never a bad thing for stars with secrets to protect.

No matter how blatantly gay the duo appeared to be, they were careful not to be publicly pegged as homosexuals. Those cute San Juan and Santo Domingo stud muffins were, after all, nobody's business. But big stars are money-making enterprises that need protection, so friendships with the police were practical and prudent for Siegfried and Roy, just as they were for many stars. Los Angeles Police historian Joe Domanick points out that Hollywood always "needed to protect [their] stars and other key players from career-destroying scandals.... Carousing wild men like Errol Flynn and homosexual stars were constantly being picked up by the LAPD, but never booked."

Hollywood wanted the public happily oblivious to the behind-the-scene antics of onscreen idols. Heterosexual moviegoers worshipped the movie stars and were attracted by their sexual appeal. As long as the façade remained intact, everybody was happy. So Hollywood studios were literally more concerned with homosexuality than murder. When actor William Desmond Taylor was killed in 1922, Paramount Pictures beat the police to his mansion and removed any possible giveaways to his light-in-the-loafers lifestyle. And they even planted evidence to suggest he'd had affairs with women.

During the 1950s and McCarthyism, the fear of a homosexual exposé equaled the terror tactic of Communist blacklisting. Studios were forced to take extra precautions when a new wave of racy gossip magazines threatened to drown the town in scandal. *Confidential* magazine, founded in 1952 by Robert Harrison, was at the forefront of rags with titles like *Whisper, Blast, Uncensored, Rave* and *Top Secret*. But *Confidential* was king, boasting a readership of approximately five million in 1957.

Harrison paid a fortune to get the most shocking exposés about A-list names, serving up lurid stories of sexual affairs, theft, drug addiction, and even murder. But all of those stories combined couldn't trump a headline about a top star's homosexuality. And with today's resurgence of the modern-day tabloid trend, there are experienced journalists constantly digging the dirt from networks of sources who come into contact with showbiz stars: sales clerks, waitresses, hatcheck girls, hotel maids, bail bondsmen, moving companies, private detectives, wiretap experts, and the list goes on.

So...did a family-friendly image and all the hard work, money and gifts that Siegfried and Roy donated to the Las Vegas community help squelch any detrimental rumors? Who knows, but their many friends in high places certainly couldn't hurt.

Smart celebrities like Siegfried and Roy are like Boy Scouts: always prepared. Because one way or another, if you believe Shakespeare, the truth will out.

"The show must go on."

I n Spring of 1984, Siegfried and Roy had been at the Frontier for three years and would extend their contract by another four. But before they reached the end of their third year, pandemonium struck Las Vegas. Contracts covering workers at fifty hotel-casinos expired at midnight on April 2, 1984. The Culinary Workers Union had decided to take action and go out on strike.

Some 17,200 culinary workers, stagehands, musicians and bartenders set up picket lines along the Las Vegas Strip, forcing all the major hotels to cancel their star-studded shows. Shirley MacLaine and Suzanne Somers' nightly performances were pulled, and Siegfried and Roy's "Beyond Belief" almost met the same fate. The only people who did not desert the stage were the show's featured stars—Siegfried and Roy—and their animals; the ever-faithful Lynette Chappell; the animals' handlers; the Feld's dancers and KC unicyclists; and the conductor of the vanished orchestra.

Although the gambling industry was not affected as much as the entertainment business, the strike froze Vegas' tourism revenue; it would end up costing the city more than $100 million. The entertainment capital erupted in a state of panic. Those who dared to work literally feared for their lives. Those who no longer had jobs faced the end of their livelihoods and lifestyles.

The strikers truly did not know what they were up against. The leading hotels' investors would fight to the bitter end before letting the union workers sabotage their income. Hotel security departments went on twelve-hour shifts to ramp up for the strike, and extra security support was called in from around the country. In order to comprehend how high the stakes were in the 1984 strike, one must first consider Las Vegas' unparalleled level of security.

By the 1980s, Nevada had evolved from its Wild West days. It was now the most regulated state in America, if not the world. Since the era of Bugsy Siegel, security had become incredibly sophisticated, and it had to be. As famed robber Willie Sutton once put it when asked why he robbed banks: "Because that's where the money is." The high-rolling big-bucks atmosphere that lured tourists also attracted the world's thieves, grifters, crooked gamblers, and worse. By the 1970s, whole sections of the casinos' ceilings were one-way mirrored glass, concealing security personnel guarding the gaming tables from a network of catwalks up above.

As technology progressed, the term "eye in the sky" no longer referred to these sharp-eyed watchmen, but to the 10,000-plus pan-and-tilt cameras monitoring and recording almost every move made within the resort properties. These closed-circuit television cameras were hidden in glass dome-shaped bubbles above the gaming tables, but their coverage spanned slot machine areas, hallways, entrances, restaurants, showrooms, parking garages, elevators, and even every other square inch that the public never saw.

In another twenty years, Las Vegas security would get downright scary. State-of-the-art surveillance systems would convert from analog to digital recordings, incorporating sophisticated facial recognition programs that allowed casino surveillance operators to scan any suspicious person on their premises and compare them to photos of known crooks and scam artists.

With the advancement of technology, it was necessary to improve the quality of security personnel. In the old days, security guards lived up to the reputation we now associate with the Mob. They took no guff from anyone; one wrong step, and two or three bulky brutes would escort a suspected troublemaker to an alley out back and rearrange his face. Or, if he was really lucky, a knuckle-breaking goon would frog-march him to a secluded room off the casino floor for a private "conversation."

But as the decades passed, major hotels got smart about security. They had too much at risk to hire staff whose main talent was busting heads. The new breed of security officers were tough but intelligent people trained to handle anything from a medical emergency to the outbreak of a major fire. By the 90s, according to local ambulance teams, the safest place in the world to have a heart attack was in Las Vegas, due to trained security staff and state-of-the-art equipment like AEDs—Automatic External Defibrillators— which can shock a heart back into beating ninety seconds after it quits. Security Departments at the major casinos participate in AED demonstrations every month to keep them sharp. AEDs are routinely available everywhere in the nation today, but statistics show that Las Vegas stands first in the world for number of lives saved, because the city's hotels insist on constant training with the device.

By 1984, before he signed on as security chief for Siegfried and Roy, Jim Mydlach had worked for the Las Vegas Hilton for four years. He'd been in the industry for over two decades, including a stint as Director of Security and Safety for the Aladdin and Dunes hotel-casinos, followed by thirteen years at the Golden Nugget.

On April 4, 1984, Jim was about to face union strikers head on. That morning, he and his partner Bobby were on duty at the Hilton. Taking their lunch break, they took off in their security vehicle and noticed that a large crowd had amassed across the street from the hotel. When Jim noticed news reporters and camera crews converging on the crowd, he told Bobby, "Looks like strikers. We've got to go take a ride down there and check out what's going on."

"If you fuck up my lunch, I'm going to kill you," Bobby groused.

But burgers and fries were put on hold when the crowd of strikers suddenly crossed the street and marched onto Hilton property. Jim pulled the security vehicle up onto the sidewalk to block their access, then stepped out of the vehicle and read aloud the official Nevada trespass warning to the front row of the strikers. He and his partner tried to block their path, but they were only two against more than two hundred. Jim called for backup as the crowd pushed past them and headed for the hotel's front entrance, where a security team of officers and supervisors had set up a barrier. When the strikers reached the security line, they were again civilly asked to stop and leave the property immediately. That's when a striker leading the crowd—later identified as a professional troublemaker from Ohio—swung and hit Jim Mydlach.

The fight was on.

All hell broke loose as a "444" call—"Officer needs help"—went out to Las Vegas Metropolitan Police. Every cop in town not directly involved in an emergency dropped everything and raced to the Hilton. The noise of sirens was deafening as the cavalry arrived, brandishing police PR24 batons. The army of unemployed strikers fearlessly joined in the battle. One of them, brandishing a picket sign stapled to a heavy stick made of oak, hit a Metro officer so hard he split his head open.

Instead of going down, the officer whirled around, knocking out several strikers in seconds with his baton. Finally, the police and Hilton security prevailed, sending a lot of people to jail in the process.

That's when everyone knew the strike was going to be really messy. Security personnel and union workers had once played on the same team, but now they were bitter adversaries. It would be many years before any modicum of trust between the two factions would be re-established.

The TV camera crews had a field day. The clash was broadcast all over the world. Jim Mydlach got more time on the CBS Evening News than anchor Dan Rather. The *New York Times* reported that "at one point the police jailed almost 900 strikers after they harassed tourists and disrupted traffic on the Strip."

It got much, much worse. Dynamite bombs were exploding in hotel parking lots and swimming pools. On a trip to the grocery store, Lynette was shaken when someone smashed the windshield and T-Top of her red Corvette. Stink bombs evacuated casinos. A swarm of bees angrily swirled up out of a suitcase left inside the MGM Grand casino.

Being forced to take time off because of a strike was extremely frustrating for Siegfried and Roy, and the hiatus was costing the hotel a small fortune every day. During the strike, the duo's animals enjoyed their time off at Siegfried and Roy's mansion, lazing around the pool inside their custom-made habitat, which looked like a snow-capped mountain range.

Summa Corporation, the owner of the Frontier hotel, desperately sought replacement workers—fast. The culinary workers' absence didn't affect the show, but Summa needed to make non-union stagehands and orchestra members magically appear out of the desert air. It wouldn't be an easy feat to recruit workers brave enough to face a city filled with thousands of enraged strikers who had nothing to lose but their careers. One of Summa's first calls was to a man named Martin Durham, who'd opened Siegfried and Roy's "Beyond Belief" show as company manager, and then moved back to his native South Carolina with his wife.

Stagehand Jimmy Lavery was vacationing at old friend Martin's lake house when an urgent call came in from Frontier hotel president Phil Arce.

"Have you heard there's a strike?" Arce asked.

"Yes," Martin replied patiently. Hell, it was national news.

"We really need your help, Martin. Is there any chance you can come back and give us a hand putting this show together again?"

Martin instantly volunteered to help out his old friends, no questions asked. Moments later, the Frontier stage manager, Todd Dougall, called to discuss the plan of action. With Jimmy standing by his side, Martin asked, "How much help do you need?"

"All the help we can get."

"I have a qualified stagehand standing right here. Do you want him to come along?"

"Definitely."

Martin and Jimmy booked tickets and arrived in Vegas the following day. Jimmy would end up sticking around for the next twenty years!

Neither Martin nor Jimmy took the strike very seriously at first. They were there as a favor for their old crew, Phil Arce, stage manager Todd Dougall, and Irvin and Kenneth Feld. Jimmy, who loved being back in Vegas, was out drinking and frolicking with the ladies every night. But the strike was intensifying, and the fun wouldn't last much longer.

Reopening the show was a formidable mission. They had the core team, but now Martin Durham, Todd Dougall and Jimmy Lavery had to hire a raft of replacements for the show's striking employees. They started by sifting through stacks of job applications. Their process of elimination was simple. Merely showing up at the interview earned a prospective employee points, but the true test came when they'd line up a group of candidates in the middle of the stage and shout, "All of you...move stage left!" Anyone who stepped to their right was immediately sent packing. Everyone else was hired on the spot.

Finally, they assembled a team of some forty unqualified stagehands. Ex-dancers worked wardrobe; furniture movers handled the props; school teachers were trained to perform illusions; and anyone who responded to the ad was considered skilled enough to operate spotlights, general lighting, or sound, no questions asked—provided they knew left from right, of course. Conductor Al Alvarez managed to put an orchestra together. Now the company was once again complete...or as complete as it could be during a strike.

Everyone involved in the original show pitched in wherever they could to make deadlines. New staff members worked around the clock to get the show up and running in record-breaking time. Jimmy recalls clocking eighteen- to twenty-hour days. He ended up in the hospital, suffering from exhaustion. Both his arms had to be injected with intravenous fluids for eighteen hours to re-hydrate his body.

Finally, after many rehearsals to coordinate the entire troupe with Siegfried, Roy and Lynette's performance, the show was ready to go—except for the animals. In those days, Roy was the only person who trained the cats, although he always maintained he's never technically "trained" them. Roy says he simply tunes into their language and improvises intuitively off their behavior, adjusting as it changes from day to day.

The show with the new crew had to be perfect before the cats were introduced, because one misstep could lead to disaster. But after the cats had just two rehearsals with the new troupe, Irvin Feld was satisfied and announced, "We're up to speed. Let's go!"

The next day, Siegfried and Roy's act opened before a live audience. The Germans had always lived by the motto "the show must go on," and despite the whopping obstacles they'd needed to overcome, it did exactly that...and more! It was a roaring success, and got huge media attention. "Beyond Belief" was one of the first shows on the Strip to continue with non-union workers. Now the next big challenge loomed: surviving the wrath of the culinary union's enraged strikers, who'd massed behind a picket line in front of the Frontier—and were literally threatening the lives of any "scab" who dared cross it. Police had to escort employees to their cars. Frontier hotel executives were moved onto the casino premises so security teams could protect them around the clock.

Siegfried and Roy received threats every single night:

"We're going to get Siegfried."

"We're going to get Roy."

"We're going to kill the cats."

In addition to residing on the premises, owners of the multimillion-dollar hotel-casinos stocked their warehouses with food to avoid any contamination during the strike. It was a total lock-down. But who could guarantee that the warehouses were 100 percent secured? At one time, the Frontier threw away thousands of pounds of meat—the animal's feed—just on the barest of fears that it might have been poisoned. (That didn't deter them from donating it to the nearest zoo, however, and the zoo happily accepted, with no unfortunate results!)

Summa Corporation, the Frontier's owners, had a lot of money invested in Siegfried and Roy's show. The stars were viewed as a long-term investment, and losing either one or both was not an option. The company founded by Howard Hughes owned most of the legendary hotel-casinos on the Strip—The Sands, Landmark, Castaways, Desert Inn, Silver Slipper, and Xanadu Princess Resort—and they did not mess around.

These hard-nosed operators started protecting their investment a week before the strike started. Bernie Yuman called his pal Jim Mydlach, the security expert, and told him, "We're going to open the show as the contract with the hotel requires us to. I need you to get your team together. Siegfried, Roy and the animals have been getting death threats."

Mydlach was still working at the Hilton, but he managed to put together the best team possible and began working two jobs: He'd finish his twelve-hour shift at the Hilton, and then drive over to the Frontier. His ten-man security group for Siegfried and Roy was formidable. Fuji, for example, was a 5'3" black belt master of martial arts. Mydlach calls him "the most deadly son of a bitch you wouldn't want to meet on a dark night. No matter how big you were, he'd take you down." There were several other martial arts experts, plus weapons and tactics experts; a former Navy Seal; a retired White House Secret Service agent, and emergency medical technicians (EMTs). The team attended every show, then escorted Siegfried and Roy home at night.

After each show, the big cats were loaded up and escorted back to their sanctuary. Even though Roy was one of the Strip's biggest stars, he personally loaded and unloaded his animals between midnight and 3 a.m., transporting them in two white trucks. The trucks were marked "Flammable" in large letters, with no mention of what really was inside, but anyone foolish enough to peek behind the doors was in for the surprise of a lifetime.

Jim Mydlach's team provided chase cars that tailed the trucks from the hotel to the Jungle Palace, then back to the hotel the next day. Roy drove one of the trucks himself, with an escort beside him. One night, Jim rode shotgun and felt an unsettling warm breath on the back of his neck. He turned...and looked right into the ice-blue eyes of a 400-pound tiger in a cage behind him. The first time it happened, the six-foot-four bodyguard froze in his seat. "It was one of those experiences when you don't know whether to shit or go blind," he recalled. Roy nearly busted a gut laughing at his supposedly fearless "hired gun."

Siegfried drove back and forth alone in his blue Mercedes. He insisted he could fend for himself. If he could survive Roy's unpredictable animals on a daily basis, he'd survive the strike. "I can ditch anybody," he assured his concerned security team. Mydlach would just nod, but the second Siegfried left the room, two team members would peel off and follow him. "Bernie wants it done this way," Mydlach would say.

It was the security team's job not to be noticed. They did this so effectively that during one show, the audience actually mistook them for part of the act when a union worker sitting in the front row leapt up during the middle of the performance and started yelling union slogans. Jim's guys flew over, whipped him upside the head and bum-rushed him out a side door so fast that the audience just chuckled like it was a comedy bit, and the show went on.

The strike got hairier. In its eighth week, at 2:15 a.m., on June 2nd—not long after that night's show had ended—a bomb suddenly exploded in the Frontier parking lot, just under Jimmy Lavery's hotel room. The Frontier went on high alert as swarms of police officers and FBI agents arrived to investigate.

The police later reported that several minutes after the explosion, a man phoned the hotel and told an operator that he'd planted the bomb, and Siegfried and Roy would be the next target. The hotel executives tightened security, but were adamant: nothing would stop the show.

Jimmy Lavery, one of the few employees who lived on the premises during the strike, was not overly thrilled when Mydlach assigned a bear-like bodyguard nicknamed—naturally—Bear, to escort him everywhere, 24/7. As an extra precaution, Jimmy was moved to a safer room on the other side of the hotel. It was all very frustrating for a man who loved to hoist a few and party with the ladies, even though he appreciated that there was real danger lurking outside. During the three months of the strike, he left the premises just twice, and on one trip, learned there's truth in the old adage: Better safe than sorry.

One night, determined to blow off some steam, he managed to ditch Bear, grabbed stage manager Todd Dougall and slipped off to the nearest bar they could find: The Four Kegs. Ahhh! Finally, an ice-cold beer after a hard day's work! As one beer became two, then three, they started laughing about weird things that had happened in the troupe since the strike had turned a well-oiled machine into a clunker in need of a total overhaul. Like the time Roy had suddenly disappeared in the middle of a rehearsal...POOF!...just like that! And it wasn't a magic trick....

It happened during a run-through of the Metamorphosis illusion, perfected twenty years prior with Chico, the cheetah, and performed nowadays with their leopard, Sabu.

Over the years, the illusion had been developed and polished on a much grander scale than ever before. Like every part of their act, the illusion depended on the audience's understanding of the duo's respective roles; Siegfried as the magician, Roy the animal trainer. Onstage, they appeared to be on the same wavelength, but they actually performed in two completely different worlds.

For the most part, Siegfried kept his distance from the animals. But audiences were never aware that he feared the wild creatures he worked with night after night. If you had asked whether they'd noticed that Siegfried never holds the big cats' leashes, they'd almost certainly have answered with a "No." Similarly, Roy's detachment from magic was expertly disguised. Although he accepted awards and appeared at events with Siegfried, he wasn't a part of the magicians' fraternity; it simply wasn't his deal. But these nuances were so slight, they'd only be noted by fellow magicians, or the show's employees.

Their roles as illusionists followed this logic: Siegfried caused the wave, and Roy surfed it. Siegfried played the empowered magician who could overcome all evil and danger; Roy was his magical buddy. And that's how the dynamic worked so successfully. As a general rule, two magicians can't perform side by side. It's like having two orchestra conductors. But Siegfried and Roy's onstage chemistry worked, due, in part, to their offstage chemistry, and with the animals, they pulled off the double act. There have been duos who tried to imitate them, like "Jonathan and David" who appeared in the movie *Casino*, but Siegfried and Roy set a benchmark that is still unmatched.

Their dynamic is perfectly illustrated in the Metamorphosis illusion. Siegfried's the one who's tied up and magically released, not Roy. When the substitution trunk was rolled onstage, Roy rotated it to show that all four sides were solid, then Siegfried climbed in. Roy would handcuff Siegfried and put him in a black mailbag. The bag was fastened and lowered into the trunk, which was then shut and padlocked.

Flashing lights and music built the excitement as Roy dramatically jumped up onto the trunk. Swinging his arms theatrically, he'd twirl the rope in the air and tie it around the trunk.

Once, when Siegfried and Roy finally saw a video of themselves performing the illusion, Siegfried was stunned as he saw how Roy ran around the box, jumping on top of it and flinging his arms like an octopus on speed. Gasped Siegfried, "Wow, you really do all that?" All it really came down to, after all, was tying rope around a box.

Once the audience was made to believe the trunk had been fastened—that there was absolutely no way Siegfried could escape—Roy took hold of the big cloth hoop, waved it around in front of him, then threw it up in the air, and by the time it fell back down, obscuring him, he'd have switched places with Siegfried in the trunk. Inside the trunk, concealed in a holding chamber, was their leopard, Sabu. Roy would quickly release the cat into the trunk and pop into the holding chamber himself.

Then, to great fanfare, Sabu would jump out of the trunk as the audience went wild. The leopard then walked to a transport box and was wheeled offstage.

That was the end of the trick, and Siegfried would stand onstage, waving his "magic sword" until Roy rejoined him and they took their bows. But in the first rehearsal during the strike, no matter how energetically the flamboyant blond Aryan waved his sword, Roy did not appear. After a few uncomfortable seconds of looking and feeling silly, Siegfried's blood began to boil...and finally bubbled over.

"Vehhrrr eeess Roy?" he barked.

The expression on Siegfried's face said it all; he has a prominent vein on his forehead that runs down to his eye and bulges whenever he's upset. The rehearsal immediately ground to a halt. No one dared make eye contact with their furious boss as he screamed, "Find Roy!" The crew searched every square inch of the theater, even fanning out into the hotel area. Finally, someone heard a tap-tap-tapping noise backstage. It was coming from the trunk. Moments later, Roy was released from the holding chamber, cracking that he'd really enjoyed his "cat nap" during the prolonged search.

It turned out that none of the new, amateur troupe members had been told that somebody had to unlatch the trunk's holding chamber and release Roy as soon as it was moved offstage. It was a wacky moment and, luckily, Roy found the humor in it. Jimmy, Todd and the crew finally busted out in suppressed laughter.

Even Siegfried cracked a smile.

But Jimmy hadn't found it quite so funny when he became the butt—literally—of a not-so-funny joke. After the union workers walked out, it was rumored that they'd sabotaged the equipment. Every piece of machinery had to be re-tested as a safety precaution, and he was elected guinea pig.

The Frontier Hotel, where Siegfried and Roy starred in "Beyond Belief" for seven years.

▲ Lynette Chappell, the "Evil Queen," backstage at the Frontier.

◄

Siegfried Fischbacher, Roy Horn, and Toney Mitchell onstage at the Las Vegas Hilton for the annual IPOF (Injured Police Officer's Fund) event in the 80s.

Siegfried and Roy with Sheriff Moran Sr. at the annual benefit held in honor of the Las Vegas police force.

Toney Mitchell and Jim Mydlach, who was Siegfried and Roy's head of security and co-producer of the IPOF event.

Louis Mydlach with Roy at the second IPOF benefit in 1983.

Sitarra, in her cage in Roy's bedroom at the Frontier, gets a kiss from Jimmy Lavery.

An example of the prison cell-like cages at South-North Trading, Inc., in Yuka Saito, Japan.

The lion cages of the South-North Trading, Inc.

The entrance to a Japanese animal dealership specializing in rare all-white animals.

A view from the parking lot of the Japanese dealership, where Siegfried and Roy purchased their rare white lions.

Lynette Chappell with the Geisha Girls on tour in Japan.

The cats and their trainers taking a break on the lawn of Little Bavaria.

▲ Siegfried and Roy's donkey (pictured). Horses, llamas, geese, roe deer, goats, dogs, big cats, and—on occasion—even Gildah the elephant roamed freely on "The Land."

▼ Roy's dream "Log Cabin" oasis in the middle of the Nevada desert.

▼ Roy's Arcadian island in the backyard of Little Bavaria.

The view from the back porch of Little Bavaria.

An example of Roy's eclectic design.

Roy Horn and staff training two of his tigers at Little Bavaria.

Monty Cox and Roy "affection conditioning" one of his cats.

A tiger playing with the deer on the other side of the fence at "The Land."

Two white lion cubs frolicking in the grass.

Roy Horn on the steps of his Little Bavarian retreat.

▲ After a long day of shooting, two cubs take a quick nap.

Siegfried and Roy in their snowsuit costumes for *The Magic Box*, shot on location at Mount Charleston just outside of Las Vegas.

Roy, lying in a gingerbread house used for the Christmas-themed shoot, shares a snack with his acting partner.

Siegfried and Roy filming on top of Mount Charleston.

▲ Cast and crew of
The Magic Box.

▲ Roy snuggles up to a trio of
white tigers.

Siegfried and Roy pose with
their tigers in front of an
American flag backdrop for the
shooting of their first feature
film, *The Magic Box.*

The "Siegfried & Roy" emblem adorns the fortress that surrounds the Jungle Palace.

The main entrance to Siegfried and Roy's mansion, the Jungle Palace.

◄ Tiger statuettes adorn the Jungle Palace wall on Valley Drive.

▲ Jimmy Lavery, Lynette Chappell, and a cub heading home to the Jungle Palace after work at The Mirage.

Lynette getting ready to put one of her precious little ones to sleep at the Jungle Palace nursery.

Monty Cox, one of Siegfried and Roy's trusted animal coordinators.

"When you work with lions, you live in a life-or-death world." —Monty Cox

A group of tigers play in their pen outside.

Steve Wynn's glitzy Mirage Hotel and Casino.

Chris feeding Gildah a snack at The Mirage's Secret Garden habitat.

A plaque dedicated to Roy's favorite snow white tiger, Sitarra, who was officially known as the matriarch of the Royal White Tigers of Nevada.

One of Siegfried and Roy's cats behind the fence at the Secret Garden.

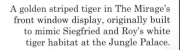

A golden striped tiger in The Mirage's front window display, originally built to mimic Siegfried and Roy's white tiger habitat at the Jungle Palace.

The Dolphin Habitat at The Mirage.

One of The Mirage's dolphins pops out of the water to say "Hello!"

A dolphin swims in one of the three interconnected pools in The Mirage's Dolphin Habitat.

Lynette Chappell and Jimmy Lavery celebrating at The Mirage.

A 600-pound tiger relaxes in the Secret Garden.

Trainers and cubs rehearse for the "Siegfried & Roy" show at The Mirage, which would go on to become the most successful act on the Strip.

Two white cubs onstage, training for their debut at The Mirage.

Jimmy Lavery and Monty Cox babysit the cubs in an apartment on The Mirage compound.

An adorable white cub models for the camera.

Three cubs play-fight over a towel in their room at The Mirage.

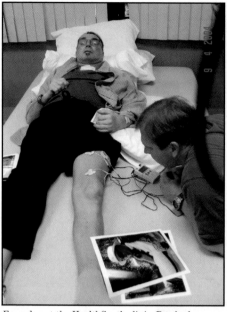

Everyday at the HealthSouth clinic, Roy had a short handwriting therapy session after lunch, followed by an hour of physical therapy during which his muscles were stimulated in a process he called "Electrocution."

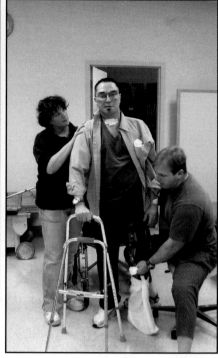

Roy Horn, several months after the incident, learns to walk again at the HealthSouth Clinic with the help of two physical therapists.

Roy in his favorite Armani beanie and Nike running shoes, undergoing physical therapy at Miss Horn's house on the Jungle Palace estate.

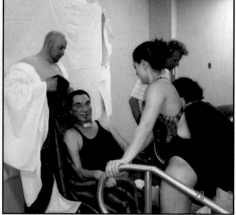

Louis Mydlach with Roy Horn undergoing swim therapy at HealthSouth.

Later in his recovery, Roy trained in the pool with his nurses.

Due to atrophy of the muscles, Roy Horn developed "claw hand" on his left side. Here, he does a muscle-strengthening exercise with his right, working arm.

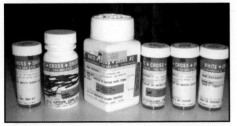

Roy Horn took pain medication shipped over from Germany in addition to his prescriptions from various doctors in the United States.

▲ One of Roy's happier moments after the mauling was getting to hold one of the newly born leopards, at the Jungle Palace.

◄ Roy, in his Invacare electric wheelchair, feeds a goat at Little Bavaria.

Roy Horn was known for his larger-than-life birthday celebrations.

Siegfried and
Roy reunite
onstage for
Roy's birthday.

 The duo and their
longtime manager,
Bernie Yuman, who
referred to himself as
Siegfried & Roy's
"Ampersand."

"Testing out the equipment" entailed such dicey stunts as balancing on the mirror ball as it dangled ten feet above the seating area. The rotating mirror ball added pizzazz to the closing act of the show. Roy and a tiger would appear standing on the glittering ball as it rotated high above the audience. Jimmy, who weighed almost as much as the tiger and Roy put together, went up on the ball and signaled for it to be rotated. It began turning, and he tried to keep pace as it turned, but he'd barely taken a step when the ball began spinning so fast he was forced to hold on for dear life.

Jimmy hollered angrily, and the ball finally stopped. At first, he figured this was just one more case of inexperienced help. But a quick investigation revealed that the controls *couldn't* be adjusted. Somebody had programmed the ball to rotate at full speed. But who?

It looked like the strike had struck again!

As for Jimmy, he could have been flung into the fifteenth row of the audience. Luckily, he only had a short fall from the ball—and landed smack on his butt.

"Wish I'd seen that!" Dougall teased his friend back at The Four Kegs.

Just then, a guy at the bar approached them.

"Hey! What are you doing here?"

"Hey man, what *are* we doing here?" Jimmy repeated nonchalantly to Todd. The beer had gone to his head.

Todd mumbled back, "I don't know, we're just talking."

Both were oblivious to the fact that the guy was a union worker. And they were drinking in a union bar. Suddenly, they were surrounded by a group of unhappy ex-employees. Jimmy looked up from his glass and muttered, "Todd, this ain't looking pretty!" Back in those days, neither of them owned a cell phone and had no way to call for help. Thankfully, a friend named Rick Prior came to the rescue at just the right moment and escorted them back to the hotel. That incident convinced Jimmy that working with lions and tigers was a hell of a lot safer than leaving the sanctuary of the Frontier—at least during the strike.

Jimmy ventured out one other time. During the strike, Lynette's dresser, Sharon Jimmerson, tried her hand at a little matchmaking. She told Lynette that Jimmy was the best new catch on the "Siegfried & Roy" team. To begin with, he had an unlimited RFB tab—free room, food and beverages—at the hotel. As Sharon colorfully put it, that meant half of the show's female dancers would immediately fall blind drunk in love with him...or just get blind drunk. "Go for it," Sharon told Lynette. Sharon then went to Jimmy and told him Lynette had a crush.

Never one to miss an opportunity, Jimmy asked Lynette out to *the* "in" place at the time: The Flame, right across the street from the Frontier. A spark was ignited that night at The Flame when Jimmy and Lynette hit it off immediately, but they agreed to keep their romance a secret.

After the strike was over months later, the show's original stagehands were re-hired. Gradually, everything went back to the way it had been. Jimmy stayed on for a couple of weeks to make sure everything was running smoothly and then booked a ticket back to Georgia. On his last day, he sadly walked backstage to wish everyone farewell. He said goodbye to Siegfried after the first show that night, but Roy wasn't around so Jimmy went looking for him upstairs in the apartment the duo used between shows. As he'd done many times, Jimmy marveled at the view from their window. It was one of the most amazing, and most valuable, in Vegas, and it overlooked the entire Strip. Countless celebrity guests—from Elizabeth Taylor, to Michael Jackson, James Brown and super-producer Aaron Spelling—had oohed-and-aahed at that view with hosts Siegfried and Roy.

It was a truly exotic apartment. A leopard lived in a cage in the bathroom. Sitarra, Roy's favorite tiger, resided in their bedroom. Once, Jimmy had taken Aaron Spelling's daughter, young Tori Spelling, to see Sitarra—showing the child that the baby cat was so docile she could pet her.

When Jimmy walked into the apartment at about 9:30 p.m., Roy was taking a shower. Jimmy's plane was scheduled to take off to Atlanta at 11:55 p.m., and he was cutting it close. He couldn't leave without saying goodbye, so he waited until Roy emerged and launched into his goodbye speech. But Roy was having none of it. "No, no. You're not going anyvehr," he barked in his Teutonic accent.

"Roy, I've already checked out...I'm gone," replied Jimmy.

Roy immediately had Bernie on the phone. "Jimmy's staying. He's going to vork for us." Astounded, Jimmy put down his bags and ended up working for Siegfried and Roy on and off for almost two decades.

After Jimmy excitedly ran downstairs to break the news to Lynette, he suddenly realized he'd already given up his room. "No problem," said Lynette. She offered to put him up for the night. Jimmy couldn't believe his luck. This beautiful dancer with the best body in the show was inviting him, a Redneck from Georgia, to spend the night in her house? How could he refuse? Naturally, he didn't, and the couple ended up living together for nineteen years.

Lynette and Jimmy finally split up in April 2003. Jimmy was thrown out of the house and the locks were changed. With incredible timing, he hired an attorney the very day before Roy's mauling, then filed a lawsuit against Roy and Lynette for what he claimed was owed him.

On April 29, 2005, just over a year into the court case, Siegfried signed the settlement giving Lynette ownership of the house. In addition, she was given the office next door, which ironically Jimmy had built before they split up.

"It is, by any measure, a Palace fit for a King."
—*Siegfried & Roy*

In 1982, before the names Siegfried and Roy became synonymous with images of exotic white tigers, India's Maharaja of Baroda, the commissioner of wildlife for his vast nation, jetted into Las Vegas to see "Beyond Belief." After the show, he visited Siegfried and Roy in their apartment, talking into the wee hours about how the duo handled their animals and of his native India's efforts to preserve its wildlife. The nobleman captivated the duo with a riveting story about his late cousin, the last Maharaja of Rewa, Martand Singh, who had been fascinated for years by rare sightings of an elusive, mystical creature he believed existed only in India. A painting of this animal was actually inscribed on his family's coat of arms, but Martand Singh had never laid eyes on the creature.

The magical beast was known as the White Tiger, or Ghost Tiger, because its faint black or brown stripes are visible only in certain light. Incredibly, as later research revealed, just one white tiger is born in every 10,000 births. The first-ever recorded sighting of one dates back to the mid-fifteenth century.

In December 1915, the father of Martand Singh, Maharajah Gulab Singh of Rewa, actually captured a white tiger cub. As Maharaja of the largest princely state in Central India, he'd hunted and killed more than his fair share of tigers, but decided to keep this pale, glowing rarity as a pet. The tiger was about two years old when captured, and it lived in luxury at the Maharajah's summer palace for five years. Then the rare animal ran out of luck. The Maharajah had him butchered, stuffed and sent as a gift to King George V of England as a token of India's deep loyalty to the crown. His son, Martand Singh, who came into power in 1951, had never seen a white tiger, and finding one became an obsession. Despite the recorded sightings, he was beginning to doubt the beast's existence. He had hunted hundreds of tigers; surely one of them would have been white, but....

Finally, the young Maharajah's prayers were answered. He was hunting from one of his jungle "hides" when a tigress suddenly padded into sight. She was trailed by four cubs. One was white. The Maharajah was ecstatic. He and his hunting party immediately opened fire. The tigress and three cubs died in a hail of bullets, but the one white cub escaped unscathed. The trackers who were sent out after the fleeing cub found a fresh kill made by the tigress and waited near it patiently. The white cub, alone and drawn back to the kill by hunger, was spotted hiding in a rock crevice nearby. The trackers set a bowl of water in a cage, and after several hours, the thirsty youngster walked into the trap. The cub was then transported to the Maharajah's 150-room palace and imprisoned forevermore in a large, enclosed courtyard.

This tiger was named Mohan, and he became famous as the inspiration for the "white tiger fever" that began with the young Maharaja of Rewa, who suddenly believed he had found his destiny: to breed his white tiger and "restore" the species. What he didn't know was that white tigers are not a separate species, but a recessive genetic mutation of the common golden Bengal. So despite years of mating Mohan to a golden Bengal tigress, only golden cubs were produced.

Then in 1958, Mohan "accidentally" mated with his own heterozygous daughter, a tigress named Radha, who carried the white gene inherited from her sire. Radha gave birth to an all-white litter of four: a male named Raja, and three females named Rani, Mohini, and Sukishi. They were living legends; the first white tigers born in captivity.

Today there are 200 to 300 white tigers in the world. Although common in zoos, they are still rare in the wild. All those in captivity are believed to be Mohan's direct descendants, and products of incest, because the only way to pass on their white genes was to mate father to daughter, brother to sister, mother to son, etc. As for the first four cubs, the Maharajah donated Raja and Rani to the New Delhi Zoo; Sukeshi remained at Govindgarh Palace in a harem courtyard to mate with Mohan; and in 1960, Mohini was bought for $10,000 by John Kluge, a German-American billionaire, who donated him to the Smithsonian National Zoological Park as a gift to the children of America.

Two keepers traveled to Rewa, India, to collect the tigress, carrying a letter from the Indian Ministry of Commerce and Industry authorizing her export. But the Ministry of Food and Agriculture in New Delhi refused to honor it, claiming the tigress was a national treasure. After much debate, officials finally conceded that Mohini's export would not adversely affect India's supply of wild tigers. Eleven men carried her to the plane, and on December 5, 1960, Mohini was presented to President Eisenhower in a ceremony on the White House lawn.

At her new home in the National Zoo, Mohini was a huge attraction. Naturally, zoo officials wanted to breed more just like her. No white tigers were available, but the zoo eventually found Radha's brother, Samson (Mohini's "uncle"), and he was imported to become her mate. Their first litter produced one white cub and two orange cubs. Sadly, only the orange male, Ramana, survived. The second litter produced two more orange cubs; one was stillborn, but a female, Kesari, survived.

Then...success! Mohini, born to her father and her sister, was mated with her orange son, Ramana, and a white female, Rewati, was born in 1970. At that time, the worldwide population of white tigers in captivity totaled just three dozen.

Mohini and Ramana's next litter consisted of two white and three orange cubs. Sadly, a tragedy occurred as Mohini produced a stillborn and soon after crushed three of her cubs. One white female, Moni, survived.

Later, during renovation of its cat habitats, the National Zoo loaned the Cincinnati Zoo the orange brother-and-sister pair, Ramana and Kesari. Ramana died shortly after the move, but two years later, in 1976, the Cincinnati Zoo found an unrelated white tiger, Tony, in Peru, and bred him to Kesari. This mating produced two white siblings, a male, Bhim, and a female, Sumita. They became mates and produced many litters of white cubs. Three of their offspring would eventually fall into the hands of Siegfried and Roy.

As the Maharaja of Baroda concluded his gripping tale on that evening in 1982, he informed Siegfried and Roy that his cousin, the Maharajah of Rewa, had stipulated just before his death that none of his white tigers could be sold to individuals; they were for the enjoyment of the public only. But even as the Maharajah of Baroda made this statement, Roy's only thought was: *How can I get a white tiger?*

Prior to the conversation, he'd barely known that white tigers existed in captivity; but now that he did, Roy fell victim to "white tiger fever." His new mission in life was to save these animals from extinction.

The Maharaja introduced Siegfried and Roy to Edward J. Maruska, chairman of the Zoological Society of Cincinnati, who welcomed their enthusiasm. After a period of negotiation, Siegfried and Roy committed themselves to preserving the white tiger and became part of the zoo's breeding team. It was agreed that they would be given a male and female from the next litter born.

They waited anxiously until a female gave birth, and when they received the call, Roy jumped on the next plane to Cincinnati. There was no way he was going to let someone else choose his cubs for him. When he arrived at the nursery, he immediately spotted the one he wanted: a snow white cub with no stripes—the first pure white tiger to be born to a zoo in the United States.

Luckily, officials considered the animal useless to their breeding program—their other pure white tigers hadn't bred and were believed to be sterile—so Roy picked out two striped cubs, paid a small fortune for them, and talked the zoo into throwing in the "useless" cub as a freebie. They also agreed that Roy could take any stripe-less white cubs born in the future, and everyone ended up happy.

Roy named his snow white cub Sitarra, meaning "star of India." She is officially known as the matriarch of the Royal White Tigers of Nevada. The other two cubs were a male, Neva, meaning "snow," and a female cub, Shasadee, or "the chosen one." Neva and Sitarra became the first breeding pair of white tigers for Siegfried and Roy, who pioneered the concept of breeding selectively to produce stripe-less white tigers. And Roy came to believe that he had single-handedly saved the white tiger species, even though they are not really a species at all.

In 1987, Siegfried and Roy launched a white tiger breeding program at Phantasialand, a theme park in Brühl, Germany. They'd been invited to Phantasialand's twentieth anniversary, and gifted the park with a pair of ten-month-old white tigers, Siegroy and Vegas. Phantasialand, after agreeing to construct a tiger habitat modeled after the one the duo had built at their Las Vegas home, was allowed to start its own breeding program.

Not surprisingly, what started as a charitable gift reaped huge promotional benefits as the two performers— amid a flurry of international press—were presented a key to the city by Brühl's mayor. Roy reported in their autobiography that the owner of Phantasialand, Richard Schmidt, "wanted to include a tribute to our career; a Siegfried and Roy museum, complete with film clips of our shows, old costumes...props, and walls of photos," much like the world-famous Liberace Museum in Las Vegas.

Despite their ego-tripping, it's fair to say Siegfried and Roy infected millions of "white tiger fever" enthusiasts when their world-famous show began featuring the exotic beasts. Suddenly, every zoo and circus wanted its own white tiger. When they introduced white lions into their act in the 90s, demand for them, likewise, immediately shot up.

The rarity of white tigers and lions made them a natural temptation for the breeding industry. Unique animals have been an attraction since the beginning of mankind. The hybridization of big cats for financial gain dates back to the nineteenth century. Lions, tigers, leopards and jaguars are among the species that were crossbred to create such hybrid varietals as Ligers, Tigons and Lepjags— oddities people flock to see.

Siegfried and Roy would eventually purchase their own lepjags, named Ali and Chico, from a breeder in Florida, although they learned the hard way that these mixed breeds are not always as friendly as full-bred tigers. Ali and Chico were big, with the muscular physique and intense ferocity of pit bulls. Unpredictable and untrainable, they could not be walked on a leash like tigers, and only one or two trainers could handle them. The upside was that because Chico and Ali were from the same litter, they looked identical, which made them ideal for one of Siegfried and Roy's most spectacular tricks at the Frontier: the Cannon Illusion.

The illusion begins as a cannon, with Chico's head poking out of the barrel, is rolled onstage. Roy, wearing a helmet, walks around the cannon. Pulling his helmet visor down, he disappears behind the huge weapon. Once Roy is out of the audience's view, one of his doubles, Danny Gross, switches with him and climbs up into the cannon barrel with Chico. Roy leaves the stage, unseen. The cannon fires, there's a flash of light, and everything goes dramatically dark. By the time the lights come up a moment later, Roy—who's had plenty of time to walk around to the other side of the stage— magically appears in a cage with Chico's brother, Ali. The illusion is that Roy and Chico have been fired out of the cannon and flown across the stage.

While this is going on, Danny and Chico disappear down a trap door. The audience is shown the inside of the cannon, but it's empty. Siegfried then joins Roy and Ali on a flat platform that's suddenly elevated straight up into the ceiling, or "fly space," in an explosion of bright stage lights. The audience erupts in applause and the stage goes black, signaling the end of the first act.

One night, the trainers mixed up Chico and Ali, so it was Ali who ended up poking his head out of the cannon barrel. Roy had no idea the cats had been swapped...until the slam-bang finale. As they hurtled up to the ceiling, Roy looked down and gasped to see that Chico, not Ali, was at his side. Putting a cat on a platform that suddenly shoots forty-odd feet straight up could have triggered a dangerous fight-or-flight frenzy.

Unlike Ali, Chico had never been trained to expect anything like this sudden ride skyward. Roy could have been clawed or bitten—or yanked off the ascending platform as the terrified cat spontaneously jumped. Fortunately for Roy and the audience, his ferocious lepjag stayed cool.

Chico and Ali had hair-trigger tempers and were notoriously hard to handle. After a show at the Frontier one night, trainers were about to transport the lepjags back to the Jungle Palace when Ali suddenly bit one guy's ankle through the bars of his cage. The injured trainer, a young fellow named Russell, was rushed to the emergency room. But while he was at the hospital, the other lepjag trainer— who was Russell's boyfriend at the time—got bitten on the leg by Chico just half an hour later. Wanting to avoid the bad press that would result from reports of two dangerous animal attacks on the same night, it was decided that the second trainer should be taken to a different hospital for emergency treatment. Both trainers recovered from the bites and were soon back at work.

Siegfried and Roy's interest in rare breeds such as the lepjag was hardly unique in the world of animal exhibition. Exhibiting rare animals often pays off bigtime. When Sea World acquired the world's only performing whale, Shamu, in the 60s, crowds flocked to see her. In the 80s, the San Diego Zoo, desperate for a pair of pandas to display since the adorable black-and-white bears didn't exist in America, turned beseechingly to China. When that nation finally loaned the United States a pair of giant pandas—for a hefty sum, of course—the zoo's profits skyrocketed. In 1990, when the giant pandas gave birth to the first surviving cub born in North America, visitors poured into the zoo.

So when Siegfried and Roy first presented white tigers—and white lions, which were added to their act in 1995—they triggered the human equivalent of a feeding frenzy among zoos the world over. The Toronto and

Philadelphia zoos quickly acquired white lions, instantly upping their attendance, while the Cincinnati Zoo sold its white cats to zoological parks across the U.S., West Germany, Thailand, Japan and other countries—or traded them for other valuable species.

But even though this sudden surge in white cat breeding seemed like a positive step towards preserving animals, it actually had detrimental repercussions. White tigers need to be crossbred with direct family members in order to pass on the heterozygous gene, but these incestuous matings also passed on such genetic defects as hip dysplasia, cleft palates and crossed eyes. Some of Siegfried and Roy's tigers experienced so much pain in their back legs they could barely walk. Their spinal cords had to be operated on to relieve pressure on their nerves so they could stand properly. Their hip problems were magnified by their confinement in cages that are unnatural for beasts meant to range in forests and jungles.

If one of these captive, inbred cats was released into the wild, it would not survive very long. Learning to hunt through experience is a two- to three-year process begun at birth; it cannot be taught by humans. Breeding animals in captivity—whether in zoos or private sanctuaries—is hardly the same as conserving them in the wild, no matter what well-intentioned "animal lovers" would have you believe. Encouraging the breeding of pure white tigers has actually had a negative effect on normal tigers. White tigers are taking up room in animal habitats which would otherwise house the better-bred gold tigers, experts charge. Knowing this, most zoos are hypocritical, keeping at least one white tiger on display because the public demands it, and the zoos need money to stay in business.

Due to the attention Siegfried and Roy have garnered because of their use of exotic animals, gaining approval from animal activists and their fans is even more important than ever before. But they're still easy targets for endangered species protection groups because their efforts have never focused on conserving endangered species in natural habitats. Animal extinction is a growing global concern.

Once, 100,000 tigers ranged free from Siberia to India, but it's estimated that at least 95% have died off in the last century. Perhaps 5,000 remain in the wild, less than half the number held in captivity around the world.

Adding to the world's tiger decline is the fact that every part of their body is valuable on the black market. Even though it's now illegal, poachers and smugglers have flooded the underground trade with tiger skins, plus organs like bones, eyeballs, and even whiskers, all of which are prized in oriental medicine or as aphrodisiacs.

For Hindus, the tiger is a supernatural force; their power makes them the ultimate trophy. Just a hundred-odd years ago, one Indian Maharaja personally hunted and killed 1,200 tigers, dispatching as many as 100 on a single hunt. Today, there is a *total* of 100 tigers still alive in those reserves.

Poaching ignited a war in the East between tiger preservationists and hunters. Seven reserves in India barely have a tiger left; one was recently exposed as having none at all. Extreme measures have been taken to save tigers from extinction: the government has even issued a "shoot on site" order for anyone seen hunting a tiger.

Siegfried and Roy, for all the affection lavished on their tigers and other cats, are exploiting creatures that should ideally remain in the wild. Their unnatural breeding of the white tiger, especially, is exactly that: unnatural. And although their veterinarian, Dr. Martin Dinnes, is world-renowned, and Siegfried and Roy are financially able to provide the best care for their animals, their benign exploitation of these exotic creatures has indirectly reinforced abuse by humans.

While the duo has always claimed they buy their lions from Johannesburg Zoological Gardens, following their endorsement by South African President Nelson Mandela, they've actually purchased many of them in Japan, where the exotic creatures live in conditions barely above the level of jail cells. Siegfried and Roy have glossed over their animals' Japanese origins, but there's evidence they bought several white lions from a Japanese dealership called South-North Trading, Inc., located in Yuka Saito, Japan. One rare animal expert—who wishes to remain anonymous—travels the world to bid on exotic creatures for her clients and claims Siegfried and Roy not only bought several white lions from this Japanese dealer but practically monopolized the company's business to ensure that no competitors would have access to their white animals.

This facility—a so-called Worldwide Zoo Animal Distributor—only sold rare white animal breeds: tigers, lions, and a weird amalgam of white owls, kangaroos, donkeys and zebras. The facility was owned by a man who'd made his fortune operating Japanese racing car circuits, and he kept his animals in a pitch-black, cement-floored cavern that resembled a filthy garage. Again, to give Siegfried and Roy their due, by contrast, they believe in "behavioral enrichment" for their animals and house them in natural-looking habitats.

Siegfried and Roy's desire to obtain white lions and tigers was insatiable. They searched every private source possible and were willing to spend freely. While competitors were paying anywhere from $80,000 to $115,000 a cat, there's evidence that Siegfried and Roy topped nearly all bids. After Roy was mauled, the Guadalajara Zoo revealed it had sold Siegfried and Roy four tigers since 1995, and wouldn't hesitate to sell them more. It was one of those tigers, Montecore, that attacked Roy. He had taken the cub from his mother when the baby was just five days old.

Although Siegfried and Roy were secretly cornering the market, the face they showed the public screamed, "Save the animals!" At the November 1996 opening of the duo's Secret Garden display at The Mirage, Siegfried and Roy were publicized as crusaders for rare white tigers and lions. As Roy deftly put it, "Our jobs as magicians is to make things disappear. One of our dreams is to make these animals reappear."

And reappear they did, forcing the duo to construct an appropriate abode for the white creatures to live. The construction of Siegfried and Roy's spectacular desert mansion, the Jungle Palace, began while they were still at the Frontier, even before they learned about white tigers from the Maharaja of Baroda. In 1980, they bought a house in West Las Vegas, near Decatur Boulevard; in 1982, they bought two more neighboring properties; by the mid-80s they'd bought the entire block. When Siegfried and Roy moved into their huge estate, they were joined by an assortment of tigers, lepjags, leopards, and two lions, Leo and Mombasa. The animals lived in the custom-designed habitat called the Garden of the White Tigers, situated behind Siegfried and Roy's sprawling residence.

The duo eventually turned the block they'd bought up into a sort of "Siegfried & Roy" Village. Roy's mother, Johanna, moved into their first acquisition on the north side of the property. The Jungle Palace, where Siegfried, Roy and the cats lived, faced east onto Valley Drive. The lovely Lynette moved in across the road, on the corner of Valley Drive and Pleasant Street. Toney, before his untimely death, lived in the guesthouse on the corner of Valley Drive and Vegas Drive. And Roy's brother, Werner, eventually lived in a Vegas Drive house just west of Toney's. To top all that, an office was built opposite the Jungle Palace, next to Lynette's house, to provide Siegfried with somewhere to rehearse.

The house Werner would live in was purchased from a neighbor, Miss Cox, under rather unusual circumstances: Leo the lion escaped the Jungle Palace one day and promptly ate Miss Cox's pet poodle. As a result of her trauma, Siegfried and Roy replaced the wooden fence separating their properties with a high concrete wall. Roy then offered to buy Miss Cox's house. She sold them the property and was allowed to continue living there until her death a few years later, at which point Werner moved over from Little Bavaria.

The original architecture of the duo's properties was Spanish-influenced, but Roy, no doubt inspired by the Maharaja of Baroda's tales of exotic India, announced that their mansion should emulate the Taj Mahal's white marble dome design and ornamentation. He wanted the mansion to overlook a domain where his tigers could roam freely, much like the Maharajah of Rewa's palace. Towering over the Garden of the White Tigers, Roy constructed a staggering re-creation of the snow-peaked Himalayan mountain range that's home to so many tigers in the wild. Roy's outdoor wonderland is described in Charles Maclean's 1991 article, "The Ultimate Illusion," as a "giant block of melting ice cream."

Roy explains, "The moment they [the tigers] went in there, they relaxed, they became different animals...as if the camouflage made them feel more secure." The white tigers had a swimming pool of their own, and, although there were two others on the expansive property, one designated for humans, and one for the other animals, all species shared pools indiscriminately.

Instead of smooth, linear designs, Roy wanted everything to be stucco, curved and stark white. Even Lynette's house across the street had to be color-coordinated, so that when Roy looked out his bedroom balcony he could see a reflection of his exotic Eastern-style empire.

Around the time Roy decided to renovate the entire Jungle Palace, Siegfried had to go to Germany for a month, leaving Roy alone on the West Coast for a few days. Roy said he planned to have a round of plastic surgery, probably in California, before jetting off to Acapulco to heal. But Siegfried suspected Roy had a few tricks up his sleeve. He warned Jimmy Lavery that no changes to the Jungle Palace were to be made while he was away. However, only moments after Siegfried's limo left for the airport, Roy called in a construction crew and started work on the estate. The daily noise was so incredibly loud that the construction team offered to put the neighbors up in a hotel.

Finally, the work was done. The Jungle Palace was magically transformed. And when Siegfried returned from his trip, he was livid. "I told you not to spend any of my money," he roared at Jimmy Lavery.

Jimmy answered, "I didn't. Roy said it was all his."

The battle never ended, but Roy usually ended up getting his way. He'd cleverly convince Siegfried to agree to his ideas—most of them, at least—by inventing flaky schemes to generate income. At one point, Roy wanted to build a huge party pavilion in Little Bavaria, mainly because he loved to host spectacular private bashes. So he told Siegfried they'd make a fortune renting it out as a movie set. Between 2000 and 2003, architectural models were designed and Roy secured the permits, but the estimates came in too high, and the project dissipated just a few months before Roy was mauled.

Another of Roy's grand plans was to turn the Jungle Palace into the next Liberace Museum, the most popular daytime attraction in Las Vegas. None of these money-making schemes materialized, but Roy continued to spend with both hands on expensive furniture and art he called "investments": a clock once owned by Napoleon Bonaparte, an original Hieronymus Bosch, an interpretation of the Mona Lisa by pop artist Peter Max. In "The Ultimate Illusion," Charles Maclean explains that "decorators have been kept at bay" because the Jungle Palace's primary decorator is Roy himself. "A house doesn't mean anything unless it's a reflection of the people who live in it," the eccentric Roy explains in Maclean's article.

The Jungle Palace's lavish interior decorations did not end at valuable artwork and fancy ornamentation. The Tiger Kings bought their very own tanning beds to burnish their glowing hides, and they commissioned an artist to paint a copy of Michelangelo's fresco from the Sistine Chapel on the domed ceiling of a central hall. Directly underneath that masterpiece replica they installed a cutting-edge coffee bar and cappuccino machine, which they never figured out how to use. Among the array of antiques and collectibles from around the world were a toilet masquerading as a confessional booth, a nightingale birdcage gifted by Japan's imperial family to commemorate their tour of that nation in 1989, an imposing Buddhist shrine, and Roy's collection of tick-tock clocks and stained glass.

The Jungle Palace boasted a large marbled Jacuzzi, located in the room where they ate breakfast, overlooking the Garden of the White tigers. The house would be kept silent until housekeepers awoke the duo at noon each day. They would invariably dine together in the grand breakfast room with Roy's mother, Miss Horn.

Roy doted on his mother and her word was gospel. When he came home each night after performances, he would awake "Mutti" and chat with her about the show. Even after her death, Miss Horn's presence lived on in the Jungle Palace. Her chair at the breakfast room table was never occupied by another. Every week like clockwork, Miss Horn's bed linen was changed, and her slippers always stayed beside her bed. After she was cremated, Roy kept his mother's ashes in an urn, which was set on a glass table in front of the fireplace in his house; every morning, fresh roses were placed beside it. Going one step further, Roy purchased a Louis Vuitton bag for the urn, so he could take his mother with him on his weekly retreats to Little Bavaria. Before setting out in his Rolls-Royce, ever-faithful son Roy would carefully fasten Miss Horn's remains tightly with the seatbelt.

Siegfried and Roy had separate living quarters in the house, with Roy monopolizing most of the space. He had an office, a huge bedroom and bathroom, and a fifteen-by-forty-foot walk-in closet almost the size of Siegfried's entire suite which was was built in his office behind Lynette's house. His bedroom was dominated by a huge black bed, where he'd lounge and meditate with his big cats for hours on end. All four corners of the bed originally sported huge elephant tusks, but Roy finally removed the ivory trophies because they marred his spotless image as an animal lover.

Roy's black marble bathroom had been designed with a cage overlooking his Jacuzzi. It was intended for Sabacca, his black leopard, but the cat's perch was finally sealed off because even Roy found it impractical to host a wild animal in his lavatory.

Siegfried's wing of the house has a domed ceiling and walls dominated by a larger-than-life painting of his favorite subject...himself. *Vanity Fair* interviewer Matt Tyrnauer described his tour of Siegfried's quarters thusly:

> Siegfried takes me on a tour of his wing of the house, which is just off the dining room. Roy's rooms are upstairs. With Yuman a few paces behind us, Siegfried leads me into his bedroom suite,

positions me at the center of the airy stucco-walled chamber and instructs me to look up. Gesturing toward a baroque fresco on the dome and walls, he announces, "This is the young Siegfried, when I was in my youthful days!"

The life-size image is that of a perfectly formed nude boy toy, leading two fierce cheetahs on a chain through a desolate moonscape. "And what happens is Merlin is with the evil, and Siegfried is the power and the strength and the good magic," he explains, pointing out the Arthurian wizard, who, in the company of a hydra-headed serpent, is shooting fire from his fingertip at the young Aryan hero. "Black magic against white magic. In other words, the evil spirit against the good spirit."

"What's that enormous crystal you are holding?" [Matt asks].

"It is the power of life and light. It's nothing special," he concludes, exhaling a cloud of blue cigarillo smoke [He smokes La Paz cigarillos.].

Matt mentions that "the young Siegfried looks not much different from the present-day Siegfried." He shrugs, "Well, the painter got a little carried away."

The Jungle Palace is easily identified by the glaring gold "SR" logotypes on its imposing, spike-topped gates. Siegfried and Roy lived together behind those gates for three decades. When their intimate personal relationship finally faded, Siegfried moved into a 7,266-square-foot home in Spanish Trail. However, their professional partnership never faltered, despite a bizarre rumor springing up that Roy had died of AIDS and been replaced by a surgically-modified brother, Ray. Even Roy's great friend Shirley MacLaine began to believe it was true when a friend insisted she'd been to his funeral.

In their interview with *Vanity Fair*, Roy dispelled the rumor of his disappearance, but the duo continued to cover up the fact that Siegfried had moved out. The interview took place in 1999, and Siegfried had long since left the Jungle Palace, but he and Roy paraded around the property as if they still lived blissfully under the same roof. There was no mention of Siegfried's separate enclave in Las Vegas, and blissful though the duo appeared to be, they steadfastly refused to confirm their alleged homosexuality. After all, why should they?

When smoke and mirrors win you your lifelong dreams, why abandon illusion?

Chapter 12
SARMOTI

"Anyone who thinks they can do what Siegfried and Roy have done should go ahead and try—it's almost impossible."

—Steve Wynn

By 1987, Siegfried and Roy had not just survived but triumphed during their six-year run at the Frontier, and they were now hailed as the biggest act in Las Vegas.

They had nearly made it to the top of American showbiz, and they had been given various honors in Europe as well, including Germany's prestigious Bambi award and Iron Cross and Order of Merit. What's more, in 1986, the boys were able to finally make their pilgrimage to Rome, during which they met Pope John Paul II, a meeting arranged through Bernie Yuman's connections at the White House.

Accompanying them to the Vatican were Siegfried's sister, Margot—a devout Franciscan nun—and her mother superior from Germany. When the group arrived, a papal emissary asked for the names of their patron saints. Roy, not being Catholic, gave the name of St. Francis, the patron saint of animals.

The most talkative in the audience was Roy, who was keen to tell His Holiness about the duo's crusade to save the white tigers. Then Roy asked the Pope to bless a favorite amethyst cross that he wore. After the blessing, Roy put the cross on and said, "This is Siegfried," in tribute to his best friend. Bernie Yuman, a Jew, also asked the Pope to bless him and his family.

Noting Roy's devotion to the saint, a papal assistant gave him a blessed fragment of St. Francis' bone. Roy later gifted it to Margot, at her request.

Siegfried and Roy, always retaining at least a fragment of the humility they had in the beginning of their careers, were extremely moved by the whole event.

Upon returning to Las Vegas, they were the hottest act in town and their contract at the Frontier was coming to an end. It was no surprise when Steve Wynn, the charming and handsome mega-casino developer, vowed do-or-die to snatch them up for his newest venture, the magnificent Mirage, due to open in three years. When Wynn approached them in 1987, they happily accepted his offer, but before becoming The Mirage's star attraction, they had another exciting adventure ahead of them: a ten-month tour of Japan.

As they plunged into a heavy rehearsal schedule for the tour, Siegfried and Roy began preparing for another important turning point in their lives—becoming citizens of their adopted land, the Unites States of America. To achieve that goal, they needed to take an INS test and demonstrate that they could read, write and speak English, plus answer random questions about U.S. history and its government. After studying a list of possible questions in the citizenship prep manual, they had Jimmy Lavery test them. Out of sixty-odd questions he threw at them, Roy managed to answer three. Siegfried scored a big, fat zero, which sounds worse than it is, because studies have shown that native Americans don't do much better.

On July 4, 1988, they took the test; and on Roy's birthday, October 3, 1988, they were granted U.S. citizenship. To celebrate the achievement, they took time out from the Japan rehearsals and threw Roy an All-American birthday party, complete with hot dogs and hamburgers.

Finally, after months of rehearsal for the Japan tour, the troupe packed up and hit the road. Everyone was full of high hopes, but the journey to the Land of the Rising Sun was daunting. They were crossing the Pacific Ocean with a herd of wild animals, a five-ton elephant, and a crew of one hundred-plus; a massive undertaking that required two 747 jumbo jets, nicknamed "Flying Tigers," and two cargo ships, facetiously dubbed "Roy's Arks." The tour was organized by impresario Dan Yoshida and Fuji Television, the show's producers abroad. Tsumura Corporation, a pharmaceutical company, was the corporate sponsor. Siegfried and Roy would become very close to the Tsumura family, especially Madame Sumiko Tsumura, the wife of the company president, who spoke fluent English, and made their stay a delight with her friendly, can-do attitude and high energy.

Siegfried, who believed everything was a "sign," was thrilled to see paintings by his favorite artist, Boris Vallejo, on the wall of the Tsumura home. "Whenever we're putting a show together, I always present our creative people with a book of Vallejo's work to give them an idea of the feel and coloring we're after," he told them.

To house their act in Japan, a truly amazing structure called the "Shiodome" was designed and built. It was a moveable unit that could be deconstructed and transported from one city to the next. The theater section, which seated 3,600 and had cost $14.5 million, boasted technical capabilities that easily matched the magicians' stage requirements. The luxuries that were built in for the comfort of the stars, their crew and the animals were astounding, and included stereo and TV sets for each animal. Siegfried and Roy had explained to the producers that "the animals enjoy music and television when they're confined because it occupies their minds."

Their show itself beat anything the Frontier had ever seen. The Japanese went wild, and upwards of two million people watched in awe as Siegfried and Roy not only performed brilliantly, but spoke Japanese throughout their act. Showing enormous commitment, the duo had hired a Japanese professor from the University of Nevada to teach them the native language before they left Vegas. Siegfried conceded that their accents were "far from flawless," but it was an amazing feat.

If experience had taught the duo anything, it was that no show ever ran perfectly. Ten months was a long time for Siegfried and Roy to perform without mishap. Two especially scary incidents involved the so-called "royal box," a V.I.P. box that sat in the middle of the Shiodome audience. One night, their close friend Michael Jackson, who'd come to Japan for a visit, was sitting in the royal box and Siegfried made the mistake of introducing him from the stage. Instantly, half the audience rushed to the box. Luckily, because it was used for an illusion called the Hangman Execution, a trap door was built into the floor of the box, and security guards sneaked Jackson through it and away from the mob.

An even scarier incident occurred when Siegfried impulsively appeared in the royal box one night to surprise its occupants—and was suddenly grabbed by several tough-looking Japanese, one of whom pointed a gun at his head. It turned out that the occupant, who'd been discreetly described by Japanese staff as a "famous man," was the local equivalent of The Godfather. Happily, the Mob boss recognized Siegfried instantly and waved his underlings away with a good-natured laugh.

In Osaka, Japan's major city in the south, Sitarra, their first all-white tiger cub from the Cincinnati Zoo gave birth to a litter of three cubs on the Fourth of July, 1989. In their autobiography, Siegfried and Roy claim that one million people entered a contest to choose their names: Tokyo, Fuji and Osaka. It was later reported on their website, however, that the same three cubs were named Red, White, and Blue, in tribute to Independence Day.

To further complicate these discrepancies, Siegfried and Roy may have actually contradicted their autobiography's original claim by describing a second birth of tiger triplets during their ten-month tour. They even claimed they had another naming competition in which 28,000 frenzied Japanese fans contacted their sponsor, Fuji Television, with suggested names. The official winners, according to Siegfried and Roy, were Ichiban (Number One), Sakura (Cherry Blossom), and Kakkoii (Cool).

After nearly a year of wowing record-breaking crowds in Japan, the time had come to say "Sayonara." Siegfried and Roy were headed for New York City and an engagement at

Radio City Music Hall. The trip home was no fun for Roy, whose plane was delayed over five hours because airport employees had loaded the livestock crates with the animals facing sideways instead of forward, which would have panicked them in the air. After leaving Osaka, Roy's plane— with his tigers and Gildah, the elephant, onboard—stopped to refuel in Anchorage, Alaska, and then took off for New York City, where manager Bernie Yuman had organized a huge press conference. Roy changed into theatrical clothes, so he'd be "camera-ready" when he exited the plane to stride dramatically toward the flashing press camera, leading his gigantic elephant. Bernie swore it would be the most unique entrance ever witnessed in jaded New York City.

Suddenly, however, the plane encountered a surprise storm and was forced to make an emergency landing at a nearby airport. Roy describes the experience as utterly terrifying: "With the captain and copilot cursing and praying, and me sitting next to them, watching and relying on the grace of God—my entire world was at stake, and in a split second it could be gone—we began our descent. Sweat was flying around the cockpit, and in a minute more, God knows where we'd be. At last, only 250 feet out, the captain saw the landing strip. Who cares that the landing was rough? ...We were alive."

Alive, yes, but at an unscheduled airport, with not a photographer or reporter in sight. Not quite a fate worse than death but close.

While Roy was having the ride of his life, Siegfried was kicking back in Puerto Rico. "As for Siegfried," Roy wrote somewhat sarcastically in their autobiography, "he's always there when it really counts!" Siegfried apparently found it hard to tear himself away from his precious island. He jetted back at the last possible minute and came within half an hour of missing their celebratory parade through the streets of Manhattan to the theater.

The duo's stint at Radio City Music Hall was a major success, and a satisfying one considering their unpleasant experience years before with the bullying agent who'd labeled Siegfried a "Nazi." This time, they sold out thirty-two consecutive shows at the most prestigious theater in New York City. The *New York Times* raved that "blasé Gothamites" should "go see Siegfried and Roy...the reason for which Radio City Music Hall was built." In the city that had embraced millions of immigrants seeking the American Dream, Siegfried and Roy were now enjoying their very own piece of the pie.

The duo had made headlines in a very different way on an earlier tour of New York City two years before: a van transporting two tigers in their crates was hijacked off the street just prior to their appearance on the CBS *Morning Program*. Security chief Jim Mydlach remembers the phone call from an agitated Bernie Yuman:

"Mydlach, get all your contacts in gear—fast! Someone stole the tigers."

"What? You're kidding?"

"No, Mydlach, honest to god. Now get your contacts here!"

Bernie's initial reaction when he'd first learned the tigers had been stolen was classic. "Get me the CIA, get me the FBI, and get me the President," he roared at a press agent as he dialed Jim Mydlach.

After "a citywide search by the police, a safety alert by health officials and a news alert by television and radio stations," as the *New York Times* reported, cops finally found the van abandoned five hours later in the Bronx. The two tigers, Siegroy and Vegas, were safe, and the five-hour tiger heist hit the headlines nationwide; Bernie Yuman couldn't have planned it better himself!

After their sold-out stay at Radio City Music Hall, the troupe headed back to Las Vegas for their spectacular opening as headliners at The Mirage. Siegfried and Roy had signed a $57.5 million, five-year contract with Steve Wynn, more than doubling their Frontier salary of $5.5 million a year. But they had their work cut out for them. Wynn had just built the biggest hotel on the Strip and landed the biggest stars in Las Vegas history for his marquee. He was dead-set on living up to the title he'd always coveted: King of Las Vegas.

Steve Wynn was born in 1942 in New Haven, Connecticut. His businessman father, Mike, had changed the family name from Weinberg. The Wynns were taking outings to Las Vegas when most Americans had barely heard of it. In 1952, when he was ten years old, Steve Wynn remembers how his dad "used to put me to bed and then sneak out at night and shoot the dice at the Flamingo and the Sands." Back then, Wynn told an interviewer, Vegas was a place where one rode horses through the desert, then hitched them to rails outside a casino's back door. "It was like stepping back into the frontier," Wynn recalled. "Casino owners were king; they owned the town. They were glamorous; they had beautiful women and lots of money."

Wynn's father opened a bingo parlor in Vegas, but was forced to close it after finally being turned down for a gambling license. He and his wife returned to Utica, N.Y., and reared Steve and his younger brother, Kenneth, in an atmosphere of affluence. Steve attended the University of Pennsylvania, and just before he graduated in 1963, his father died of a heart attack.

Wynn had considered a medical career but instead decided to take over the bingo business his father had started in New York. It wasn't an easy decision because his father, a longtime gambler, had died owing money to illegal operators. Luckily, he'd made a lot of important contacts in his life, so Steve wasn't left entirely without assets. To pay off the family debt and make money, Steve—ambitious and smart—looked for a future beyond the family business and chose the real-estate market. In 1967, one of his father's connections called with an offer to invest in a hotel in Las Vegas. According to unauthorized biographer John L. Smith—who's been sued unsuccessfully five times by his subject—Steve Wynn "enjoyed a discount on his purchase other investors did not receive and was made a working officer in the Frontier."

At the age of twenty-five, Wynn secured a loan to buy five percent of The Hotel Last Frontier for $75,000. Just days later, Howard Hughes snapped up the joint for $24 million. Robert Maheu, Hughes' official alter ego and financial advisor, recalled meeting Wynn after the deal was struck. The final signing of documents was scheduled to take place that night, and Maheu and his son were waiting in the boardroom to close the deal when a confident, young man walked in and introduced himself as Steve Wynn. Never one to hold back, Wynn told the two men about his ambitions to be a key player in the future of Las Vegas.

In 1967, when Robert Maheu had acquired the Desert Inn on behalf of Howard Hughes, he bought the first limousine ever purchased by a Vegas hotel. People around town rebuked him for being too ostentatious. Steve Wynn thought otherwise—and told him so. "Mr. Maheu, I was so peeved that you were criticized for buying a limo. When I'm done with this city, there will be more limos per capita in Las Vegas than any city of its size, and the hotels will be bigger than anywhere else in the world." After that conversation, Maheu told his son, "Poor Steve, he's working too hard."

But when "poor Steve" opened the most expensive hotel in the world two decades later, Maheu ate his words. On The Mirage's opening night, Wynn received a telegram reminding him of the conversation in the boardroom. It ended with this observation: "Steve, it is now obvious that it is I who had been working too hard. –Bob Maheu"

In 1973, after a series of career-building investments in bingo, liquor and a parking lot next door to Caesars Palace, Wynn took over the Golden Nugget downtown, and transformed it from a sleazy, failing casino located in a high-crime area into a white-marble-and-brass castle; a millionaire's paradise.

By 1977, the Golden Nugget had expanded to 1,907 rooms. It was rated as the only Four-Star, Four-Diamond resort in downtown Las Vegas and became the only hotel-casino to win the award consecutively for over twenty years. Under Wynn's watch, it was said that the Nugget was so clean, you could eat off its floors. Years later, Wynn kept similarly high standards at The Mirage. Jimmy Lavery describes Wynn as being very particular about every minute detail and rated him "the smartest guy I have ever met."

Wynn sweated for his customers and made sure his employees were inspired to do the same every single day. A gifted orator, he could mesmerize his staff with motivational speeches; and if he noticed that an employee was down, he'd launch into a rousing pep talk and get that person jazzed about work and life. To make sure every customer in his hotels was taken care of, he was careful to *over*hire; if he had a Four-Star Four-Diamond hotel, he would hire like it was six stars, guaranteeing no customer was without.

In 1978, Wynn used Golden Nugget profits to buy another aging hotel, this time in Atlantic City. Gambling had just become legal there and he jumped at the opportunity to cash in. He tore down the old building, and built another Golden Nugget with 506 rooms.

Wynn never stinted on big-name talent. One year, he paid his pal, Frank Sinatra, $10 million to star in both the showroom and Nugget commercials. And even though he owned a fleet of jets, helicopters and limousines to ferry his high-rolling customers from coast to coast, he was wary of scaring away ordinary folks and downplayed his wealth and power. In one of the most successful marketing schemes in history, Wynn starred in his Nugget TV commercials, playing himself as the humble hotel owner, star-struck by the glamorous guests who frequented his hotel. He'd appear with marquee names like Frank Sinatra, Kenny Rogers or Dolly Parton. In one commercial, Wynn greets Ol' Blue Eyes and says, "Hi, Mr. Sinatra, I'm Steve Wynn. I run this place."

"You see I get enough towels," Sinatra deadpans, pushing a tip into Wynn's palm as if he were no better than a bellhop.

With this caliber of celebrity endorsement, Wynn predicted viewers would eagerly lap up every shtick-filled line. And they did. By 1984, Wynn's net worth was estimated at $100 million; he'd become a Las Vegas celebrity in his own right.

A decade later, Wynn wowed the entertainment capital yet again by demonstrating the full capacity of junk bonds: high-interest loans secured by speculation of future success. He used Wall Street to finance the construction of the first new resort on the Strip since Kirk Kerkorian opened the MGM Grand—which was half its size—sixteen years prior.

Wynn eventually came to realize that Las Vegas was starting to surpass the gambling industry that had put it on the map, and in response, the hotelier was quick to build the Golden Nugget in Atlantic City for Easterners who didn't have the time or inclination to fly across the country and gamble away their mad money.

The sense of doom deepened for the Vegas gambling industry when President Ronald Reagan signed the Indian Gaming Regulatory Act, sparking a nationwide casino-building frenzy. The city needed to invent something bigger and better to reignite the dwindling tourist industry, and Steve Wynn had the perfect solution. He'd give the people what they wanted, even if they didn't know it yet: a luxurious "mega-resort" so fully equipped its guests would find no reason to leave. Better yet: there wouldn't be a tacky neon sign or bare-breasted girl dancer in sight.

His city's future lay in providing classy, clean entertainment for families and children. As he put it, "Topless women marching up and down a staircase should have gone out in the fifties, that was an antiquated idea imported from France after the Second World War. In Europe that kind of show was done with taste and flair; in Vegas it was just T&A."

Siegfried and Roy felt the same way about topless dancers, and their collaboration with Steve Wynn was the natural next step in their careers. Roy writes of Wynn, "His vision was so far beyond what anyone had ever done in Vegas that if you wanted to compare him to anyone, you'd have to say he was like Walt Disney. Except in his fantasy there was no kiddie park."

Actually, there may as well have been: In the 1990s, Las Vegas beat out Orlando's Walt Disney World as the most popular tourist destination in the United States, due in part to the city's family-friendly makeover. With three million square feet, 3,049 rooms, real gold-tinted windows, thirty stories, and costs approaching a reported $640 million, The

Mirage was the most expensive resort of its time—with the biggest hotel, the biggest casino, the biggest guest rooms and biggest man-made lake. The Mirage was a fitting investment for the biggest man in Las Vegas. Junk bonds were used to raise $565 million of the costs, a huge gamble. The new hotel would have to make $1 million a day to service the debt.

It did.

With Golden Boy Wynn's Midas touch, the hotel exceeded expectations from the moment it opened on November 22, 1989. Within its first month, rugs in the lobbies and casino reportedly had to be replaced as more than a million people had marched through and worn them out. During its first year, The Mirage claimed over $200 million in profits.

Within two weeks of opening, Wynn hosted an old-fashioned Las Vegas sport: world champion-level boxing. He paid a reported $8 million for the highly anticipated third boxing match of a trilogy that had begun in 1980, establishing himself as a key player in the boxing/casino world in a matter of days. Throughout his life and career, Wynn has always walked a fine line between family- and adult-friendly entertainment; his boxing soirees were a perfect example.

The fight was a huge and highly publicized affair, drawing a packed, star-studded audience. It was preceded by an all-out firework display, and the energy circulating through the crowd was simply electric. Despite all the hype, however, the actual match was anticlimactic and a huge disappointment for avid boxing fans, many of whom booed and left the arena before the decision was announced. The *New York Times* reported, "As spectacles go, this one had the garish excess of a typical Las Vegas production number. But who knew there would be more snap, crackle and pop in the pre-fight pyrotechnics than in 12 rounds of Sugar Ray Leonard vs. Roberto Duran? Dull bout."

But the critics couldn't slow The Mirage's instant success. From the moment it opened, there were endless lines outside. And even the much-maligned boxing match was a big winner financially. According to the *New York Times*, the money spent on advertising plus the boxing purses—totaling a whopping $35 million—was recouped through "sales to cable television ($16 million); closed-circuit television ($3 million); foreign television ($4 million); gate tickets ($11 million), and merchandising agreements. The real money, however, comes from the casino. On fight night, $5 minimum tables become $50 tables. The hotel is sold out the entire week of the fight...on the three days surrounding the Sugar Ray Leonard-Roberto Duran middleweight fight at The Mirage, the 'drop,' or the amount wagered at the tables, was around $70 million—a record. About 20 percent of the drop is kept by the casino as its 'win.'"

Wynn invested a fortune to feature heavyweight champions such as Buster Douglas, Evander Holyfield and Mike Tyson. And he made it impossible to drive past The Mirage without gaping at the fifty-four-foot manmade volcano, which erupted every half hour into a Gilligan's Island-themed, five-acre lagoon of grottos and waterfalls, by situating the attraction strategically between the hotel entrance and passing traffic. Wynn also added a tropical rainforest stocked with ninety-foot-high trees; a twenty-thousand-gallon, saltwater aquarium featuring small sharks; $3-million villas, equipped with their own private pool and a miniature putting green; and luxury apartments which cost more to build and decorate than most American homes.

Despite all his success at seeing far into the future, Wynn was struck by a tragic twist of fate. He gradually started losing his sight after contracting a degenerative retinal eye disease called retinitis pigmentosa. His biographer, John Smith, noted: "There was bitter irony attached to Wynn's persona as a sightless visionary."

Six feet tall, well-groomed and trim, Wynn looks like one of the celebrities he mingles with, and like them (Siegfried and Roy included), he has an ego to match his fortune. That's why he treats himself to any and every self-preserving measure his money can buy, attempting to beat back the ravages of age.

It's rumored he's had face lifts, the first when he was in his early forties, plus liposuction when his rigorous sports regimen wasn't delivering the physical improvement he wanted. Biographer Smith calls it: "Wynn's carefully crafted image. Intense workouts and constant dieting help keep him looking more like a lifeguard than the chairman of a billion-dollar casino company."

Supposedly, the billionaire's beauty routine was inspired in part by his endless pursuit of women. In business, he's the family-fun king; but in his personal life, he's a traditional Las Vegas guy. In Smith's exposé, one of Wynn's former employees, Ron Tucky, claimed the boss probably had "300 [women] a year." It is most likely that these allegations are grossly exaggerated, and Steve's wife Elaine, former Miss Miami Beach, still appears to be happily married to her sweetheart, whom she met during his sophomore year at college.

Long before The Mirage opened, the future King of Las Vegas knew his crown would never be secured if he didn't find a larger-than-life act to star in his showroom. In order to stay in the game, Las Vegas' showrooms needed to compete by producing costly, lavish stage productions. However, they lost money doing so—an estimated three to five million dollars a year—even with the pull of featured celebrities.

Wynn explained: "Revues such as the Folies-Bergère at the Tropicana or the Stardust/Lido lost less per show because of their reliance upon production rather than famous stars."

So why not hire famous stars?

"With the advent of rock acts in the early seventies, the phenomenon of the one-night concert tour arose. And with it came a fundamental change in the entertainment business. It started with the rock stars, but it took over and included all kinds of entertainers; even Frank Sinatra started doing one-nighters. Entertainers could now go to a city, play to five, ten, or even twenty thousand people for two hours, and earn up to two hundred thousand dollars for the evening."

In order to come up with a solution to this impasse, Steve Wynn had to think outside the box, and way beyond.

He needed a show centered on both the production and the entertainer, knowing that no single star would have the clout to draw in thousands upon thousands of people on a long-term basis.

And finally, Steve Wynn found his answer. He says, "For me there was only one sure bet: the biggest act in the history of Las Vegas: Siegfried and Roy.... Any other entertainer would have burned out, but Siegfried and Roy were wrapped in their magic and a production show. With them I knew I had the best of both worlds: the sustaining value of the production and the marquee value of their magic."

Wynn gave the duo carte blanche. He offered them $40 million to design their own performance space in the hotel. This seemingly unlimited budget gave them free rein to hire the best set, lighting and sound designers, creating the most impressive spectacular show Las Vegas had even seen.

Although the pair had figured out much of their Mirage act before leaving for Japan, a unique set design had eluded them. Then, in London, they saw a stage play designed by John Napier, the Tony-winner who'd also mounted *Cats* and *Les Misérables*. They knew immediately that he was the right man for their show. Next, they brought in writer-director John Caird of the Royal Shakespeare Company, and collaborated to create the show Napier tags "Marvel Comics meets the Met."

Napier worked extensively with the two illusionists, flying back and forth from Japan before he even made an initial model for the set. Once the set design was approved and actual construction began, tinkering with the complicated effects—a giant animated dragon, rows of marching, life-size metal puppets, and other such high-tech toys—was a nightmare.

Their rehearsals were long and arduous, but the new show was starting to blow everyone's minds. Siegfried and Roy, and their Limeys from London, had transformed their magic circus act into a phantasmagorical theater production. The Las Vegas-based culture critic David Hickey described it as "a seamless...conflation of Warner, Barnum, Houdini,

Rousseau, Pink Floyd, *Fantasia, Peter Pan,* and *A Midsummer Night's Dream."* The new elements would ensure rave reviews for the show, but the newly expanded spectacle presented a few problems.

The proscenium at The Mirage had tripled from what they were used to at the Frontier. The dome-shaped stage was big enough to house an elephant farm, and the duo almost became lost in the elaborate production design. Siegfried and Roy were too far away from their audience to communicate with them as spontaneously as they had at the Frontier. The joke was that they could have been replaced by impersonators with few the wiser! They even had to jettison a few of their illusions that just didn't work in the huge space.

Much of this was due to Wynn's influence. He always wanted everything grandiose and amplified. He'd helped establish Cirque du Soleil as a permanent fixture in Las Vegas, taking what had made them a success and reproducing it on a much grander, more awe-inspiring scale. He'd say, "That's beautiful, but give me ten times as much," and he kept insisting on adding more and more acrobats.

When Siegfried and Roy became a permanent fixture at The Mirage, they had an advantage over performers who still had to tour. David Copperfield has been known to tour over 200 days of the year. Siegfried and Roy didn't leave their auditorium for thirteen years. But sticking to their comfort zone meant that they'd never match the international recognition David Copperfield won by touring cities around the world. The duo, especially Siegfried, didn't want to tour other countries, and except for long runs in Japan and at Radio City Music Hall, they didn't tour at all.

Bernie Yuman and Steve Wynn both bragged that Siegfried and Roy were the world's No. 1 entertainers, of course, but that wasn't really true. Limiting themselves to a specific niche had limited their potential fan base. That's why Wynn was correct to heighten every stimulus and visual in the show, ensuring that even when fans came back to see the show a second or third time, something new would jump out at them.

One perk of having such a large-scale production was that the illusionists could make mistakes, and no one would notice. Working with wild animals, plus a maze of wiring and technological equipment, meant that Siegfried and Roy often had to improvise when something went wrong. On certain nights, magical numbers would get adjusted or switched out entirely due to a technical hitch or if an animal was acting up. But one mishap that was so glaring, even on the huge stage, occurred when Siegfried came back from a vacation in Germany. Every time the duo visited their homeland, they celebrated like it was "Oktoberfest," and during a trip in the mid-90s, Siegfried gorged so heavily on food and drink that he came back a couple of sizes larger.

One night, performing the Hangman Illusion, Siegfried literally couldn't squeeze in the fitted narrow space that was designed to conceal him from the audience's view, and he ended up with half his body hanging in plain sight! Mortified, he immediately went on a strict "schnitzel verboten" diet-and-exercise regimen. He'd committed the worst crime in magic: allowing the illusion to be broken.

Siegfried and Roy were dead serious about never letting anyone penetrate their aura of mystery and magic. Even John Napier, their stage designer, was not allowed to know the secrets behind their illusions. Instead, he was forced to invent their now-legendary stage machinery based on his perception of their performance from the seating area, just like any other audience member. As every good magician knows, it is the *un*knowing that entices the audience in the first place, so Siegfried and Roy couldn't let their illusions be exposed—ever! During photo shoots, for instance, their photographer and his team would be told to wait outside while Siegfried and Roy set up their illusions. Their cast and crew of 164 were the only people who had to be let in on some of the mysteries, and they had to sign confidentiality agreements.

No one ever cracked the secrets of Siegfried and Roy, and what valuable secrets they were. The show opened on February 1, 1990, and nine years later, it had "sold out at 104 percent for every show at $90/seat," accumulating a gross profit of more than half a billion dollars. Kenneth Feld called it "the most popular and lucrative production in the history of Las Vegas…. There are no live performers today who can draw over 700,000 people a year except Siegfried and Roy."

Steve Wynn says that when he picked Siegfried and Roy to open The Mirage, they were already "the all-time greatest attendance attraction in Las Vegas history." Taking Feld's statement up a notch, the billionaire noted that "by orders of magnitude, nobody has ever drawn the kind of attendance that they have. Really, in terms of numbers of people who have witnessed the act, nothing has come close— Elvis, Frank Sinatra, Martin and Lewis, Steve and Eydie, and Wayne Newton all put together don't approach Siegfried and Roy."

By 2001, the duo had grossed $1 billion and broken every box office record. They'd been named Magicians of the Decade by the Academy of Magical Arts in Los Angeles. They'd grown so popular they had their own TV cartoon series on the Fox network. It was called "Siegfried and Roy: Masters of the Impossible." Its acronym, SARMOTI, became the duo's version of "abracadabra" and, eventually, the motto for their empire.

*   *   *

Siegfried and Roy went on to complete several other projects for the TV and Silver Screen, some more prosperous than others. In 2003, what would be one of their last endeavors in this arena, the duo starred in a new cartoon called *Father of the Pride*, produced by Jeffrey Katzenberg of Dreamworks fame. It was due to air that year but was postponed until 2004 after Roy's near-fatal mauling on October 3. They had hoped they would have success as cartoon characters and weren't much interested in branching into live-action film or TV after their wild-and-wooly experiences shooting a movie called *The Magic Box.*

Opening in late September 1999 in 160-plus IMAX theaters, the film had V.I.P. premieres in Los Angeles and

New York, followed by global premieres in München, Berlin, Tokyo, Montreal, and Toronto.

Siegfried and Roy *needed* a celebration after filming *The Magic Box*. The film shoot had been rigorous, draining, and even dangerous. In one scene, Roy was supposed to ride a big, male white lion with seven other lions chasing behind them. Monty Cox, the Hollywood animal trainer who'd given the duo their first lion, Leo, was there to help choreograph the animals, and he had his hands full with a cub named Montana and a few other youngsters.

In the wild, once lion cubs become adolescents, they are considered to be competition for the older males and are driven out of the pride. Wandering male lions form their own pride called "ronin," a Japanese word that means master-less samurai warriors with no clan affiliation. These young lions turn macho and vicious because they need to find another pride with males old enough or sick enough to kill or chase off.

Only then can they can mate with females. Ronin will even kill off cubs in their new pride to get the females back in heat. The sex drive of the young males is awesome. When a lion's ready for action, he'll mate more than 100 times in 24 hours!

Monty Cox says that "when you work with lions, you live in a life-or-death world." When Monty trains lions for movies, his goal is simple: make sure they don't kill or maim their human co-stars. "You have to know lions, get in their minds," he explains. "Tigers are more predicable. You can train them by creating a world of displacement and make sure that if the cat is going to eat anything, it will go for the trainer."

When the director called "Action," according to the plan, one lion would be let loose and Roy would jump on his back. Two beats later, the lion pack would be released to chase Roy playfully. The camera crew had to run to keep up with the action. It was simple enough, but Monty started feeling uneasy when strong winds suddenly swept the set. Wind puts lions on edge, making them "high." And when lions are high, they become dangerous. Monty conferred with Roy, who decided they'd go ahead with the shot regardless. It still might have been okay with experienced trainers like Monty and Roy running the show, but Siegfried suddenly decided he wanted to be in the shot, too.

Knowing Siegfried's general uneasiness around the big cats, who were already nervous, Roy sensed danger and flat-out told him, "You can't."

Siegfried refused to back off and snapped, "Monty, make it happen."

After taking a few moments to revise his plan, Monty decided to keep Siegfried positioned close to the camera, where he could rescue him quickly if a cat went wild.

When shooting started, Roy mounted the white male and rode it into a meadow. Siegfried was dancing around ten feet in front of the camera, just as Monty had instructed. But suddenly, Monty heard Roy shout his name. Roy, now on foot, was being stalked by a white lion in a corner of the field. Making a quick choice, and knowing Roy's experience, Monty yelled back that he couldn't leave Siegfried alone. Roy continued yelling for help as another lion joined the first. Now two of the beasts were lying flat on the ground, eyeing Roy and poised to pounce.

Monty broke from the camera, leaving Siegfried to fend for himself. As he ran toward Roy, he pulled a stick from his pouch, threw it at one lion and hit him on the hindquarters.

The startled cat backed away from Roy. Monty ran full-speed at the other lion, yelling like a wild-man. The cat spooked and streaked off. Now Roy was safe. Monty quickly looked back to make sure Siegfried was okay—and his heart-beat accelerated. A lioness had just launched herself at the blond magician, leaping four feet in the air and snapping her jaws shut just as agile Siegfried dodged away from her dagger-like teeth. But the lioness turned, gathering herself for another charge. Monty, still halfway across the field, knew he couldn't get there in time to save Siegfried, and thought, *He's a dead man.* Siegfried recalls thinking the same thing, but just in the nick of time, another trainer, John Brown, came running and slid in front of the cat, shutting her down.

Siegfried, thoroughly frightened, walked off the set as he raised his hands in the air and shouted, "That's it. No more."

Not surprisingly, there were also many tiger mishaps during Siegfried and Roy's heyday. Tigers have a totally different gut reaction to disturbances than lions. Compared to their maned brethren, tigers don't have expansive minds; their narrow focus is kill, eat, mate—period! As apex-predators, they are the biggest felines, at the top of their food chain. The word tiger is derived from the Greek word for arrow, and the beasts can hit speeds of thirty-five miles per hour. They are capable of hunting and taking down any prey in the wild and pose a serious threat to human beings unlucky enough to encounter them. Their three-inch canine teeth alone can inflict puncture wounds equal to the depth and diameter of an adult finger. And, great hunters that they are, tigers sense immediately that humans are much easier targets than agile wild animals.

A nasty tiger attack injured an employee named Chuck Flannery in 1985. Chuck, a welder, and trainer John Brown, were doing maintenance work on a cage at the Jungle Palace. Roy was sunbathing in the courtyard, and had let the tiger, called Magic, out of his cage for some exercise. Magic was lying in the courtyard, out of sight behind the fountain, when Chuck came walking through to fetch some spare parts. When he jumped over a two-foot-high fence by the fountain, making a short cut to the workshop, he startled Magic, who instantly lunged from behind and punctured Chuck's neck with all four canine teeth. Roy quickly jumped up, pulled Magic off Chuck and put the tiger back in its cage.

Chuck was out cold on the ground, bleeding profusely from neck, back and throat. Luckily, paramedics arrived at the Jungle Palace in just two minutes, because they'd been nearby on a call. Chuck was rushed to the same hospital Roy would be taken to after his attack in 2003, and his injury was nearly identical. Fortunately, Chuck survived his awful mauling, but ended up paralyzed and wheelchair-bound for the rest of his life. Tragically, his young wife deserted him.

Immediately after the incident, the "Siegfried & Roy" spin machine and lawyers went into overdrive. The tragedy was minimized and described as a case of Chuck being in the wrong place at the wrong time. Chuck sued Siegfried and Roy for letting a tiger roam free and unsupervised while maintenance workers were onsite, but he lost the case. Years later, he told the press, "I can't be mad at the guy [Horn]. Hell, I can't be mad at the cat, either. It happened. He was playing, that's all."

Ironically, Magic didn't survive. The tiger, being treated for kidney disease at the time of the attack, was quarantined for ten days and stopped eating. He died of kidney failure shortly after.

Another attack occurred when a trainer named George was walking a white male tiger near the front habitat at The Mirage. As they strolled past a female tiger in heat, George got in the way when the male started toward the female. In a split second, the tiger's deadly bite tore George's stomach muscles loose. He was rushed to hospital and luck was on his side; he recovered fully and was back at work a few weeks later.

The strangest tiger incident occurred one Easter Sunday morning. Siegfried and Roy had a hotline set up at the Jungle Palace for themselves and Miss Horn so they could call Jimmy and Lynette's house directly. Activity at the Jungle Palace never began before midday, so when the hotline jingled early that morning, Jimmy Lavery picked up quickly, sensing bad news—and he got it.

A staffer reported that a man had jumped into the white tiger habitat, right by the cats' swimming pool. Although there was a fence around the pool, it was only about four feet high—intended to keep tigers in, not people out. The fence wasn't tall because that end of the pool was too deep for the tigers to stand in, much less jump out of. Nobody had anticipated that a human being in his right mind would jump a fence to join a pack of wild carnivores.

Apparently, this man had done exactly that. He'd parked a van on the other side of the wall and jumped over into the habitat, falling into the pool. Jimmy and other

Jungle Palace staff rushed to the site—and could hardly believe their eyes. A man holding a Bible was preaching histrionically to three mesmerized white tigers, Shasadee, Sitarra and Neva. Recalled Jimmy Lavery, "It was like everything was happening in slow motion. We thought of calling the police, but what could they do? Come and drag the tigers away from the bible-thumper? We were all worried that we were about to witness a gruesome attack."

After a while, the "Preacher" finished his sermon and prepared to leave. Shasadee and Sitarra, as if finally bored by it all, walked away. Neva apparently wanted to hear more of God's word, because just as the guy went to jump back over the fence, the cat chomped his ass and yanked him back into the habitat. She looked slightly disappointed and puzzled moments later when an ambulance arrived to rush the man to the emergency room.

At the hospital, things got seriously weirder when the Preacher jumped out of a top-floor window. Perhaps it was his unfaltering faith, however, that saved his life, because a canopy he hit on the way down broke his fall and saved his life. Incredibly, when the Man Who Moshed the Tiger Pit was released from the hospital, he threatened to sue Siegfried and Roy!

In addition to all the human victims of tiger attacks at the Siegfried and Roy compound, several tiger-on-tiger injuries occurred at the Jungle Palace. On one occasion, when Roy had two of the biggest tigers out of their cages by the pool—one weighed around 670 pounds, and the other 550—the larger cat wanted to get in the water, but the smaller one didn't...so the big cat grabbed the smaller one and flung him violently into the pool like a stuffed toy. While the aggressor was speeding away from the scene, no one dared encroach on his territory. After feeding time, he was finally calm enough to be put back in his cage.

Dr. Dinnes, who was in California at the time, was called. Just five hours after the incident, the doctor arrived on the scene with his fully equipped veterinarian's truck to operate on the injured tiger. The beast was too heavy to move, so Dr. Dinnes stitched him up on the spot. During the operation, as fluid was being flushed into the wound to sterilize it, Jimmy Lavery, who was assisting, suddenly felt fluid dripping down his leg. When he asked Dr. Dinnes where it was coming from, the vet discovered another puncture wound. The measured distance between the two wounds was seventeen inches; that's how wide the cat's jaw had extended.

Considering all these dangerous close-calls—animals attacking man, animals attacking animals—it should have come as no surprise when Roy Horn was attacked and nearly killed by his beloved tiger, Montecore, in 2003, just two years after the German duo had won their biggest prize yet: a lifetime contract at The Mirage.

Chapter 13
DAY OF THE DOLPHIN

"Not even marine mammals in the desert seems far-fetched in Las Vegas."
—Time Out Las Vegas, *2005*

In the summer of 1983, Steve and Elaine Wynn vacationed at a health spa in upper-crusty Rancho La Costa, California, and visited Sea World in nearby San Diego. Steve instantly took a strong liking to the park's magnificent dolphins and started thinking about installing a school of Flipper look-a-likes in his own back-yard. After they returned home, Mrs. Wynn recalls, she looked out a window and saw her husband pacing around outside. He told her he was measuring a site for his future dolphin pool. As it happened, no sleek sea mammals actually ended up living in Steve Wynn's garden, but he made his dream come true by creating a beautiful habitat for them in his hotel.

The Mirage was not the first mega-casino in Vegas to feature aquatic life. The Riviera had imported sea lions to the desert for a show called "Splash," and the MGM Grand had staged a show featuring a single dolphin. Somehow the horrible living conditions the animals endured at those hotels were never exposed, and today's sophisticated animal rights organizations would have crucified them in the press. The poor sea lions were cramped for weeks on end in a trailer, and MGM's solitary dolphin was kept in a tiny tank in the basement, deprived of sunlight.

The more Wynn thought about creating a Mirage dolphin habitat on a grand scale, the more he liked it. But getting a permit to own dolphins would be tough. He needed to come up with an angle that would persuade the proper governmental authorities, and he finally hit on it: a dolphin exhibit constructed to advance science by educating children. "Dolphins are special and different...their effect on all humans is overwhelming and unique," Wynn told the powers-that-be. "How wonderful it would be if all kids in Las Vegas could experience them."

According to biographer John L. Smith, "The process took many months and a shark-like lobbying effort that involved not only the superintendent of Southern Nevada's Clark County School District, but also the state's congressional delegation...."

Nevada Governor Bob Miller staunchly championed the program. His spokesman stated, "They are not going to have six dolphins in a Mason fruit jar. Some people back in Washington don't understand this. It will be top rank."

Needless to say, Wynn got his dolphin license.

The ball got rolling when Julie Wignall, director of The National Aquarium in Washington, DC, got a phone call from The Mirage's architect who inquired about dolphins and then asked her to meet with Steve Wynn in Las Vegas. She'd never even heard of him, and recalls, "People in Las Vegas kept talking about gaming. I thought that hunting must be very popular there."

The King of Las Vegas flew Julie Wignall into town and spent three hours with her, outlining his dream of dolphins in the desert. Then he offered her the job of making it all happen. When Wignall accepted, the billionaire gave her virtual carte blanche to create the most advanced dolphin habitat on the planet. In January 1989, she moved to Las Vegas and immediately added two world-renowned vets to her team: Dr. Lanny Cornell, the former vice president of Sea World and a pioneer of preventive care for cetaceans in captivity, and Dr. Martin Dinnes, the first veterinarian to devote his practice to non-domesticated animals—and who was also Siegfried and Roy's private vet. Both experts were consultants for aquatic parks and zoos around the world.

As usual, Wynn accepted nothing but the best. He wanted to dazzle the public, not appall them with a tacky attraction like the notoriously cruel Japanese bear parks, where dozens of bears are confined in small concrete pits, often don't get fed unless tourists toss them bear biscuits, and rarely get medical treatment for injuries sustained during all-too-frequent fights. He wanted a naturalistic dolphin habitat dedicated to environmental science that would enhance his philanthropic image and, of course, attract more paying guests.

He ended up investing $17 million to create the world's most advanced animal research program for marine mammals. His 1.5 million-plus-gallon saltwater pools were upwards of nine times larger than government regulations required. A filtration system cycled and cleansed the man-made "seawater" every two hours. State-of-the-art equipment included a special underwater research observa-tion post and a monitoring system that allowed 24/7 viewing by staff members, security, and Steve Wynn himself.

Construction workers had already started digging a huge hole for the pool in early 1989 when Julie hired Jimmy Lavery, who'd worked with both Dr. Dinnes and Dr. Cornell at the Frontier. Both experts had recommended him for the job, and when Julie met him for the first time at The Mirage Coffee Shop, Dr. Cornell grabbed one of the Keno cards scattered around on every table for players of the Bingo-like game and sketched a schematic of the dolphin filtration system with a crayon. Dr. Cornell showed the sketch to Jimmy and asked if he'd work on constructing the pool. Jimmy made an instant decision and wrote "yes" beside Dr. Cornell's sketch with the crayon—that was to be their contract.

While the pool was in progress, Julie Wignall, Dr. Cornell and Dr. Dinnes began the daunting task of finding suitable dolphins. Steve Wynn had made a bold pronounce-ment, stating that only dolphins already in captivity would be acquired; they'd never be taken from the wild. Collectors who worked with marine mammals immediately began fretting that if The Mirage emphasized obtaining dolphins in captivity, animal rights groups would force all exhibitors to stop wild captures.

Julie began contacting every marine mammal facility with dolphins, but most weren't interested in working with The Mirage. Then she got an inspired idea. Animal rights activists were constantly regaling the press with stories about "terrible roadside attractions housing dolphins," so Julie sent out the word: "If you know where these facilities are, let me know." Her idea paid off when she got a tip that a facility was about to close down in Galveston, Texas.

Julie immediately headed to Galveston, where Dr. Cornell and Dr. Dinnes joined her. The trio found two dolphins suitable for The Mirage: a healthy, robust three-year-old female named Haley and an older dolphin, Sigma, sadly covered with cuts inflicted during a swim under a "gate" connecting two pools. Conditions at the facility were deteriorating rapidly, so calls requesting emergency transport were made to the USDA/APHIS (U.S.D.A. Animal Plant Health Inspection Service) and NMFS (National Marine Fisheries Service).

Meanwhile, Dr. Dinnes got a promise from Six Flags Texas to serve as a temporary holding facility for the animals until The Mirage habitat was completed, if they got government approval. USDA gave an immediate thumbs-up, but the NMFS dragged its feet, saying that the case would have to be reviewed. A local veterinarian with a marine mammal background was hired and, with two of Dr. Dinnes' animal trainers assisting, mounted a daily watch over the animals while negotiations with the government continued.

Less than a week later, Haley was discovered dead one morning. According to necropsy reports, she'd died from ingesting poisonous oleander leaves. Stunned by this turn of events, and knowing that Sigma wasn't in the best shape to begin with, panicked phone calls went out again to the NMFS, begging for permission to move her quickly.

On a daily basis, the local vet and Dr. Dinnes' trainers reported on the Galveston facility's deterioration as it neared final shutdown; of especial concern was the lack of adequate water filtration and the declining morale among the few remaining staff members. About a month later, approval to transport Sigma to Six Flags finally came through.

Next, Dr. Dinnes offered to sell The Mirage four dolphins he owned in the Florida Keys. A few weeks before the pool opened, Jimmy Lavery was sent to the East Coast to check up on the dolphins with a warning from his bosses: Don't talk to anybody about your mission. Animal rights activists like the hardcore PETA were complaining loud and long about The Mirage's plans and harassing Wynn and his hotel employees. Someone had phoned in a death threat against Julie Wignall *and* her dolphins. Even though the Dolphin Habitat was being designed to serve as a model of man-made environmental quality, with the best specialists in the world involved in its creation, PETA was dead-set against it and still is today. Their position is unequivocal: dolphins should not be kept in any kind of captivity facility, and those in captivity should be released into the wild. According to Wignall, their extreme belief is that dolphins in captivity should be killed, as "death is better than captivity." The foundation of these beliefs is that no matter how well-run or well-intentioned the habitat is, it still can't produce the same conditions the dolphins experience in the wild.

While Jimmy Lavery waited at the Miami airport for his connecting flight to the Florida Keys, his cell phone rang. A stranger on the line started asking for details about the dolphins' transportation.

Jimmy cut the guy off with, "I don't know what you're talking about." To which the stranger replied, "Don't you work for me?"

"I'm not talking about anything on the phone," Jimmy snapped, and hung up.

A few minutes later, Julie Wignall called and gasped, "Did you just hang up on Steve? You need to call him back right now, Jimmy. That was Steve Wynn. The boss."

Sheeeaht! That's the end of my job, thought Jimmy. He quickly returned the call and asked for Steve Wynn's office. Joyce, Wynn's assistant, picked up, then put Jimmy on hold for about twenty minutes, giving him plenty of time to stew over his future as an employee. When Joyce reconnected, she told the Georgia redneck that the boss wanted him on the next plane back to Vegas. No questions, no dolphins—NOW!

Jimmy flew back to Vegas, called Wynn's office from the airport and was told to meet the boss right away in The Mirage's French restaurant. When he arrived, the maître d' took Jimmy to Wynn's table. Ten elegantly attired people were crowded around the billionaire. Jimmy, ever the Georgia hick, was in his standard duds: Jesus sandals, shorts and a t-shirt. He didn't exactly blend in with Wynn's crowd of jet-setters sporting dark suits and flashy dental work that had probably cost more than his house. Knowing Wynn's reputation for hot-headedness, Jimmy figured "Mr. Vegas" was about to get payback for the phone hang-up by shouting at his employee in front of his guests before firing him.

Instead, Wynn calmly questioned, "So, what size plane are we using to transport the dolphins?"

Is this the foreplay before the big explosion? Jimmy wondered.

He grunted a brief explanation of how he'd proceed with the animal transportation. Wynn got it like he always does—fast! Said Jimmy: "Wynn is a visionary. He is so sharp. He took the few details I told him and filled in the blanks himself. He turned that into a narrative for his friends at the table. And his spiel was accurate."

Jimmy told Wynn they'd use a medium-sized aircraft to transport the dolphins, but Wynn ordered him to use the biggest plane that would fit the runway. Moments later, Wynn asked Jimmy, "Don't you need to go somewhere?"

"Yessir."

And Jimmy flew 2,000 miles back to Florida.

Transporting the dolphins to The Mirage was a tremendous feat. Not only was it necessary to find a way to get the four 500-pound mammals into specially designed, water-filled transport containers in the Florida Keys and then fly them to Las Vegas, but arrangements had to be made to pick up the dolphin named Sigma in Texas. To add to the challenge, animal rights activists were threatening sabotage.

Evergreen, one of the world's largest transportation companies, was hired. A 727 was chartered. On the day of the transport, each dolphin was supervised by a separate veterinarian. They were hoisted by stretcher and gently deposited into custom-made containers filled with water and ice so their body temperatures wouldn't escalate. The plane refueled when it stopped in Miami, and a new stock of ice— from, ironically, the "Dolphin Ice Factory"—was brought aboard.

The plane took off and landed a few hours later in Dallas, where according to a Steve Wynn tipster, PETA's shock troops planned on blocking the entrance to Sigma's habitat with trucks. As always, Wynn was one step ahead of the game. Two locations in Dallas housed dolphins, and he had publicly announced the name of the facility where The Mirage's dolphin would be picked up. The information Wynn gave was bogus, so PETA was faked into watching the wrong facility.

Finally, Jimmy spotted flashing red and blue lights approaching the plane. Sigma the dolphin had a police escort. Her transport container was hoisted aboard and fastened into place as the pilot got an "all clear" for takeoff. Julie Wignall phoned Steve Wynn to tell him they were all on their way home.

Dolphins and crew entered Las Vegas airspace at 2 a.m. As they neared the airport, lights began to blink off like dominos. For safety and security, a blackout had been arranged between airport administrators and Steve Konig, Steve Wynn's director of security. As the 727 descended, every light at the airport switched off. Once on the ground, the dolphins were loaded onto two huge semi-trucks. The city's streets were blocked, and there wasn't a car in sight.

Operation Dolphin had concluded...flawlessly.

Happily, all the animals thrived as they became acclimated to The Mirage's just-completed Dolphin Habitat, and it opened to the public in November 1990. Visitors were given tours to introduce them to the animals and to share information about their biology, their behavior, and their importance in our oceans.

The dolphins swam among three connecting pools, around a huge artificial coral reef system. Some visitors became "regulars" and started learning the antics of specific dolphins. For example, the dark gray coloration of Merlin's back met with the white coloration of his belly, forming an

"M" near his groin. It was very easy to recognize Merlin, as he had a habit of swimming around the pool on his back; something these animals will do only if they feel comfortable in their surroundings. Hotel reservation staff got used to visitors asking for rooms that overlooked the dolphin pool so that they could watch Merlin from their room.

School children came during morning hours for age-appropriate programs that taught them about marine mammals. Annually, 60,000 students take field trips to the facilities. Steve Wynn created a separate entrance for the facility so kids didn't have to enter through his casino. And even though it lost him revenue, Wynn decided to not open the Dolphin Habitat to the public before 11 a.m. so his educational programs for youngsters would take place uninterrupted.

Even though Wynn's programs and research into dolphin behavior won awards, and his water filtration protocols were used as models around the world, his dolphin habitat remains a source of controversy. While the hotel claims to have a very low dolphin mortality rate, it's been criticized by some animal welfare groups because eleven of sixteen dolphins housed at the habitat have died since it opened in 1990. These critics say dolphins shouldn't be kept in habitats. In the wild, dolphins can live forty-five years. In captivity, the lifespan ranges from five to twenty years.

While a sign beside the dolphin lagoon states that none of their dolphins have been captured from the wild, the World Society for the Protection of Animals (WSPA) disagrees. On their website in May, 2003, the group cited a federal Marine Mammal Inventory Report (MMIR) released that year, claiming that three of The Mirage dolphins had been captured from the wild.

Additionally, the WSPA claims that although The Mirage facility is billed as a "research and educational" center, the dolphins interact with the trainers for public display and are trained to perform such tricks as tail-walking, vocalizing, ball-playing, flipper-waving and towing their trainers around—just like dolphins at traditional tourist attractions.

There was, however, good news along with the bad: within a fairly short time of the habitat's opening, the dolphins began to have babies. Steve Wynn immediately added another 900,000-gallon pool. Clearly, the huge tanks must provide a healthy environment or the dolphins wouldn't breed regularly.

Wanting to keep a constant eye on his dolphins, Wynn had cameras installed in his office that would allow him to view all underwater activity. When the camera system was first installed, Jimmy Lavery—at a friend's house enjoying a quiet drink one night—got a call from the big boss, who was saying he suddenly couldn't view the Dolphin Habitat from his desk. Puzzled, Jimmy tried impromptu trouble-shooting, telling Wynn to "press the button on the right" and "try Command 74," etc. Wynn insisted he still couldn't see anything in the tank. Frustrated, Jimmy raised his eyes and peered up at the night sky through a window.

Bingo!

"Um, Mr. Wynn," he said carefully. "There are, uh, no lights on in the pool. So, the reason you can't see is because it's now past...dark."

One day in the early 90s, Steven Wynn and Jimmy Lavery were taking a dip with the dolphins when the idea arose of building a major tiger habitat for Mirage superstars Siegfried and Roy. The billionaire, in his usual extravagance, had built a small apartment for himself just off of one of the dolphin pools. The room was built so that his dolphins could visit him while he was at work; or, on a moment's notice, Wynn could step into the shallowest of the Dolphin Habitat's three inter-connected pools, which consisted of the main pool, medical pool, and holding pool.

After their swim that day, Wynn offered Jimmy a cup of coffee and got down to business. It was time, he said, to start building a proper tiger habitat for Siegfried and Roy, like the one at the Jungle Palace. The Mirage front entrance already boasted a white stucco habitat, equipped with a pool, where two or three tigers were visible to the public through a glass window. It had been built in 1990 (and would survive until 2007, after Roy's mauling by Montecore, when it was finally converted into a BLT Burger joint). But now, Wynn told Jimmy, the time had come to build something big enough to hold the legendary white tigers and all the big cats: something to rival the Dolphin Habitat. One of the names Wynn had been kicking around was "The Secret Garden."

Jimmy nodded enthusiastically until Wynn told him about his one reservation: he didn't want to start the project if he had to constantly consult and get approvals from Siegfried and Roy's entourage. He'd been down that road before. Wynn didn't want to jump through hoops. He wanted it his way. No Bernie Yuman, no high-strung architects, no lawyers.

Wynn said to Jimmy, "How can I get this going with just Siegfried and Roy?"

Jimmy replied, "If you can get Roy to shake your hand, you'll have his word and that's all you'll need."

"How do I get that to happen?" Wynn queried.

Jimmy thought about it for a minute. How could Wynn squeeze in a quick conversation with Siegfried and Roy with no managers or lawyers around? Then he remembered: it was Lynette's birthday, a perfect time to distract everyone so Wynn could get some alone time with his stars.

Jimmy told Wynn, "Meet me backstage right after the first show, before the second starts."

Incredibly, just as Lavery himself walked backstage that night, Wynn's assistant Joyce was there to meet him, bearing bad news: "Your mother was in a car accident. You need to get in touch with her."

"What?"

"Your dad's in the hospital, too."

Before Jimmy had a moment to absorb Joyce's news, Siegfried and Roy came offstage. As everyone began singing "Happy Birthday" to Lynette, Jimmy said urgently to Wynn, "Quick go in there," practically shoving him into Lynette's dressing room. The slick redneck then grabbed Siegfried and

Roy and told them Steve wanted to speak to them. Now! After the three were together in Lynette's room, alone, Jimmy locked the door.

None of them emerged for nearly an hour and a half. Finally, just thirty minutes before showtime, the triumvirate invited Bernie Yuman into the dressing room. By now, the troupe was getting ready for the second show, except for Siegfried and Roy, who still hadn't eaten, and Lynette, who was still locked out of her dressing room. Just five minutes before showtime, Siegfried left the meeting and went upstairs to the apartment. Then Roy came out and disappeared to change for the show.

Then...Steve Wynn emerged. Jimmy knew instantly the deal was done; the billionaire was grinning like a Cheshire cat.

Lynette, who had yet to change her costume, snarked at Jimmy, "Thanks a lot for shoving them in *my* dressing room!"

Finally, Jimmy could catch a plane back to Atlanta to check up on his parents, who were recuperating in different hospitals. His dad, who'd been recovering from an earlier stroke, had suddenly come down with pneumonia. His mother, who'd been in a serious car accident, was in a hospital on the other side of town.

Jimmy flew to Atlanta to see them, but returned to Vegas within twenty-four hours.

In due course, the Secret Garden habitat was built under Jimmy's supervision and opened in 1997. It turned out beautifully. The animals included white tigers, golden striped tigers, lions, birds and other creatures—and even the huge elephant, Gildah. The habitat was a new wonderland for the animal-obsessed Roy.

Julie Wignall, the animal behavioral expert who was in charge of Wynn's dolphin habitat, recalls that Roy truly had a special talent with animals. He had a mystical connection with them on a primitive level, as opposed to expertise springing from formal schooling in animal training techniques and behavioral patterns.

Roy didn't look at animals as biological specimens, which was touchingly naïve, but it was an attitude that was bound to have repercussions. Among other things, Julie specifically told Roy it wasn't good to have just one elephant; they're herd animals that need companions. But Roy believed he was the only family Gildah would ever need.

Even though Roy ignored the "rules," animals responded to his strange behavior. He purchased companion animals for Gildah that included turkeys, chickens, and a donkey, but never an elephant playmate. One of these companions, a turkey, hilariously took a liking to Julie and was extremely protective, following her everywhere. Julie always told people how mortified she was that of all the animals at The Mirage, it was a turkey that had latched onto her.

Then a group of Navajo Indians came to see the Secret Garden, and the leader of the tribe chastised Julie for being embarrassed about the turkey's devotion. He told her that one of the greatest honors someone can have is for a turkey to bond with her, because turkeys can identify a potential shaman or visionary in any group of human beings. In Navajo lore, the turkey is second only to the eagle. Hearing this, Julie started treating the turkey with respect, but from that moment on, the bird haughtily ignored her!

Roy had such a way with the animals that whenever he walked into the Secret Garden, every single animal would jump up and get excited. Like "Ace Ventura: Pet Detective," Roy would walk into the Secret Garden and shout out "Good morning!" to his animals, startling them out of sleep.

But life with wild animals is rarely like a Hollywood movie. On a fateful day in 1997, when Jimmy Lavery happened to be far away in Mexico—hand-delivering, believe it or not, Gerber's baby food for three of Siegfried and Roy's newborn tiger cubs (because the Mexican brands just don't cut it)—a catastrophic incident occurred at The Mirage.

The Secret Garden had just opened to the public. Hollywood animal expert Monty Cox was on hand to teach trainers how to handle the big cats in the new habitat, but on January 17, Roy suddenly insisted that Monty and all the trainers accompany him to Little Bavaria for a photo shoot. It was certainly not the wisest idea to leave The Secret Garden completely unattended by animal trainers with hotel guests roaming around, but Roy was the boss.

During the photo shoot at Little Bavaria, Monty suddenly got a panicked call from Steve Wynn. One of the tigers had killed another tiger, and Mirage guests had actually witnessed the slaughter. Even now, sputtered Wynn, an audience was gawping at a tiger corpse lying limp in the habitat. Where the hell was a trainer to remove the killer tiger from the cage?

According to a tourist who witnessed the savage attack, the male tiger bit into the female's neck, then held on tight for at least twenty minutes, but "nobody did anything...no animal trainer was on hand" to intervene.

Monty was immediately rushed to the scene and all of the rubber-neck tourists were quickly ushered out of the Secret Garden. When Monty realized what had happened, he was furious...and sad. These two tigers, Baroda, a male, and Nirvana, a female, should never have been left alone together. Like any expert, Monty knew that when you put tigers in a cage, you have to know their psychological dynamic and team them up judiciously, making sure they're compatible. Monty had assigned two females and one male for this cage because Baroda—a very feisty male—needed more than one female to keep him at bay. But someone had removed one of the females, leaving Nirvana alone with Baroda.

Eyewitnesses said Nirvana, a playful female, had approached Baroda and started slapping at him. Baroda, who'd been lazing in the sun, snarled at her, so she coyly walked away. But being a frisky female, Nirvana persisted. As Baroda dozed, she teasingly pawed at him again. He snarled, she walked away, but this time it was too late. The cranky male casually stood up, padded over to Nirvana...and lunged, sinking his fangs into her neck.

Tigers are solitary creatures who like to be left alone, so being trapped in a cage with another tiger can get on a cat's nerves. As Monty puts it, "It's like a man having to put up with his wife's nagging all day long; after a while you can't take it any more."

In their natural habitat, tigers have endless terrain to explore. At The Mirage, the biggest cage is 6,000 square feet. The one housing Nirvana and Baroda that day measured about 2,500 square feet. "Imagine being in a small cage with no escape route...you get cabin fever pretty quickly," explained Monty.

On this day, death was the awful result of cabin fever. Men, women and children watched in horror as Baroda clamped his powerful jaws on Nirvana's neck and slowly, slowly suffocated her to death.

Monty was blamed for the incident. The Secret Garden was immediately closed. Jimmy Lavery jetted back from Mexico and swore to a furious Steve Wynn that this would never happen again and that competent animal experts would always be on hand at the habitat. It was not a good beginning for the Secret Garden, but it re-opened the next day. The incident, involving no human death or injury, was quickly forgotten.

But potential for danger always lurks when wild animals live in the world of man. Just a few years later, KLAS-TV news in Las Vegas reported that a former Mirage employee had revealed that "in 2000, the tigers chewed through the fence at the Secret Garden and security guards used emergency procedures to get a hold of the tigers before animal handlers stepped in. This was apparently minutes before the Secret Garden opened to the public."

Imagine several tigers running loose among the milling crowds at The Mirage. How bad would it have been? Compare it to a fatal attack that occurred at the San Francisco Zoo on Christmas Day, 2007, when a single Siberian tiger leapt over a twelve-and-a-half-foot-high fence, killing one teenager and injuring two others. Or compare it to what can happen when even an experienced person has casual, friendly contact with the powerful beasts, like the time Jimmy Lavery brought back the three cubs that had been thriving on Gerber's in Mexico.

Lynette adored the babies and would let them suck on her finger like a pacifier after she removed her fake nails. One day, the cub named Vishnu was sucking on her finger like a baby cat, but nobody noticed that baby's teeth had suddenly started to grow. To her credit, Lynette did not scream or flinch when she abruptly pulled back her finger, now bleeding and stripped of her entire real nail.

Lynette, not wanting Siegfried or Roy to know she'd been careless, told no one except Jimmy. He figured the bosses didn't need to know. The next day, however, a staffer called Lynette and Jimmy's house and inquired, "There was blood outside Vishnu's cage. Do you know if anything happened?"

"No, nothing happened. Somebody just cut their finger or something," Jimmy responded.

To this day, Siegfried and Roy don't know about that bite.

Lynette had another little secret. Stored in her freezer were ziplock bags full of claws she'd kept from cubs de-clawed over the years, not wanting tiger body parts to be slipped to the black market. Ironic, of course, when you consider that Lynette had just been "de-clawed" by a cub. Interestingly, Lynette's "little secret" covered up another Siegfried and Roy fairytale. The duo has told the public for years that they *never* de-claw their cats, fearing, accurately, that animal protection groups would be up in arms.

Siegfried and Roy were fanatical about keeping secrets from their employees and the public. Even to many of their closest friends and staff, their personal life is an enigma wrapped in mystery.

"After living and working with some of the world's most magnificent creatures, we have felt the threat of their loss. So we felt compelled to create a safe environment—an environment in which these animals could live in serenity."

—Roy Horn

Siegfried and Roy shared a strong bond with Mirage owner Steve Wynn: an absolute addiction to animals. Not surprisingly, considering Wynn's huge assets, the billionaire topped even the German duo with his animal ventures—some that made great business sense and others that revealed him as a dyed-in-the-wool eccentric. Whether he was creating the world's most exclusive golf course—with many exotic birds and animals ranging over its greens, and others resting beneath it in a pet cemetery dedicated to his beloved dolphins—or fussing over the bottle-feeding of a baby kangaroo in his offices, Wynn repeatedly proved that his love for animals was deep-seated...and very rewarding.

Although it's difficult to separate fact from legend in Wynn's storybook life, the alleged impetus for building the world's greatest golf course was The Mirage's harpooning of a "whale," the Las Vegas nickname for high-rolling multi-millionaires who aren't afraid of seven-figure gambling. In this case, the whale was the CEO of a Japanese company who lost several million dollars at The Mirage gaming tables. Wynn decided to use this whale's sudden windfall for a project he'd been mulling. So in 1989, he carved yet another larger-than-life playground out of the desert sands: Shadow

Creek Golf Course. Ignoring the utter improbability and impracticality of constructing an 18-hole, 250-acre golf course in the middle of water-desperate desert, Wynn went ahead and created yet another venue for well-heeled guests to enjoy life and spend their money. Wynn's investment? A whopping $48 million-plus!

He hired golf course architect Tom Fazio to help design the layout for the lakes, cascading waterfalls, rolling hills, and 200 varieties of trees that he envisioned. As a demonstration of Wynn's affection for animals, exotic birds and beasts often outnumbered guests and staff combined. According to one Shadow Creek patron, Michael Konik, "It feels as if you have wandered into some sort of bird sanctuary. There are thousands of them: quail, pheasants, flamingos, chukars, and snow white swans. They have a wallaby, too."

Shadow Creek Golf Course is shrouded by an air of mystery. Its celebrity guest list is studded with boldface names of the rich and famous—people who demand and expect total discretion. The club's seventy employees are sworn to confidentiality and warned not to breathe so much as a whisper about what happens behind the walls of this fortress dedicated to privileged duffers.

The golf course was dug deep into the sands, with a ten-foot-high chain link fence that obscured it to onlookers. With tighter security than the White House, the Shadow Creek club has been known to turn down an ex-President or two, which certainly hasn't harmed its swankier-than-thou public image. The inconspicuous signage at its entrance is a tiny gold plaque next to an intercom: you speak, and security staff decides if you're worthy of admission.

Once inside, cameras are forbidden. To play at the Shadow Creek Golf Course, or even to see over its high fences, you have to stay at one of the MGM Mirage resorts. Michael Konik wrote in *Cigar Aficionado*, "It's the greatest golf course you'll (probably) never play."

How exclusive is Shadow Creek? It has a membership of one: Steve Wynn. Here's why:

In 1993, the then twenty-six-year-old daughter of Steve and Elaine Wynn—a tall, attractive blonde with the rather bizarre name of Kevyn—was suddenly kidnapped and held for a $1.45 million ransom. Wynn paid the money and picked up his daughter, unharmed, from a car at McCarran International Airport. The ringleader of the kidnapping team, one Ray Cuddy, was arrested in due course at Newport Beach, where he stupidly tried to pay cash for a Ferrari. Cuddy was sentenced to twenty-four-and-a-half years in prison. Shaken by the incident, and determined to protect his family forevermore, Wynn built a mansion on the secure grounds of Shadow Creek Golf Course, where he and his family could live peacefully and privately.

In *1001 Golf Holes You Must Play Before You Die*, Shadow Creek is described as, "perhaps the most magnificent man-made golf-wonder found anywhere on earth...(its) 17th hole certainly is one of the most dramatic at Shadow Creek. The tee show is hit from the top of a ridge and over a lake to a tiny green that's surrounded by huge rocks and four deep bunkers—two at the right, one at the left front, and one at the rear. But the hole's most spectacular feature is the large waterfall that drops into a small pool behind the green."

Few golfers teeing off on that 17th hole know that just below their golf shoes lies Shadow Creek's very own dolphin cemetery. The top of the ridge drops straight down, and its steep slope is dotted with tombstones concealed by long grass. Steve Wynn loved his dolphins so much, he wanted them close by always. What better place for them to rest in peace than on his idyllic hideaway golf course.

The first time a dolphin died at The Mirage habitat, no one knew what to do with its remains. It was a question that had to be addressed for the future. Although Wynn had the money and commitment to keep his dolphins healthy with every safety precaution possible, all animals inevitably suffer fatal illnesses or accidents, or simply die of natural causes. Regardless of how that first dolphin had died, the real question was: where and how would its remains be disposed of?

First order of business, of course, was removing the dolphin's corpse so as not to unsettle Mirage guests. Overnight, Jimmy Lavery had the in-house carpenter build a coffin; then he phoned Shadow Creek and ordered one of Wynn's employees at the golf course to start digging a hole. But when Jimmy arrived with the coffin, the employee got spooked by the morbid job and flew the coop, leaving Jimmy to dig the hole. Thus was the dolphin cemetery born. Since 1990, eleven of Wynn's prized dolphins died and were laid to rest there. Sadly, however, for all those folks who became fans of Merlin, Sigma, Squirt, Bugsy, Banjo, Darla and the others, there are no guided mourning tours of Shadow Creek.

In 1991, Steve Wynn hit the headlines when he famously shot off his index finger while handling a gun in his Las Vegas office. It was a bad day for Steve: no sooner had he left The Mirage to undergo an operation to save his finger, when he was told that one of his baby dolphins had died. Wynn—a fastidious man, who's congenitally incapable of leaving any question unanswered—had to know exactly why the dolphin had died. He ordered his staff to spare no expense and demanded that every test possible should be performed to determine the exact cause of death. Wynn knew he'd need bulletproof evidence to prove the dolphin had died of natural causes to thwart animal activists who were salivating for any excuse to close down the Dolphin Habitat.

When the initial necropsy didn't produce definitive results, more tests were needed. Jimmy was sent back to the cemetery with the local vet, Dr. Simon, to dig up the dolphin three weeks after its internment and get all necessary tissue samples. Although the investigation seemed excessive, even by Steve Wynn's standards, the process was imperative. He loved the dolphins like they were his children, and he'd keep them near him at any cost.

Although the second necropsy yielded nothing new, Wynn felt confident that the dolphin had not died because of defective environment and animal activists were not able to prove otherwise.

When Siegfried and Roy hired Dr. Dinnes as their personal veterinarian, they ended up sharing him with virtually every animal-owning celebrity in America; notably, their friend Michael Jackson. And because Dr. Dinnes was one of the world's most revered vets, Steve Wynn simply had to have him on his team. He was hired along with Dr. Lanny Cornell of Sea World around the same time that Julie Wignall was commissioned to spearhead the Dolphin Habitat.

Dr. Dinnes lived in Los Angeles, but constantly traveled the globe. He had offices in London, Japan, and Africa. In the early 90s, Dr. Dinnes was called to the New Jersey Zoo to help an ailing newborn baby kangaroo because its mother had rejected it. When joeys are born they're less than an inch long and weigh about 0.04 ounces. After birth, they immediately claw their way up the mother's body and enter the pouch. They attach their mouth to a teat, which enlarges and holds it in place until it's fully developed. In this case, instead of letting her joey stay in the pouch, the mother had expelled it, leaving it to fend for itself.

Steve Wynn happened to be on the East Coast when Dr. Dinnes told him about the abandoned joey. Next thing you know, Wynn was on his private plane back to Vegas, cradling the tiny female he'd named Bonnie. The staff at The Mirage was overjoyed to have a cute little joey to keep them entertained. Wynn's assistant, Joyce—who was also Dr. Dinnes' girlfriend—ended up taking care of Bonnie, who had a baby bottle filled with milk glued to her mouth every minute of the day. And Wynn gave the joey her very own room at The Mirage. When Joyce worked in Steve Wynn's office, she would tie a sweatshirt onto her chair and stick tiny Bonnie into the makeshift pouch.

Eventually, stuffed-toy-sized Bonnie shot up to a height of four feet eleven inches—with a three-foot tail—so she ended up living at Dr. Dinnes' ranch in Los Angeles, within driving distance of Las Vegas. Sadly, because kangaroos usually live in their mother's pouch for the first seven to ten months of their lives, and because her mother had disowned her, Bonnie kept falling ill. Finally, there was nothing more Dr. Dinnes could do for her. A year later, Bonnie died on his ranch.

Human beings who love animals know that their lifespans are typically much shorter than our own. Animal deaths are as inevitable as the grief their owners feel, and there's always the practical matter of how to deal with a pet's remains. Over the course of their thirty-plus years in show business, Siegfried and Roy needed somewhere to bury deceased members of their own menagerie, and like Steve Wynn, they decided to keep their animals close, interring them in the "dirt" they'd acquired over the years around Little Bavaria. It would be their very own pet cemetery.

One Christmas, during the holiday break from The Mirage, one of the show horses named Favorito, the duo's favorite stallion, contracted colic, a bothersome affliction for a human child but a potentially fatal condition for a 1,000-pound horse. The veterinarian told Lynette and Jimmy to bring Favorito to his clinic, but he couldn't save the horse and had to put him down. He was too big to cremate, but another horse had already been buried on The Land, so Favorito was laid to rest right next to it after Jimmy Lavery and a team of workers dug the hole. Favorito remains there to this day.

Roy, who loved horses and owned many in the course of his career, was devastated. In his grief, he started reminiscing about his life with horses, and recalled, in his and Siegfried's autobiography, a magnificent steed named Grandissimo. One day, when Roy lay down on the sand to rest briefly after hours of riding his horse through the desert, he heard, and then actually saw, a rattlesnake poised just inches from his face. Instantly, Grandissimo came to Roy's rescue, rearing and stomping the snake until it was dead. Then, Roy recalled, Grandissimo made a touching gesture after the snake had been killed. "Still foaming at the mouth, his large black eyes still flashing and blowing air through his nostrils, he came over to me and nudged and nuzzled me with his head.

"Now, I ask you…is that friendship?"

Gildah, Siegfried and Roy's famous "disappearing" elephant in The Mirage show, died in August 2005. Considering how long the elephant had been a part of Roy's extended family, it's likely she too was buried in The Land's cemetery, but the duo's always kept silent about it.

After burying many of his animals, Roy eventually became committed to the cremation of remains. He had shelves of urns lined up in his bedroom, each containing the ashes of his dogs and big cats; and strangely enough, his own mother! In the case of the big cats, Roy knew cremation was the best answer. The demand for illegal wild animal fur was still high, and he feared the animals' graves might be robbed.

Jimmy's first experience with cremating Roy's animals occurred when the tiger Sahra died in the mid-80s. Sahra had been one of the boys' favorite cats; she was the first exotic animal, after Chico and Simba, that Roy had trained for the show. Around 1982, while Siegfried and Roy were still at the Frontier, Sahra's health slowly began to deteriorate. At one point, she had to have daily kidney dialysis. During the procedure, she'd lie on the laps of Roy, or Jimmy, or Dr. Dinnes for hours on end while she watched her favorite cartoon, *The Jetsons*, with dialysis tubes protruding from her neck. Like any child, Sahra loved her cartoons.

Sadly, six months after Sahra's dialysis treatment, Jimmy went to the Jungle Palace one day to check on the tigers. The moment he entered the habitat, he noticed that they were all on high alert and standing at the front of their cages. Jimmy walked past the cats and found Sahra's lifeless body. She must have died just moments before his arrival because she was still warm. Sahra was Jimmy's favorite cat. He stood in shock for several minutes, trying to absorb the fact that she was no longer alive.

With the assistance of a few men at the Jungle Palace, he put the cat in the van and drove her to the local animal crematorium. It was of modest size, but the only one in town. When they arrived at the crematorium, the owner broke the bad news to them: "That big cat ain't gonna fit in our crematorium. Not in that little thing."

"Oh, man," groaned Jimmy. Not sure what to do, he called Dr. Dinnes and said, "Doc, I...uh...I got Sahra with me...and I don't know what to do...."

"What's wrong with it?"

"It's dead."

By this time, Sahra had gone into rigor mortis, so there was no hope of somehow stuffing the huge animal into the tiny furnace. But Roy, who'd been called, didn't want to hear it. He wanted the cat cremated and brought back to the house as soon as possible, and he insisted that the ashes had to still be warm when he got them. Furthermore, he'd instructed Jimmy to make sure the furnace was clean before Sahra's body was put into it. Roy didn't want any other animal's ashes mixed with his cat.

There was only one thing to do.

"Cut her up," Dr. Dinnes told Jimmy.

"Oh man, Doc, I can't go cuttin' up this tiger."

"Well, you call me back when you come up with a better way of getting her body into that furnace."

Jimmy had no choice. He dismembered the tiger's corpse, cutting off its legs. He called it one of the worst experiences of his life.

Times with the animals weren't always so sad. Jimmy remembers a hilarious interaction between Bernie Yuman and Leo, the lion. Bernie never liked going near the cats, or any animals. For one thing, he was always dressed in black, which didn't work well with white cat fur. Plus, Bernie was afraid of the cats. Even though he managed an act employing hundreds of animals over the years, for Bernie Yuman it was strictly business, not a labor of love, when it came to a creature big enough to eat him.

One day, Jimmy decided to play a joke on Bernie. Roy called Bernie to the Jungle Palace to discuss "business," and they met outside in the garden. What Bernie didn't know was that Leo had been hidden under the bench he and Roy were sitting on. What Bernie also didn't realize was that Leo, in his old age, was like a big, harmless puppy and posed no threat to anyone. Suddenly, in the middle of his conversation with Roy, Leo's tail snaked out from under the bench and flicked one of Bernie's cowboy boots. At the sight of that gigantic tail, Bernie's jaw locked wide open in mid-sentence. He froze, a look of sheer panic flashing in his eyes. It took a few minutes to calm him down before everyone had a big laugh—everyone except Bernie, that is.

While Leo the lion had always been a friendly fellow from the first moment Siegfried and Roy were introduced to him by Monty Cox, many of Roy's other cats were not so easygoing. Especially those, says Roy, who came to him as adults. "As the father figure to my animals I love the rewards I reap from nurturing them," he explains. "All the time, love, and effort I put into an animal come back to me tenfold. It's much more difficult...when I adopt a fully grown one. Then I have to undo fears, insecurities, and mistrusts that have developed in his past." One of these emotionally wounded cats was an adult panther named Macumba who came to Roy through Dr. Dinnes. Macumba, the vet explained, had become heartbroken when his owner died. Now the cat was lashing out at anyone who approached. "Because a placement in a zoo couldn't be arranged, it was only a matter of time before the specimen would be put down," said Roy, who couldn't bear the thought of a beautiful black panther's life being wasted and decided to give him a shot.

After Macumba was delivered to the habitat, he acted like a depressed child, remaining hunched in the dark corner of his cave all day long. Roy knew he had to break the spell, so he began sitting in the cave with him. Finally, Macumba reached out: "Suddenly I felt a paw on my knee and then something heavy on my legs. I opened my eyes. Macumba had laid his weary head in my lap.... Macumba had returned to life."

Macumba joined the duo's act, replacing Sabu, who was retired from performing because of arthritis. So the cycle went on.

Roy loved his animals; they loved him back. He had hundreds of lions and tigers over the course of his career and knew each one intimately. But just as tragedies can occur when even a well-meaning father neglects a child, Roy's progressive absorption with his celebrity status would have tragic consequences.

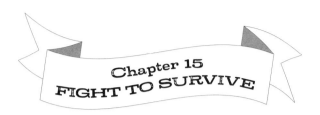

Chapter 15
FIGHT TO SURVIVE

"Everything was the show. My life was the show and the show was my life."

—Siegfried Fischbacher

Montecore's attack on Roy, on October 3, 2003, was shocking, but hardly surprising. Put simply, the golden boys were now in their golden years. And as their strength and stamina ebbed, so did the tight discipline and attention to detail that had driven four decades of success. Exhausted after their monumentally grueling Mirage shows, they yearned to relax, party with pals, and enjoy the fruits of fame. They began taking more vacations, and Roy tacitly acknowledged he was spending less time bonding with his jungle cats when he admitted he could no longer remember all their names.

Although the aging Tiger Kings had been awarded a lifetime contract at The Mirage in 2001 to commemorate their thirteen-year tenure at the hotel, Siegfried and Roy, the world-famous performers, were expected to retire imminently. But not "Siegfried & Roy," the brand name. That would live on and on, continuing to draw tourists and sell tickets to the Secret Garden and Dolphin Habitat. Already, the duo had begun diverting the spotlight onto the next generation of illusionists. In 2000, they discovered twenty-four-year-old singer/magician, Darren Romeo, and introduced him onto the magic circuit. Romeo's show headline changed to: "Siegfried & Roy present Darren Romeo, The Voice of Magic." In an eyeblink, just two years later, their protégé had nailed down a gig at The Mirage.

The "Siegfried & Roy" name was still strong, no question, but the German supermen were slowing down. At The Mirage, they were gradually reducing their weekly number of performances and taking increasingly longer holidays. And why not? They'd worked hard and bounced back from injuries and illnesses over the years. But the *Las Vegas Review-Journal* reported that a decade before the mauling, in October 1994, "when [Roy] was a mere lad of 50 and still working two shows per night, the duo took a two-month vacation—the longest in their career—after Roy was sidelined by knee surgery." The cartilage had been irreversibly damaged after many physically strenuous years of bouncing back and forth across their gigantic stage. Even after he'd had surgery, Roy's knees caused him incredible pain, forcing him to intermittently cancel shows.

Roy wasn't the only member of the troupe whose physical condition had slowly deteriorated. Lynette Chappell, their female star, was on the wrong side of fifty and still competing—in a revealing spandex body suit—with showgirls half her age. She'd suffered a serious injury when she'd fallen during a levitation illusion and crashed down on the stage. The showgirls said they actually heard the "crack!" of bones breaking when she hit the floor. The show had to be stopped because Lynette had collapsed on the passerella in front of the stage curtains in full view of the aghast audience members, and she couldn't be moved until medics arrived twenty minutes later. Despite the fact that she'd injured herself severely, Lynette insisted on going back to work the next day, but the pain sent her to the hospital, where she learned she'd cracked two vertebrae and was in near-paralysis.

Like most dancers, Lynette tended to ignore pain and always pushed herself to the limit. Incredibly, at the very moment Montecore had attacked Roy, Lynette was running hard on a treadmill backstage to keep her energy up for the evening's final performance.

The show itself suffered from old age, prompting writer A.A. Gill of *Vanity Fair* to brutally term it "without hesitation, the worst specialty show I have ever seen.... They do tricks so ancient and so bad that they must think we were all born yesterday. But then, compared to them, we pretty much were."

Ironically, and sadly, A.A. Gill's article was published in the October 2003 *Vanity Fair*, which hit the newsstands just before the tiger attack that finally ended the duo's Las Vegas stage show. With uncanny foresight, Gill mentioned in his article how exciting it would be for the audience if one of the performers actually *was* attacked: "Everyone's really here to see the white carnivores, hoping against hope that just maybe, just once, the tables will turn and Siegfried and/or Roy will get to see the inside of a big pussy."

As Siegfried and Roy had aged, so too had the cats and their other animals. The show was gradually losing its once unparalleled spark. Audience members were heard questioning whether the animals were sedated. It was alleged that the cats had to be zapped with electric prods to get them to move and look animated onstage.

The Secret Garden display area could house only about twenty of the sixty cats rotated in and out of the show. The rest were crammed in kennels out back. Over the years, lack of exercise took its toll on the animals. It also had an effect on these sensitive beasts when their human "leader of the pack" began spending less and less time bonding and showing them affection; actions that Roy himself had always deemed crucial to the act's success.

Incredibly, by 2003—just before Montecore snapped—Roy had openly admitted he couldn't remember all of his animals' names; and worse, that he was no longer attuned to each individual personality.

Condsidering all of these factors, and the innate nature of tigers and lions, it's hardly surprising Roy was mauled on that fateful night in October 2003. The wonder is that it didn't happen sooner.

In a 2004 article in *People* magazine, Siegfried confessed that the attack had actually come as a relief to him. He said they'd been considering retirement, but had too many people depending on them to end the show. He admitted that as he'd watched Roy fall in 2003, he felt a strange detachment. "It was not panic. It was in my mind:

'He needs help.' But my first thing was, and it sounds strange and I feel strange to say it, but I was relieved. In my mind, I'm saying, 'We have to stop.' It was positive. 'We have to stop....'"

But even though Siegfried and Roy were expected to retire and had discussed it, it was hardly an easy thing to contemplate stepping out of the limelight once and for all. Siegfried told *People*: "Everything was the show. My life was the show and the show was my life."

After so many years of being inextricably entwined as a famous brand, would Siegfried and Roy have given up their show if events hadn't forced them to? Even today, years after Roy's mauling, the duo are still seeking new life in the spotlight as they tout the incessant, but hard to believe, claim that they will return to the stage.

The abrupt end of the German duo's career deeply affected Siegfried. Suddenly, their fate had been snatched out of his hands; his inability to control the situation was a severe frustration. He didn't know if his lifetime partner would survive, never mind fully recover, and all his money and power couldn't change that. But strangely enough, the unforeseen tragedy had an upside; after incredible turmoil and a terrible clash of wills, it eventually would have the effect of bringing the two performers even closer together than they had been for years.

For a while....

After the tiger attack in November 2003, Roy had been rushed to the Las Vegas University Medical Center (UMC). Siegfried visited him there every day. Roy had suffered paralysis on his left side, but fortunately his right side, which controls speech, thought and memory, wasn't affected. He could comprehend what was going on around him, although even a month after the accident, he could barely speak and had to rely on a respirator to breathe. As far as friends and family could tell at that moment, Roy Horn was not expected to live.

Incredibly, he hung in there. And the great animal communicator found ways to communicate with human beings, via such techniques as hand signals and blinking.

Siegfried would tell Larry King on TV that his interaction with Roy after the incident was comparable to "how we communicate on stage. Just by a touch of his hand.... Sometimes we just have to look at each other, and I know exactly what he means." He said Roy had wordlessly signaled in this manner for his "special pet dog" as soon as hospital staff had removed a breathing tube just three days after the accident. The staff brought Roy the dog, Piaf—which had belonged to his mother, the late Miss Horn—into the ICU, hoping it might boost his morale.

Sadly, seven months later, when Roy was still in rehabilitation, Piaf grew ill and Lynette had to have him put to sleep. Nervous about breaking the bad news to Roy in his sickened state, Lynette waited and asked Louis Mydlach—Roy's bodyguard, and the son of the duo's longtime head of security, Jim Mydlach—how she should tell him. It was decided she'd speak to Roy by phone while Louis Mydlach was with him. Later, after Roy had taken Lynette's call and heard the bad news about his beloved Piaf's death, he grew quiet. He then told his bodyguard that he'd sensed one of his animals had passed away that morning, he just hadn't been sure which one.

While Roy remained at UMC, vigils continued outside the hospital and the Jungle Palace for days on end. Hoards of fans gathered, waiting and praying for good news. The hundreds of candles used in a ceremony organized by magicians Penn and Teller lit up the night sky, a spectacular, unforgettable sight.

Roy's fans erected shrines outside the hospital, covering them with hundreds of poster boards, cards and flowers, and lighting dozens and dozens of candles to illuminate their signs. One police officer was approached by a fan who said his grandfather insisted he personally deliver a package to Mr. Horn. Inside the package were White Castle hamburgers. The officer shook his head, told the man he'd make sure Roy knew about the gift, and then escorted him to the bus stop, giving him a dollar to get home. This was just one of many ways fans displayed their support and warm wishes for Roy's recovery.

As news of the tiger mauling spread, Siegfried and Roy's personal refuge, the Jungle Palace, teemed with uninvited guests: bus lines, limos, taxis, and even helicopters were swarming around and above their home. Camera crews and journalists bombarded Roy's bodyguards with endless questions, hoping for news or a glimpse of him, even though he was still at UMC. Roy's die-hard fans were very upset when no updates were offered in the wake of the accident. Nearly 1,500 people an hour drove by the Jungle Palace to drop off cards and eyeball the ailing performer's abode. Employee Louis Mydlach would patiently shake fans' hands, letting them know Roy wasn't on the grounds, a ploy to keep the German's actual whereabouts under wraps so UMC wouldn't be inundated.

By the night of October 6th, the Jungle Palace's white walls and gates were completely papered over with fans' offerings. The security detail that constantly patroled the crowd was made up of former federal agents, bodyguards, and retired police officers, but even these highly trained professionals couldn't control the mob scene. Finally, the Metropolitan Police Department had to step in to assist Roy's staff in shooing away the hordes of fans and locking the place down. From that point on, while Roy was at UMC, no one was allowed in or out unless on a pre-approved list authorized by Jim Mydlach.

The security staff soon got organized, and all activity at the Jungle Palace was logged carefully, twenty-four hours a day, in a book the security team referred to as The Bible, maintained by Jim Mydlach. There were perimeter checks performed on the grounds every fifteen minutes to ensure no overzealous fans got past the gates. The rooftops to the lion and tiger cages were checked for intruders. Nothing got past Mydlach's security team.

On October 7th, Siegfried was interviewed by CNN's Larry King. According to the *Las Vegas Review-Journal*, he'd already sat for separate interviews at the duo's Jungle Palace with CBS, NBC and ABC, plus a pool of three print reporters. The interviews were more personal and probing than ever before; in light of the tragedy that might take Roy's life at any moment, the questions about their personal, intimate relationship seemed especially valid and natural. Still, Siegfried refused to admit he and Roy had anything more than a platonic, although very close, relationship.

Roy's condition remained critical. He was placed in Intensive Care at UMC. Bernie Yuman arranged for a nun to visit and pray for his recovery, but Roy Horn's future was looking grim.

Weeks went by. Finally, it was announced that Roy was able to breathe on his own, and his condition would soon be stable enough to transport him to UCLA Medical Center for further treatment, evaluation, and brain surgery. There, doctors would re-attach the piece of skull that had been sewn into his stomach lining at UMC.

On October 28, 2003, Roy was taken to the North Las Vegas Airport, where a private G5 jet was waiting to transport him to UCLA. A Flight for Life helicopter nurse joined the entourage to attend to Roy on his first plane ride since the attack. The press was unable to sneak a glimpse of fragile Roy as he was hustled aboard because his security team used a favorite ploy—opened umbrellas—to shield him from cameras and prying eyes.

At UCLA Medical Center, Roy drifted in and out of consciousness. He suffered blood clots and brain swelling. Unable to speak, he struggled to express himself in writing. Yet, he improved. Released from UCLA, he arrived back at the Jungle Palace on December 22, 2003, nearly four months after he'd left it, just in time for Christmas.

Roy's security team had been tipped that the paparazzi were flat-out determined to get a snapshot of him as he was being taken out of the ambulance at home. Since the mauling, only one image of Roy had been released. The night the accident happened, someone had managed to capture a shot of the star through a window. The photo, which showed him lying on a stretcher with an IV bag, had made the cover of the *National Enquirer*. Months later, despite strict measures by his security staff, the paparazzi snapped another shot of Roy as Louis Mydlach wheeled him out the back entrance of HealthSouth, the clinic he'd attend for many weeks after his return to Vegas. Again, that picture hit the front page of the *National Enquirer*.

Would the paparazzi make good their boast and snap Roy yet again? Just a few minutes before 2 p.m., on Monday, December 22, an ambulance flanked by four motorcycle police officers escorted Roy to the Jungle Palace for the holidays. This time, the paparazzi, despite their kamikaze threats, were foiled. Not one of them got within clicking distance.

Roy was much better, but obviously far from out of the woods. His high blood pressure had skyrocketed after the tiger's bite, because the massive wound had impeded blood flow to the brain, resulting in a stroke that had paralyzed his entire left side. And due to atrophy of his muscles, Roy had developed what's called "claw hand," or "wrist drop." His hand had to be placed in a splint to keep his fingers, hand and arm stretched out. Although he'd never be able to flex his fingers completely, Roy eventually was able to open his hand—just marginally—years later.

He was unable to climb the stairs to his second-floor bedroom in the main house, so once back at the Jungle Palace, he moved into his mother's single-floor home next door. Miss Horn's front windows were frosted, so no one could see inside, even with a telephoto camera lens. A huge white tent was built to cover the entrance to the house as an extra precaution, even though the paparazzi had been led to believe Roy was in the main house.

Although Roy looked nervous and frail, he was surprisingly coherent and alert. He waved to greet his bodyguards on his first day back and shook Jim and Louis Mydlach's hands. He said it was good to be home.

Roy hardly slept when he first returned from the hospital, lying awake most of the time, mindlessly watching TV, staring blankly at the screen. His neck was causing him a lot of pain, and he needed someone to constantly adjust his pillow. A nurse's station was set up next door to his room so he could call out to them 'round the clock if he needed anything, and they regularly checked his blood pressure, oxygen stats and temperature. Most of these "nurses," however, weren't nurses at all. They were actually aides provided by a commercial healthcare company, and many were completing their nurse internships, getting hands-on training working for Roy!

Louis Mydlach was in charge of keeping a sharp eye on the aides and caring for Roy. During much of Roy's rehabilitation, he and Louis were inseparable. Louis' father, Jim, had worked for Siegfried and Roy for twenty-five years, so the younger Mydlach had been raised around the duo and had looked up to them since boyhood. Before the accident, Louis had been working security for Michael Jackson. When his father contacted him after Roy's attack, he immediately made himself available and worked as Roy's bodyguard on-and-off for fifteen months.

During the early days of Roy's long and complicated recovery, he complained that his healthcare aides were ignoring him, so a TV camera was installed next to his bed. Still Roy grumbled, complaining to Louis that at one point he'd motioned at the camera for about an hour, yet none of the staff had appeared. Once, he had wet the bed by the time an aide materialized. Other times, only one aide would show up, and—being too heavy for one woman to carry to the bathroom—he was actually dropped several times, ending up riddled with bruises. Louis Mydlach recalls that when he started to check in on Roy more frequently to see if the aides were doing their jobs, he discovered caretakers sleeping during shifts, knocking back glasses of wine, or sneaking a smoke outside, all of which they had been forbidden to do.

But however disappointed Roy was with his caretakers, the constant staff turnover and recurring negligent behavior, he'd bribe them with presents to motivate kinder treatment. He gave one woman a large, valuable jade stone, but Lynette had demanded its return, arguing that Roy had been heavily medicated at the time.

Concerned about the quality of care his boss was getting, Jim Mydlach told Lynette he wanted to use other security measures in addition to the video recorder in Roy's room, which would allow him to keep track of what transpired behind closed doors. Without the aide staff's knowledge, the equipment was hooked up to a secret monitor in another room of the house.

As for the aides, they often claimed they couldn't hear Roy calling them, so Jim's security team also installed a baby monitor next to his bed, directly wired to the aides' station. Despite all these measures, Roy still complained that they were ignoring his calls. In desperation, he ordered a large, old-fashioned bell with a wooden handle that he'd clang vigorously to get attention.

Other complications arose due to the absence of registered nurses at the house. While Roy's caretakers were charged with checking his blood pressure and oxygen levels every hour, they could not legally administer Roy's medication; only Lynette and Siegfried were authorized. The caretakers did, however, notate each pill and the dosage administered to Roy in a special journal. One of them complained to Louis that Siegfried was treating her badly ever since he'd ordered her to give Roy a scheduled pill. Even after explaining she couldn't administer medication because she was not a registered nurse—she'd been told that only Lynette and Siegfried could give Roy his meds (which Siegfried had to know)—the assistant claimed that the blond Tiger King continued to be unpleasant.

Tensions were rising. Lynette and Siegfried, who'd hired the healthcare staff Roy constantly complained about, were actually considering cutting back on his twenty-four-hour care, according to Louis Mydlach. But Bernie Yuman vehemently fought them on that idea, so the 'round-the-clock system stayed in place. But no matter how much Bernie argued, according to Louis, he couldn't persuade the two to hire qualified nurses. Siegfried remained adamant that the current employees would be just fine, however much Roy complained. Lynette, wanting the best for Roy (and not willing to give up her position as his sole caretaker), stayed neutral in the fight against Roy's subpar aide staff.

In order to supervise the caretakers more closely, and to make sure there'd be no news or photo leaks, Bernie ordered Louis and his team to set up tighter security: cell phones of all aides would be confiscated at the beginning of their shifts; purses would be searched for weapons or cameras; IDs and badges had to be displayed to gain admission. In addition, the name of each person reporting for a shift had to be on a pre-determined list, and no swapping shifts or last-minute changes would be allowed. And to really tighten the ring of security, *all* caretakers had to be escorted in and out of the area, even after they'd cleared the checkpoint. Bernie's main concern was Roy's safety, but he also wanted to avoid any media exposure. The "Siegfried & Roy" publicity machine had been cranking out cheery press releases hinting that Roy's recovery was imminent, and the last thing Bernie needed was a photo or story that might expose the real truth.

As the days and weeks went by, arguments and bickering arose among the inherently temperamental personalities of the team that had spent so many years together. The dynamic among them all—Siegfried, Lynette, Bernie, Roy and their regular staff—fluctuated constantly. At first, Lynette took charge of the household, and Siegfried seemed happy enough to step back and take a breath after the trauma and upheaval brought on by the tiger attack.

But after a while, as was his nature, the control freak gradually seized control. In-house staff members were appalled when he began to undermine Lynette, making her the scapegoat for almost everything that went wrong. When Roy complained the nurses couldn't hear him, Siegfried reprimanded Lynette for not checking up on them enough. When Roy wanted to sleep in because he wasn't feeling well and missed his therapy, Siegfried would go ballistic, blaming Lynette. Louis Mydlach remembers how Siegfried would rant and belittle her in vicious confrontations as tears rolled down her cheeks. Never once did she raise her voice in response to the controlling German, until he wasn't around to hear her shriek in frustrated anger.

Of them all—Bernie, Siegfried, and Lynette—Louis Mydlach states unequivocally that it was Lynette who stayed by Roy's side the most, always making sure that he got whatever he needed. According to Louis, Lynette wanted Roy to get better and recover but would often confide in him, secretly, about Siegfried's arrogant interference, telling Roy angrily that "goddamn Siegfried was at it again." The friction kept intensifying, and Louis, along with his dad, security chief Jim Mydlach, was right in the center of it all. Worried about Roy's welfare, Louis even began pulling longer shifts.

Louis had been given keys to all of the locks on Siegfried and Roy's property. As Roy's shadow, he was on call 24/7 and was also given the responsibility of ordering whatever was necessary for Roy's comfort. But first, Louis had to give Roy's wish list to Lynette; she, in turn, had to get it authorized by Siegfried. And more often than not, says Louis, Siegfried would capriciously deny one thing or another. At Christmastime, Roy, who loved watching cartoons, got agitated when his DVD player gave up the ghost. Roy asked Louis to get him another one. Louis went through the chain of command, but after more than two weeks, the request had not been approved by Herr Siegfried. In the end, Louis bought the DVD player out of his own pocket, and Siegfried was furious. Why? Who could say what went through the mind of that constantly self-involved personality. Who could explain, for instance, why Siegfried invited Lynette to Thanksgiving dinner in 2004, leaving Roy by himself with a meal the staff brought to him.

While Roy went through his agonies, Siegfried continued to make personal appearances and give interviews, wanting to convey the appearance that, despite everything, Siegfried and Roy were simply taking an intermission and had everything under control. On December 1, 2003, for example, before Roy was even moved home from the hospital, Siegfried made an appearance on the *Today Show* to talk about Roy and his health. But after Roy was moved back into the Jungle Palace, Siegfried and Bernie Yuman clamped the publicity lid down tight, so Roy would have space to recover away from the public eye.

In January 2004, Roy began getting treatment at the HealthSouth clinic, not far from the Jungle Palace, where Louis says Roy received the best therapy he's ever had. Before his transfer to the clinic, Louis and dad Jim Mydlach took a tour of the facilities and inspected the accommodations. Roy would stay in the brain unit at HealthSouth where there were only ten rooms, and it was completely "locked down" so that no unauthorized persons could enter. Even the center's front windows were frosted. The elder Mydlach posted agents at both entrances to the ward, and he made sure all members of the HealthSouth staff signed confidentiality agreements.

While Roy was in care at HealthSouth, his routine rarely altered. At around 9:00 a.m., Louis would arrive at the Jungle Palace to greet Roy, who was typically already awake and being dressed by his morning caretakers. Louis made it a habit to always shake Roy's hand in the morning, to test his strength at the start of the day; if it was a strong handshake, he knew it would go well. Then, at the start of each day, without fail, Louis would repeat his mantra for Roy's recovery:

"I will keep my promise. I will never give up. The journey begins...."

After those words of encouragement, Louis would load Roy—in his wheelchair—into the van. On Roy's very first trip to HealthSouth, he made one thing clear to his personal aide staff: "Excuse me," he said respectfully to the caretakers, his thick German accent fully intact, "No one but Lou-ee drives my wheelchair."

On his trips to the clinic, Roy typically dressed in a black Armani beanie, a Nike jogging suit, black and white Nike running shoes, and black Armani sunglasses. Even though he was wearing what amounted to a total disguise, Jim, Louis, and Lynette carefully shielded him from the public eye. But that wasn't always easy, thanks to Roy's irrepressible spirit. He'd sit up front next to Louis—in the space where the passenger seat had been removed—and sometimes he'd order him to "Beep the horn! Beep the horn!" at passing drivers, or he'd wave at the cars next to them. Once, when they pulled up next to a car, Roy demanded, "Roll down the window."

Sighed Louis, "I can't roll down the window!"

But Roy kept insisting, so Louis rolled it down...and Roy started waving out the window, saying, "I have to wave to all my fans." The woman driving the car looked over at

Roy, but all she saw was a strange man covered up in sunglasses and a hat—not *the* Roy Horn of "Siegfried & Roy"!

Louis recalls that on his first day of therapy, Roy was "cheerful and tired, but ready to rock 'n roll." However, he appeared to take a turn for the worse after a quick talk with Siegfried, in their native German, just before they drove off in the van. Louis didn't know what Siegfried had said, but Roy's legs suddenly began shaking, and he grew visibly nervous. Louis calmed him down once he'd loaded him into the van by rubbing his legs—a trick he'd learned when he first went to work for Roy. Whether it was the young man's calm and caring personality, his youthful energy, or the fact that he was the trusted Jim Mydlach's son, Roy always sparked whenever Louis was around.

At HealthSouth facility, Roy spent his days submitting to tests and taking rehab courses, including speech- and physical therapy. After lunch, he'd sometimes watch TV, usually in German, and he loved having Louis read to him from the *Robb Report*, a high-end car magazine. Roy was passionate about cars. Then he'd often meditate to a CD called "Buddha Temple."

Siegfried would join Lynette, Roy and Louis for lunch most days—although he never stayed longer than an hour. But if Siegfried walked in on Roy having lunch with Lynette, and he had not been called and invited, he'd get angry. Louis recalls that at these lunches, a new problem reared its very ugly head. Siegfried began bringing over various medications—not prescribed by Roy's personal doctor, Dr. Miller, or any of the doctors at HealthSouth—and he'd insist that Roy take them. This always upset Roy, who'd respond by asking to go to the bathroom. Roy and Louis had a code for the bathroom: "I have to go let the dogs out." For Roy, the bathroom was his safe place. If he felt something was wrong, if Siegfried was going to come by, or if there was an impending medical procedure that worried him, he'd ask to go to the bathroom every two minutes. It was Roy's way of coping with stress.

While Roy's bathroom issues were largely psychological, he also had actual physical problems with his bowels. Louis recalls that Dr. Miller, Roy's doctor for nearly a decade, often grumbled that the medications Siegfried was feeding Roy were possibly causing ongoing problems, including constipation. In order to jump-start Roy's digestive tract, he gave him suppositories. Unfortunately, the side effects of laxatives and colonics affected Roy's intestines and kidneys adversely, causing a general weakening of the body. He ended up contracting pneumonia several times because his immune system was debilitated by growing dependence on the extra medications, apparently painkillers, that he told Louis Siegfried kept giving him.

Finally, Louis says, after months of Dr. Miller's playing middle-man between Siegfried and Roy, the doctor resigned in 2005.

This didn't stop Siegfried. When a therapist mentioned that swimming was often helpful in the rehabilitation process, Siegfried seized on the idea—ignoring the doctor's warnings that Roy's recovery was not far enough advanced for such strenuous exercise. In reality, swimming could actually be detrimental to his health. Nevertheless, Siegfried had Louis bring Roy to his house for his first swimming "therapy," but when Roy realized Siegfried was about to make him go into the pool, he got nervous: "Oh no, no, no—Lou-ee...Lou-ee!"

But Louis Mydlach could not disobey Siegfried's direct orders, so into the pool they all went. Instead of a short introductory session, Siegfried kept Roy struggling in the pool for over an hour. Toward the end of the ordeal, Roy's face was turning red, even though Louis was in the pool with him and supporting his body, using his legs to kick beneath Roy's so that Siegfried would think progress was being made and end the ordeal. Shortly after his "rehabilitating" swim session, Roy developed pneumonia and was rushed to the Valley Hospital emergency room.

Whether justified or not, Roy now feared Siegfried. Lynette and Louis secretly provided him with an emergency cell phone, and only the three of them had the number. Louis also carried an emergency phone—unbeknownst to Bernie or Siegfried—in case Roy should ever need him. But aside from whatever "secrets" Louis and Roy kept from him, Siegfried literally controlled every aspect of Roy's life after the mauling. Eventually, even caretakers at the Jungle Palace, who were unauthorized to dispense medication, were ordered by Siegfried to start giving Roy the drugs he wanted him to take, Louis recalls. And although he was seeing less and less of Siegfried, Roy felt his partner's powerful presence more and more.

Louis did the best he could to help. He'd challenge Roy to play little games that would exercise his brain and his muscles, motivating Roy by joining in himself. As he described it, "If Roy kicked a ball, I kicked a ball."

But it was a constant battle.

Louis says, "I never knew what therapists did, and I didn't know anyone that had any kind of brain trauma...so I had no idea what that was like. Every day was a challenge; every day was different. Roy got tired of everything so fast. As soon as he got bored with it, he'd want to start talking and he'd be through."

Louis kept trying to create fun activities. One day, he invented a game that challenged and delighted Roy. He got a grapefruit and some toy plastic bowling pins and created a makeshift bowling alley. Roy finally was able to roll the grapefruit with his left arm—the paralyzed arm—and send it crashing into the pins. "Those were the good days," Louis sighs. When Roy played "grapefruit bowling" his dormant athletic instincts kicked in and his muscles were able to function properly.

Another good day was when Roy—accompanied by Louis and dad Jim—left the Jungle Palace and went to a movie theater near Little Bavaria, where they saw a newly released animated film. Louis and Jim had Roy surrounded by so much security that no fans could get close to him, but the people waved and smiled. Louis always carried postcards and pens for Roy to sign and give out, so Roy was able to scrawl a few autographs. The fans were happy; Roy was even happier.

One of Louis Mydlach's favorite memories of Roy after the mauling came when the two of them were alone in the gardens of the Jungle Palace. Louis, pushing Roy in his wheelchair, mentioned that he was a bit upset because his young son, Gianni, had back-talked him for the first time ever. Roy smiled and pointed to a huge palm tree with a rose bush next to it.

"I planted that tree," he told Louis, "and it grew fast and tall with hardly any watering. But that rose bush took me a little more time. I had to mix the soil gently, water it every day, prune it once every two weeks, and then mist the leaves once a day so it would bloom beautifully in the spring.

"But there was a secret ingredient to caring for the roses. I also talked, watched and listened until they were not infants anymore, but beautiful, adult plants, smiling at you in the morning sun as they waited for you and relied on you for care and nurturing...as children do...and as your son does with you."

"Thank you Mr. Roy," Louis said with understanding.

"Thank you, Louis," Roy replied "for trusting me enough to share your thoughts about your son with me. The pleasure is mine."

It was just one of many memorable, quiet walks that the two were able to enjoy when they were alone.

Another good day was when a litter of leopards was born at Little Bavaria. Holding the tiny cubs had an enormously positive impact on Roy's mental state. He loved his animals more than anything, but rarely got to see them now—much less touch them.

Still, the bad days were very bad. One of the worst came when Roy needed an MRI. Almost immediately upon arriving at the hospital, the famously claustrophobic trainer began throwing a fit, refusing to go into the narrow tunnel of the MRI machine. Finally, Louis had to squeeze into the tunnel with Roy, an impossibly tight fit, but somehow they did it.

The strain of caring for his gravely wounded boss was beginning to wear Louis down, despite his youth, energy and affection for Roy. Things came to a head when Roy finally made a rare public appearance as a presenter at a 2004 K-9 awards show. Nervous about being out in public after his attack, Roy wanted to go to the restroom: his safety zone. But he had a hard time with the nurses, who were impatient with him, saying he needed to stay near the stage. They didn't want to let him move, so Louis finally intervened and started to push the wheelchair to take Roy to the men's room. A caretaker slapped Louis' hand and said, "You get out of the way!" before seizing the wheelchair.

Roy went nuts. He told her, "No, no, no. I don't want you, I don't trust you." The caretaker snapped that she didn't care and continued to push him to the restrooms. Louis followed and watched in disgust as the nasty nurse refused to let Roy wash his hands afterward. Until they left the awards show, the nurses wouldn't let Louis near Roy. Later, as Louis put him into the car, Roy said, "I'll see you at home."

But Louis didn't go "home." Frustrated and angry, he quit.

No one dared tell Roy what had happened. When Louis didn't return to the Jungle Palace that day, he grew increasingly nervous. As one day turned into the next, and still no Louis, Roy refused to do his therapy or even leave the house without his friend and protector. After much cajoling from the staff, including dad Jim Mydlach, Louis finally agreed to come back to work for Roy again. In his absence, everyone had lied to Roy, telling him Louis had taken his little son, Gianni, to Disneyland. When Louis got back, Roy asked, "How was Disneyland?" But later, he told Louis, "I know you didn't go to Disneyland. But it's okay because now you're back."

Roy's recovery progress was maddeningly slow. Even though publicists kept making optimistic claims to the press, the truth was that even after one year had passed, there was not much advancement to report. Still, in March 2004, Roy told the German magazine, *Bunte:* "You know I nearly had both feet in the ground. But I am doing fine again." Later that year, he told *People* magazine, "I'm going to show everybody that I will come back. That I *am* back."

But in March 2004, the *Las Vegas Review-Journal* got closer to the truth when it reported: "Signs of strain surfaced last week when Siegfried & Roy's publicist in

Germany, Claudia Dressler, told news outlets Roy walked 500 steps with the aid of a wheeled walker. TV stations reported that Siegfried & Roy's local management was 'distancing' itself from the report.

"Dressler, sources say, would not have given such details without the approval of Siegfried & Roy. That signals a serious shift in protocol at a time when insiders say Yuman now must schedule appointments to see Horn.

"'Something's definitely brewing,' said a source close to the situation."

Bernie Yuman would not comment, and it was obvious that mixed messages were being released from the Siegfried and Roy camp.

One month after the publication of the *Las Vegas Review-Journal* report, columnist Norm Clarke wrote: "Siegfried & Roy's longtime manager, Bernie Yuman... brushed off rumblings that his role has been diminished."

In a subsequent column, Clarke wrote: "During lunch at the Palm restaurant...I asked Bernie Yuman, Siegfried & Roy's manager, to address the report that Horn was walking on his own, even conquering stairs, no less.

"Yuman raised his hand and made a circle with his thumb and forefinger.

"'Zero steps on his own,' Yuman said.

"And the e-mailed photographs of a hale and hearty Horn?"

"Yuman shook his head. 'Not true.'"

In August 2004, the *National Enquirer* reported that Roy was suicidal, stating, "his mental condition has grown worse in recent weeks as his physical condition shows no signs of improving."

Despite a grueling rehab regimen of up to six hours a day, Roy had not regained any feeling in his left arm; he still struggled to focus his right eye; and he needed to wear the splint that allowed his arm to stretch out. He was also extremely sensitive to cold and always wore a blanket over his $10,000-plus Invacare electric wheelchair.

On August 10, 2004, Roy was admitted to Craig Hospital in Denver, Colorado, for intensive therapy, and to learn to walk again. The Colorado hospital catered to patients in much worse shape than Roy, and he didn't like the place to start with. When Siegfried ordered Louis back to Vegas after he had moved Roy to Denver, it was the final straw. Days later, feeling little encouragement and missing his friend Louis, Roy insisted on returning home to the Jungle Palace.

According to the *National Enquirer*, "He arrived August 10, but didn't have his formal evaluation until August 12. On August 14, Roy decided he had had enough and left."

Back in Las Vegas, Roy transferred to the Hogan Medical Center to continue his rehabilitation. After three months there, Roy finally began to walk again. A rare moment showed that the spark of the old Siegfried and Roy relationship was still alive. A group class was passing a big ball back and forth and Louis took Roy over to play. Then he told Siegfried, who'd stopped by that day, "Join in!" Siegfried refused at first, but after Louis playfully pushed him into the scrum, he laughed and started having a good time. Finally, the two close friends and former lovers were smiling and laughing together again.

Roy was now able to make limited public appearances. One of his first was at a performance of the new show "Havana Night Club" at the Stardust hotel in August 2004. Incredibly, Roy had found the energy to help co-produce the extravaganza with Siegfried and Nicole Durr, a German-Danish blonde who'd created the show. Nicole, who'd come to be known as "Siegfried's girlfriend," was always at the Jungle Palace and apparently had a very rich father who'd helped subsidize the Cuban-themed production. For the first time since his accident, Roy felt like he was back in the showbiz he loved, creating designs for the show and managing the lighting and stage set-up. What's more, Roy had spent his own money on the show, which gave him back the feeling of responsibility he'd lost along with the physical feeling on his left side.

At the show, wrote gossip columnist Norm Clarke, "A stunned crowd broke into applause as the wheelchair-bound Horn was escorted to his table."

Roy's appearance at the show was a landmark—the first time he'd been seen standing on his own in public. And it was one of the most brilliant illusions he'd ever sold to an audience: in actuality, Louis Mydlach was standing close behind Roy, surreptitiously holding him up by his pants!

After the show that night, Louis, Siegfried, and Jim Mydlach were standing in the back of the theater when Louis told Siegfried, "You guys had a great show tonight. I mean, it's your show too, you know...."

Siegfried looked at him strangely and said, "Yes, but I'm not the center of attention anymore." Then, incredibly, the aging performer burst into tears in front of his bodyguards.

Louis told him, "It's alright—you guys are legends. Don't worry about it. You'll always be here, Las Vegas is your town." However saccharine it may sound, it was the truth.

After "Havana Night Club," as a thank-you for all of his hard work, Roy gifted Louis with a watch, and a card that read: "Thank you very much for all of your help. If it weren't for you, we wouldn't be here. People like you make a big difference. —Mr. Roy Horn" Then he gave Louis the oversized watch, saying, "You're a big person, you need to have a big watch." When Louis thanked him, Roy replied, "You don't have to thank me. Everyday you're here, but you thank *me*? No, I thank you."

Right after Roy's first public appearance at "Havana Night Club," the duo's much-hyped autobiographical animation TV series, *Father of the Pride*, was set to premiere on August 31, 2004. As this was the only project in the works that didn't require the athletic Roy of old, the team focused on hyping *Pride* hard, beginning with a television special hosted by Maria Shriver. Roy had always idolized fellow-immigrants Maria and her husband, Arnold Schwarzenegger, but he tried to beg off because he didn't think he was up to doing a major interview for national TV. After pressure from Bernie and Siegfried, Roy finally agreed.

Maria had arranged to meet the duo at the Jungle Palace to film a segment with the white tigers. It seemed simple enough but turned into an occasion fraught with potential high drama: it was the first time Roy would come face-to-face with Montecore, the tiger that had taken him down. As soon as he arrived at the Jungle Palace, Roy told Louis, he suddenly felt sick. "I don't know if I can do this today," he said.

Louis made a call. Five minutes later, Siegfried and Maria Shriver entered Roy's room. Siegfried screamed, "I don't know what the hell your problem is, but we're doing this shoot. You need to get out of that bed right now." Maria Shriver lost her trademark patience, pressuring Roy to get up, insisting she hadn't come out in vain. As Siegfried screamed and cursed, Roy, ghost-white on his bed, exploded and yelled at Louis: "Get them out. Out, out, out, out!"

Louis immediately walked Siegfried and Maria out of the room and locked the door, then calmed Roy down. After meditating with him for about an hour, Louis made another call. "Roy's good to go." And he was! The interview went off without a hitch. Even Siegfried was happy. But it was back to the hospital for Roy; the trauma had brought on a new bout of pneumonia.

Father of the Pride, pushed back several times after Roy's horrific mauling, finally aired. The production was a first-class effort. Each episode reportedly cost $2 million. Such major talent as John Goodman, Cheryl Hines, Orlando Jones and the legendary Carl Reiner, then 82, voiced the leading roles. But despite it all, *Pride* took a fall, shot down by a barrage of scathing reviews.

New York Times reviewer Virginia Heffernan commented on the ethics of airing a "lively and fanciful" cartoon version of a real-life man who was partially paralyzed and wheelchair bound, perhaps forever. Siegfried and Roy are out of commission in real life, carped Heffernan, yet on TV "the Siegfried and Roy show is still up and selling out, as in days of old."

For a man so ambitious and determined, Roy's painfully slow physical progress and the failure of his animation series was too much for him to bear. A smoldering depression captured his soul....

On November 15, 2004, the *National Enquirer* claimed that Roy Horn had repeatedly attempted suicide after Montecore's attack. According to one of the magazine's insiders:

> When Roy tried to kill himself he "was at the lowest point of his life. He couldn't walk and could barely talk, and no one could seem to reach him." ...Twice nurses found that he somehow managed to pull out his breathing tube in attempts to end it all.
>
> Another time he pulled out his IV.
>
> He was doing anything he could to stop living, and he was placed on a suicide watch by his caretakers. Finally his wrists had to be restrained with straps so he couldn't injure himself.
>
> Then for a while he stopped eating. The staff tried to force-feed him, but he wouldn't take nourishment. A feeding tube had to be reinserted.

Perhaps the most shocking revelation, according to the *Enquirer* source is that:

> One time [when] Siegfried was reading a letter to him from a fan telling Roy to hang in there. Roy croaked, "Tell the truth. I'm dying. Why won't you let me kill myself?"
>
> When he was finally able to hold a pencil, he would scrawl the words "help me die" and "stop the pain."
>
> ...Later when his depression had lifted somewhat and he could talk, Roy admitted he was trying to do himself in. He told Siegfried, "You have no idea what I've been through. I tried to pull the plug on myself, but it just didn't work. I guess God still has plans for me."

Louis Mydlach claims that the so-called "suicide attempt" was completely overblown by the magazine. Roy pulled out his IV tubes, says Mydlach, because he was highly medicated and had no idea what he was doing. Moaning "I want to die!" occurred during an emotional outburst, the way anyone might cry out in pain.

Just a month after the report of Roy's alleged suicide attempt, on September 21, 2004, a bizarre and potentially deadly incident occurred: a drive-by shooting at the Jungle Palace.

Louis Mydlach clearly remembers the call he and his father got from Bernie Yuman at 1:30 in the morning. "The Jungle Palace has just been shot at," Yuman told the Mydlachs. Staffer Joe Clark had been outside working late when gunfire erupted from a passing vehicle—and what sounded like bullets whizzed by him. Unharmed, Clark took cover. The shots fired were from a shotgun, it was later learned—and the buckshot pellets smashed through two windows and bored a big hole in the house itself.

Driving at break-neck speed, Jim and Louis Mydlach arrived at the Palace just as a phalanx of police cruisers surrounded the property, sirens screaming. Moments later, a Metro helicopter was search-lighting the grounds from overhead. Police officers swarmed the Jungle Palace, and Las Vegas Sheriff Bill Young himself appeared on the scene.

Meanwhile, Louis checked tapes from the estate's ubiquitous security cameras and found exactly what the cops needed: footage of the vehicle that showed such crucial details as the license plate number. Sheriff Young shook the hands of Louis and Jim Mydlach, congratulating them for running a tight ship and making law enforcement's job easier. It was a prophetic statement; just days later, an officer from the Las Vegas Police Department dropped off a photo of the shooter, informing Siegfried and Roy's security team that the culprit was one Cole Ford, a former NFL football player for the Oakland Raiders. Louis and Jim's security measures had paid off.

Cole Ford was a weird character. He'd played for the Raiders as a kicker and had a couple of good seasons before his skills deteriorated, and he was eventually fired in 1997. He'd been working in Las Vegas as a day laborer and appeared to have become obsessed with Siegfried and Roy.

First reports from police after the drive-by shooting stated that Ford was yelling out his window, "Go back to your country!" That sounded like a hate crime, but it turned out to be far more bizarre than that. When Cole Ford was arrested six weeks after the drive-by shooting, the *Associated Press* reported that a psychiatrist's evaluation found he'd fired at the Jungle Palace because he wanted to "warn the world of the illusionists' unhealthy danger to them and to animals."

Incredibly, Ford was convinced that Siegfried and Roy were responsible for the AIDS plague. As stated in the report: "Mr. Ford was completely unguarded in his report of his beliefs of unhealthy sexual contact being committed by the illusionists against their animals."

A judge ruled Ford incompetent to stand trial, and remanded him to a mental health facility.

But in the six weeks before Ford was finally apprehended, Siegfried and Roy's security team went on high alert. An armed and dangerous criminal had targeted them; who knew if he'd strike again? Cole Ford's photo was given to all personnel, and a copy was posted in the front office. A bodyguard would examine every package for bombs or contaminants. These safety precautions stayed in place until Cole Ford was finally arrested.

Insiders say that during this period, Roy was so out of it that it's doubtful he'd even been aware of the drive-by shooting. Louis Mydlach, a daily eyewitness to his boss' struggle, became disheartened as Siegfried intensified his efforts to control every detail of Roy's rehabilitation. During 2004, Siegfried—who hadn't allowed Louis to stay with Roy at the Denver hospital—issued a new edict decreeing that Louis, who'd been at Roy's side through his darkest hours, was no longer allowed to stay with him during therapy sessions. He had to wait outside in the car. At this point, he had little to no contact with Roy during the day and had been all but pushed out of the picture.

It was the final straw for Louis, who informed Siegfried, "I'm not going to be here anymore, I'm done."

Still not wanting to upset Roy, Louis invented another fairytale and told his boss: "Okay, I'm going on vacation for a while. I'm going to go check out the resort at Cabo for you."

Roy, immediately concerned, said: "Okay, so you're going on vacation for a week—and then you're coming back with us, right?" Not knowing what to answer, and caught between two masters, Louis promised he'd return. But when Siegfried heard about this, he phoned Louis and told him bluntly: "We don't need you anymore." Louis hasn't seen Roy since then—and he thinks Roy believes to this day that "Lou-ee" let him down.

In the summer of 2005, Siegfried flew Roy to München, Germany, for three weeks of treatment and a special operation at the Leonardis Klinic. As part of the treatment, Roy would be injected with stem cells from pig embryos, intended to restore damaged nerves and allow him to walk again. The head of the clinic, Dr. Scheller, firmly believed stem-cell therapy offered a glimmer of hope. But as "hopeful" as the surgery was intended to be, the *National Enquirer* quoted an informed source who revealed that Roy "complained after the first round [of treatment] that he was in pain and had trouble sleeping. He was airlifted by helicopter to another facility for a CAT scan and I'm told the results showed neurological deterioration."

Just ten days after arriving at the Klinic, Roy returned to Vegas, before undergoing further tests or surgery. The Klinic said Roy had departed because he was homesick for his animals. It was also later reported that he had backed out of a scheduled operation at a hospital in Graz, Austria. Dr. Peter Panzenböck, an orthopedic surgeon at the Graz hospital, told *Bild* magazine, "We had reserved the entire floor for Roy and his entourage."

When Roy returned home, he told the *Las Vegas Sun* that he'd checked into the German clinic because he was "getting too much pain medication here and I needed to cleanse my body." While it would make sense that Roy had been taking more than his prescribed medication, especially after the reports of his suicide attempts, Louis Mydlach read this report and his first thought was that it had to have been Siegfried feeding his partner extra pills to ease his pain.

In October 2005, firmly believing Roy needed protection from Siegfried's high-handed control, Louis Mydlach filed a lawsuit claiming that the blond Aryan's behavior was "so extreme and outrageous as to be regarded as atrocious and outside human decency." The court papers gave a very detailed account of Siegfried's alleged "outrageous" behavior in the aftermath of Roy's attack. In his lawsuit, Louis charged that Siegfried was reveling in newfound power after decades of playing second fiddle to Roy.

Louis maintains that he filed the suit, which asked for a mere $10,000 in damages, "to save Roy's life." Based on knowing the duo since he was a boy of eleven, Louis called his relationship with Roy Horn "close and almost familial"—and said that their relationship had clearly ignited the jealousy of Siegfried Fischbacher. Although insiders insist that the lawsuit described the situation accurately, it went nowhere and was dismissed without prejudice.

Despite power plays behind-the-scenes, Siegfried and Roy apparently reached a new accommodation and went back to being intimate—if occasionally contentious—friends. By 2005, Roy was spending less time at the Jungle Palace, and more at Siegfried's Spanish Trail abode. In a 2005 *Globe* article marking the two-year anniversary of Roy's mauling, he was reported to be upbeat and positive that he'd walk normally again. Speaking of his near-death experience, he said: "They were not ready for me to do the show upstairs. Not yet."

Three years to the date after that fateful October 3rd tragedy, Siegfried and Roy got their star on the Las Vegas Walk of Fame. It's not far from their statue outside The Mirage, where they'd reigned for more than a decade. Roy told fans at the ceremony that Las Vegas was "a spiritual home.... I'm feeling great and I'm feeling strong, and we will perform again at some point in the future. Maybe only once, but there will be another show. It is our life."

His obviously sincere optimism was in amazing contrast to those disturbing reports of depression and suicide attempts just two years earlier.

The scars of tragedy, including a scary white slash on his neck, remain. But despite all the physical pain and mental torture he's endured, Roy—and Siegfried, as well—will never stop defending their beloved Montecore, who snapped one night under the merciless glare of a spotlight and the eyes of a curious human audience.

Even Siegfried has found solace in the positive aspects of his involuntary retirement. He revealed to *People*, "In my life, the more successful I became, the more empty I got. Now my heart is filling up again, and it's a wonderful feeling.... I'm doing things that I haven't done before. Even putting gas in my car."

And Louis Mydlach? Looking back on it all, he wants Roy to know just one thing:

"I'll never give up. I'll keep my promise. The journey continues...."

> **"***But we are married. We are married to our profession. We are married to what we believe, and we are married to the whole substance of our beings.***"**
>
> —*Roy Horn*

Similarities between Siegfried and Roy and their closeted Las Vegas predecessor, Liberace, are uncanny. The kitsch Tiger Kings were gay icons internationally, and their preference for men was as glaringly obvious as their German heritage, yet Siegfried and Roy kept their homosexuality locked safely in the closet for decades. As veteran Las Vegas activist and columnist Lee Plotkin put it, they were "passively gay."

So in August 2007, the world was titillated—but hardly shocked—when the flamboyant lads finally confessed "We're Gay!" on the cover of the *National Enquirer*. The tabloid paper, renowned for its sardonic humor as the self-styled "tabloid of record," naturally jumped at the chance to break the "news"—but it fell just short of a ho-hum. The duo's sudden frank revelation was regarded either as a joke or a publicity stunt; but whatever the reason, they'd finally let it all hang out, so to speak, in a bold stroke that prissy Liberace never had the courage to make.

To be fair, it was a different world that Liberace reigned over as a major American star. His amazing forty-year career unquestionably would have been ruined if he'd been exposed as a homosexual. Even though fans guessed at his secret, it was the era of "don't ask, don't tell" for all gay stars.

Even by today's standards, Liberace ranked as a major superstar. His TV show received better ratings than *I Love Lucy*. He sold more than two million albums in 1953 alone. The *Guinness Book of World Records* listed him as one of the world's highest paid musicians and pianists. And he was awarded one more star than Siegfried and Roy on the Hollywood Walk of Fame.

Liberace gloried in publicity but was extremely guarded about his private life. In 1957, *Hollywood Confidential*, the notorious magazine that sparked today's tabloid craze, headlined their July issue with: "Exclusive!" ...Why Liberace's Theme Song Should Be 'Mad About the Boy'!" It detailed the star's sexual escapades with a young male press agent, providing a fact sheet detailing exactly where and when they'd had sexual intercourse. All the information published—except for one encounter—was established as being accurate. But that one discrepancy gave Liberace's high-powered legal team a victory in their libel lawsuit against *Confidential*.

Two years later, the London *Daily Mirror*—ignoring the obvious lesson that Liberace was rich and litigious—got their head handed to them by a British judge who agreed that the paper's snarky, popular columnist "Cassandra," a.k.a. William Conner, had libeled Liberace when he dragged him out of the closet with a vicious piece that read, in part:

"(Liberace) is the summit of sex—Masculine, Feminine and Neuter. Everything that He, She and It can ever want. I have spoken to sad but kindly men on this newspaper who have met every celebrity arriving from the United States for the past thirty years. They all say that this deadly, winking, sniggering, snuggling, chromium-plated, scent-impregnated, luminous, quivering, giggling, fruit-flavored, mincing, ice-covered heap of mother love has had the biggest reception and impact on London since Charlie Chaplin arrived at the same station, Waterloo, on September 12, 1921."

During the court hearing, Liberace testified a total of six hours in two days. On the stand he lied outright. Despite protests from the defense counsel, the star's aggressive attorney,

Gilbert Beyfus, didn't beat around the bush. He asked his client point-blank on the stand, "Are you a homosexual?"

"No, sir," Liberace replied.

"Have you ever indulged in homosexual practices?"

"I am against the practice because it offends convention, and it offends society."

The flamer had shot the *Daily Mirror* down in flames. Had the editors researched their subject, they'd have known he'd fight tooth and well-polished nails against allowing his sexual inclinations to become public. Virtually everyone knew Liberace was homosexual, but for the sake of his career, he had to be in a position to deny it—and with his money and power, he probably could have proved the Pope was not Catholic. Liberace settled for $22,000—a hefty sum back then—plus compensation for his legal fees. It was in celebration of this victory that he coined the witty *bon mot* that's become a cliché: "I cried all the way to the bank!"

Liberace's statement that homosexual practices offend convention and society is not quite as true today as it was back then, but even as we begin the 21st century, gay marriage is outlawed in most American states. In Siegfried and Roy's heyday, homosexuality was still, if not taboo, a touchy subject—so they chose to stay *schtum* (or tight-lipped) over the years.

In the 1950s, of course, sodomy was illegal criminal activity in all of the United States. Liberace was correct in thinking that published allegations left unchallenged would erode his popularity and income—or even land him in jail—so he always took decisive action. The irony of Liberace's "fear" of falling from grace is that his showbiz persona, his shtick, was acting blatantly effeminate, tickling the ivories at a piano adorned with an ornate candelabra; and, oh, how he loved his nicknames, like "The Glitter Man" and "Mr. Showmanship." But never, ever, would he tolerate being labeled "gay."

Liberace prided himself on being a mama's boy, and he sued the *Mirror* on behalf of all those middle-aged housewives and grannies who loved him. He knew where his bread was buttered and didn't want to alienate his audience. And yet, *he* gave the game away single-handedly, so to speak, sporting rows of gold rings on his fingers long before straight men began doing the P. Diddy bling thing; and his blow-dried hair, makeup and glitter projected anything but a masculine image. But it hardly mattered. After his stunning victory in court, Liberace was "officially" heterosexual.

...Heteroxesual until 1982, when Liberace's "chauffeur" Scott Thorson sued him for palimony and published a book about their five-year affair, titled *Behind the Candelabra*. Still, Liberace admitted nothing. And even as he went to his grave, exposed by the *National Enquirer* as a gay man dying of AIDS, the Candelabra Queen kept repeating the pathetic lie that his shocking seventy-five-pound weight loss had been caused by a strict watermelon diet.

Like Liberace, Siegfried and Roy's sexuality was never really in question. They arrived on the showbiz scene as a packaged deal and were always quick to point out—as Roy's tragic accident demonstrated—that the show could never go without them standing together as a team. Their public sensed that this interdependency applied to their personal lives as well and that the relationship was much more than a just a "working friendship."

Like Liberace, their spectacular performances telegraphed clues to their predilection—dramatic gestures, gladiatorial silhouettes, blow-dried mullets, plucked eyebrows. The preening Germans were too flamboyant and over-the-top to be anything but homosexual.

In an article in *The Advocate*, writer Steve Freiss began, "The trick to a good illusion is that it all happens right in front of you, and you know you're being fooled. But you can't figure out how, no matter how carefully you watch.... It's the way that the pair have managed over the years to become the world's most openly closeted celebrities that's truly awe-inspiring."

When people went to see Siegfried and Roy, they embarked on a journey into another realm, where men played with exotic animals and women were sawn in half. The audience knew they were part of a magical show and that disbelief must be suspended. So the public didn't question whether the Evil Queen had actually been cut into two pieces or ask how that huge elephant had disappeared. People just sat back and watched the buffed illusionists prance like peacocks as they conjured up an unparalleled extravaganza, combining animal interaction with cutting-edge technology, theatrical set designs worthy of Broadway, and upwards of six costume changes per performance. Their sexual preference and extra-curricular activities barely concerned the public.

Siegfried and Roy gave the illusion that they loved sharing their *private* world with fans. They commissioned beautifully produced publications showing their harmonious, homey life in a palace surrounded by gardens and teeming with exotic beasts. In these pictures, dark Roy is always smiling, blond Siegfried looks pensive. They say, "Our life is the show.... When the curtain comes down, we are the same onstage as we are at home. Our home is the stage, and the stage is our home." They present their home and their lifestyle as an earthly paradise devoid of sexuality. Because of this ambiguity and tight control, no unsavory scandal has ever been confirmed.

On the rare occasions manager Bernie Yuman allowed Siegfried and Roy to be interviewed, they masterfully beat around the bush and confessed nothing. In August 1999, Matt Tyrnauer addressed their sexuality in his wittily titled *Vanity Fair* article, "Married with Tigers." Roy's response to the obvious question was, "But we are married. We are married to our profession. We are married to what we believe, and we are married to the sole substance of our beings. I mean, I have a family—not only of humans, but of animals. I feel that I am part of a family in many, many ways."

When asked point blank to refute rumors that they were formally married in their days aboard the good ship *Bremen*, the boys bristled. Roy feigned surprise saying, "Oh, my God. That's a new one! So, I guess the public is intrigued, huh?"

Siegfried interjected, "Listen, when we were on the ship, at that time, if you had just mentioned we had got married, they would have thrown us off the ship, you know what I mean? ...What can I tell you? Many people say, 'Oh,

Siegfried and Roy, this is almost like a marriage, and the animals are the kids.' ...Well, what Roy's private life was is not my business; what my private life was is my business. You understand? Roy is his own man, and I am my own man. And Siegfried and Roy, who are friends, respect each other and we are there without being married.

"...So you go deeper and say what is going on in my bedroom and in Roy's bedroom? I don't care. I don't know. I tell you this because this is me, and I wouldn't ask you what you do with *your* dick, either."

Siegfried's snappy retort begged the question. After all, who cared what Matt Trynauer did with *his* dick.

Their interviewer countered, "Do you realize that Siegfried and Roy are perceived, if not as lovers, as homosexual icons?"

Siegfried responded in puzzlement. "A cult figure? A cult?"

"Icons," Tyrnauer repeated.

"Gay icons? For these people? Well, I am very honored," said Siegfried. "In my life I have a lot of friends who are gay, and I made a lot of friends in show business, and I found out that they are always interesting, intelligent, and good people, and fun to be with. They are very open-minded. They are not narrow-minded. If I am an icon to them, it is wonderful, because gay people are always very vocal.... And, you know, when you go back in history, there are great names in the arts and in every field, so be my guest."

Agreed Roy, "They are very generous! And I think it is a wonderful thing, because I care for everybody in the public. Everybody is an audience to me.... And I am flattered to think that people think that I am versatile. You don't have to define everything, and I don't want to disillusion people. Besides, I'm not a guy who kisses and tells."

In the press release for the *Vanity Fair* article, Bernie Yuman called it "their most candid interview ever." In reality, the question everyone wanted answered was expertly swept under the carpet. Although Siegfried and Roy had long since stopped living together when the interview was conducted, readers were subtly led to believe that they still shared living quarters; and at the end of the twelve-page spread, the true nature of the duo's relationship remained a mystery.

In 2003, after Roy's mauling, Siegfried continued to protect the fortress. In a heartbreaking interview with Barbara Walters, he insisted that their relationship had never been anything more than brotherly. In one of her trademark third-person asides to viewers, Walters looked soulfully at the camera and said, "Their personal life, like their magic, has always been a mystery"...then she hit Siegfried with, "Tell me about your relationship with Roy, because it is a very unusual one."

Agreed Siegfried, "It was very unusual. And it is strong, and it was unbelievable. We are brothers. We are actually more than brothers."

"Are you lovers?"

"Nnn...." Siegfried began, then interrupted himself. "I love Roy like my brother. Even more, because, you know, 44 years...."

Siegfried, overcome, continued with tear-wrenching sincerity and said, "Now I realize how important he was in my life."

The interview was highly emotional. Siegfried discussed Roy's belief in miracles, recalling that when Roy moved for the first time after the mauling, it was he who finally witnessed a miracle.

"You know what that did for me? ...He moved!"

Despite their differences, and drifting apart sexually, Siegfried and Roy, partners for forty-four years, have shared more highs and lows than most married couples. In his first solo interview after the mauling, Siegfried confirmed on *Larry King Live* that his connection to Roy "is a relationship second to none."

And on the night of the attack, MGM Mirage spokesman Alan Feldman shrugged and said frankly to insiders, "It's well-known that they were lovers at one time."

In the 1999 *Vanity Fair* piece, a close friend of the duo, movie star Shirley MacLaine, offered a juicily candid insight when she casually revealed, "I mean, they used to be lovers a long time ago, yeah? In this day and age, who cares?" MacLaine attributed their insular private life to their German naiveté. "It's likely they're living in old Germany, where one would never do such things as ask about one's life! The way they deal with the perception of them as a couple is as much sleight of hand as their act...."

Longtime friend Penn Jillette, of Penn & Teller, explained, "They are as out and as truly themselves as Snoop Dogg.... They're living outside the law in a very real way, because they are who they want to be without compromise. Deciding what you want to be and being that openly doesn't necessarily put you in jeans and a work shirt. It can also put you in a glittery Nehru jacket.... If you say to them, 'You look like crazy fairies onstage in your glitter outfit prancing around,' they don't even know what you're talking about."

So when Siegfried and Roy finally confirmed publicly in the *National Enquirer* what most people had always assumed, the question in everybody's mind was.... Why now?

The most obvious answer: we live in an age when "gay" is no longer synonymous with "taboo." The world's not what it was when Liberace first made his name, or even when Siegfried and Roy debuted four decades ago. Homosexuality in showbiz is now viewed as an acceptable quirk. Today, gay bars have proliferated even in smaller towns; new anti-hate crime laws have been written; and even though same-sex marriage is still outlawed in nearly all U.S. states, many of the archaic anti-homosexual sodomy laws have been overturned. In Nevada, the law was repealed through legislative action in 1993. A decade later, it was invalidated in federal law by the U.S. Supreme Court decision *Lawrence v. Texas*. Until as late as 2003, the land of the free permitted gay men the right to conduct sexual relations—but only with a woman.

In recent years, such stars as Elton John and Rupert Everett have survived, and even thrived, without concealing their sexuality—a giant leap from the not-so-distant times when Oscar Wilde and Liberace were forced to lurk in the lavender shadows. Wilde was sentenced to jail and exiled to France. Singer George Michael's career crashed in the U.S.

after he was busted for soliciting sex in the men's room of a Beverly Hills park frequented by children. It's easy to see why George was disgraced, but Elton and Everett are more beloved than ever after strutting out of the closet. Apparently, it's because their sexuality is non-aggressive and non-offensive. These are family-friendly queens, and they pose no threat to their fans.

Liberace's non-confrontational, mama's-boy persona made him a star long before homosexuality was socially acceptable or legal, even in show business. With his permanent, incandescent, effeminate grin and non-stop interaction with the audience, as his elegant fingers twinkled across the ivories at the speed of light, the brilliant pianist could do no wrong in the eyes of older females. Sniggering and winking shamelessly, Liberace actually exaggerated homosexuality to the point that it could be passed off as a fabricated gimmick intrinsic to his flamboyant act.

Had his audience thought long and hard about it, reality might have smacked them in the face. But who wanted to shatter a beautiful illusion? The fans were there to see a show. Liberace delivered the goods. Everybody left happy.

Siegfried and Roy's audiences react just like Liberace fans. As an eighty-year-old woman told an interviewer for *The Advocate*: "They were the one of the last wholesome things left to see in this town." For devout, church-going old ladies, it was a matter of being in blissful denial as to Siegfried and Roy's obvious homosexuality and clinging to the comfort of their "wholesome" presentation.

Siegfried and Roy's show was, of course, tailor-made for families and old ladies. Theirs was a show you could take your mother to, as Bernie Yuman did long before he even managed the lads. Their performance was designed to bypass confrontational issues like homosexuality—or any sexuality, period. Even in their early days in Vegas, the act's topless dancers stayed fully clothed during the first performance of the evening so kids could join in the fun. Nude breasts were strictly a late-night treat.

One theory behind the duo's long-postponed declaration of their homosexuality in the *National Enquirer* is that they wanted to lay their cards on the table before somebody else exposed their hand. It's even possible that they were warned about this unauthorized biography. Or perhaps they shrewdly calculated that a front-page "Yep, we're gay!" confession would put them back in the public eye bigtime! Since Roy's mauling in 2003, Siegfried and Roy have racked up more newspaper and magazine articles than they did in their heyday. Insiders say Roy's always yearned to be featured on the covers of the top-selling tabloid magazines, such as *People* and the *Enquirer*, and—in a fateful way—the tiger attack made his life-long dream come true.

As this is written, it's rumored that the duo are shopping a new "tell-all" autobiography, anxious to show publishers they can still command the public eye. There have even been numerous press releases announcing an imminent return to the stage, although it's a mystery how Roy, who still spends most of his days in a wheelchair, could ever stand up to the physical demands of a grueling show regimen.

And even if dreams of a triumphal return to superstar glory never materialize, Siegfried and Roy will always have the exciting memory of what it was like to be the hottest act on the Strip, with star-struck fans—men and women—offering up the sinful pleasures of the flesh....

...which brings us back to the Queen of Las Vegas, Siegfried and Roy's good friend, Liberace. Before he contracted AIDS and died in 1987, the gay maestro often teamed with the Tiger Kings for boy-hunting expeditions, and it's said that the three men had quite similar tastes when it came to sex partners. "Lee," as he was known to pals and lovers, gravitated more to what's known in gay circles as "rough trade"—muscular young laborers, preferably foreign—or young boys well below his own social status. Liberace biographer Darden Asbury Pyron points out that the pianist actually "preferred inequality" over hook-ups with his glamorous "equals" in Las Vegas and Hollywood.

"The stories are of cruising Mexican boys on Sunset Boulevard, picking up weightlifters, or taking on young people out of a chorus line, or in the case of [longtime lover

Scott] Thorson...and his successor, Cary James, latching onto unsteady teenagers."

Jimmy Lavery recalls ducking a close encounter of the kinky kind with Liberace in the early 80s. It was New Year's Eve, and after Siegfried and Roy's last show, Jimmy drank a toast with his German bosses, who were swilling bottles of Dom Perignon with the troupe; then he and Lynette headed out to a party at Liberace's restaurant, the Tivoli Gardens, located next door to his Las Vegas museum. The eatery's bar was piano-shaped, like the front entrance to his museum, and Liberace often held court there.

When Jimmy and Lynette strolled in that night, the joint was jumping. Liberace and guests were in a festive mood and *beaucoup* bubbly was flowing. But later that night, Jimmy experienced Liberace's attraction to working-class types—firsthand. As he and Lee, well into their cups, were having a drunken chat, the grinning ivory-tickler leaned over and simpered, "Do you want to go down to the cellar and pick out a bottle of wine?"

Jimmy, suddenly realizing he was being cruised—he was, after all, fresh meat from "Hotlanta," Georgia—instantaneously sobered up. His first thought was to respond, *Dude, in the South we don't go to no cellars!* Instead, he politely thanked "the old flamer" for his hospitality, grabbed Lynette and headed off to a safer party.

Siegfried and Roy shared Liberace's taste in men, with a preference for young boys and stagehands. They often gallivanted off to Puerto Rico and Santo Domingo to pursue conquests but partied heavily in Vegas as well.

Scott Thorson, who was Liberace's live-in lover from 1977 to 1982, reminisced about life with Lee to the *National Enquirer*, recalling the times they spent together with Siegfried and Roy.

> I met Siegfried and Roy in 1979 backstage at the Las Vegas Hilton after one of Liberace's performances. I was living with Liberace at the time and appearing in his show. When I first met them, they both commented about how young

and good-looking I was. I was embarrassed. And
from then on every time I saw them Roy would
openly flirt with me.

As Liberace and I became better friends
with Siegfried and Roy, they began to invite us to
parties at their estate. Their parties were there if
you were a gay man. The place would be crawling
with young, good-looking guys. In fact, the only
women around were the ones who worked in
their show.

One night Siegfried and Roy invited me
over for a party without Liberace. During this
period Liberace and I were fighting all the time. I
was using a lot of cocaine and it didn't set well with
him. Liberace didn't use cocaine. He smoked marijuana and used amyl nitrate "poppers" that gave
him a voracious appetite for sex.

When I arrived at their house I was a little
high and I freaked out over all the lions and tigers
roaming around.

Eventually I grabbed a drink and
settled in. After my drink, I found Siegfried and Roy
in a corner of the house and they were smoking a
marijuana joint with a few other people.

Appearing on *Larry King Live*, Thorson revealed he
was just sixteen years old when Lee's producer, Ray Arnet,
introduced him to the superstar in Vegas. Thorson said, "We
went to his house the following day. And Liberace loved
animals...and I was working for a veterinarian at that
time—I was a licensed health technician—and I was
thinking about becoming a veterinarian. And what happened
was that one of Lee's dogs had an infection in its eye, and I
think Lee just saw the way I responded toward animals."

Thorson moved in with the much-older star within a
year. "I've always wanted a son," Lee told him. "I'm going to
adopt you." And although the adoption process was never
finalized, Liberace paid for the not-even-barely-legal boy to
undergo plastic surgery—with the creepy goal of making the
kid look like his natural son. After his two-stage operation,
Thorson says, he "looked like a young Nordic version
of Liberace."

In his autobiography, Thorson wrote that Liberace often referred to him as his son and lover, and "during my years with him I was variously described as chauffeur, bodyguard, and secretary/companion.... My predecessors had been called valets, protégés, yardboys, or houseboys, depending on their individual talents. Some, like me, wound up in the act."

Siegfried and Roy had their very own Scott Thorson-type in gofer Toney Mitchell. It's rumored he had affairs with both Siegfried *and* Roy!

Then there was Joe Clark, a prop artist at the show and at their house, an effeminate, introverted man who was good with his hands. The whisper on the Jungle Palace grapevine was that he and Roy were lovers—and one night, Jimmy actually caught Roy smuggling Joe Clark into the Palace in the middle of the night after Siegfried had moved out to live in his Spanish Trail house.

It happened when Jimmy came to the Palace late one night with Lynette to check on a tiger that had undergone a medical operation that day. When they arrived, Jimmy unlocked the front gate, then locked it behind him and headed for the White Tiger Habitat. After making sure the tiger was recuperating normally, Jimmy and Lynette went back to the front gate—but were shocked to find it unlocked. Jimmy couldn't believe it, and would have sounded an alarm, but just then he spotted Joe Clark's SUV drive by the house. He locked the gate again, went home and dropped Lynette off. Suspecting something was up, he went back to the Jungle Palace—and found the front gate unlocked...again.

Jimmy re-locked the gate, and then hid near the house to see if someone would unlock it again. His cat-and-mouse game paid off when Roy suddenly emerged from the house, headed for the gate.

Bingo!

Jimmy stepped out of the shadows and "bumped into" Roy, telling him that after he'd checked on the tiger, he'd discovered "someone" had left the gate unlocked. Jimmy had figured out that the "someone" was Roy, and that he kept unlocking the gate so Joe Clark could slip into the Jungle

Palace for a late-night hookup. Roy, no dummy, realized that Jimmy knew he was the guilty party. Both men, naturally, pretended nothing was out of the ordinary. Jimmy said goodnight and left...chuckling over his spy tactics.

Siegfried had suitors of his own, and they weren't always employees. He'd swooned over a handsome and very young magician named Darren Romeo, who became known as the duo's protégé. Young Romeo was something of a joke in the magic community, where it was rumored that sexual prowess with Siegfried—not his talent as a magician—was the secret behind his suddenly flourishing career. After all, not just anyone can play the Mirage, but lucky Romeo got booked there a mere two years after meeting Siegfried and Roy. Siegfried and Romeo turned up together at all the magic conventions, and rival magicians twittered that the German illusionist's best new trick was making the young star materialize in his bed.

Darren Romeo, allegedly named in tribute to Bobby Darin, was a seasoned stage performer and singer. His foray into magic was a new development, and his act had a "Phantom of the Opera" hook. In every show, he'd sing "Music of the Night" in the Phantom's trademark half-mask. He'd paid his showbiz dues during years of singing and performing, looking for his big break—and finally nailed it in the off-Broadway production of "The Fantastiks." After deciding to venture into the world of magic, Romeo caught another big break—he met Siegfried and it was rumored that sparks flew. Suddenly, Siegfried was boldly promoting his alleged lover's show, hailing it as a "roller coaster of powerful magic, breathtaking music, and on-the-mark impressions...all emanating from the persona of an entertainer unlike any other who has performed in Las Vegas."

Although his act was considered more theatrical than magical by the Las Vegas showbiz community, Romeo's show—under Siegfried's tutelage—became popular with the public, and he went on to tour big venues. He even won the coveted Merlin Award, an honor he shared with such past winners as David Copperfield and Siegfried and Roy. Whether or not Siegfried orchestrated these wins is a matter of conjecture, but if there's anything better than famous friends and lovers, it's famous friends who are also lovers!

Like Liberace, Siegfried and Roy surrounded themselves with an extensive network of their gay friends and staff, an ideal ring of protection around them that kept their sexual secrets...secret. (It also guaranteed that a "quickie" was within arm's reach most of the time.) And there was one kinky, shared passion that Liberace, Siegfried and Roy would have wanted to keep discreet. The three men apparently shared a liking for pornography, which was legitimized by the Supreme Court rulings in 1980. Suddenly, porn shops sprang up everywhere. Scott Thorson recalled frequenting these new establishments with his excited father figure, Liberace:

"There was a series of viewing machines, like old-fashioned nickelodeons, where you could watch sex flicks to your heart's content—heterosexual, homosexual, sex acts featuring animals or children; they had it all.... The bookstores also had private cubicles in the back with what are known in the gay world as 'glory holes.' For a small fee a man could rent one of the cubicles, put his penis through the 'glory hole,' and wait for a response."

Jimmy Lavery discovered what a "glory hole" was when Roy Horn approached him one day and handed him a brass token. It was the size of a quarter and had a hole in the middle. Roy told Jimmy he'd found the token in his car and figured Siegfried had dropped it there. He told Jimmy, "Find out what this is and where it came from."

Jimmy was bemused. How on earth could he find out where a coin had come from?

"It could be from anywhere," he told Roy. "Where do I start?"

Roy was insistent.

"It's from some place in town."

Jimmy shrugged. He made a few calls and got a tip. A friend directed him to East Charleston, a seedy area bristling with porn shops. Roy drove down there and discovered that the brass token fit perfectly into...a coin-operated glory hole.

Even though they're officially out of the closet, Siegfried and Roy's sex lives remain impenetrable which is just the way they like it. There are rumors galore about their relationship, and whom or what they bedded. Ironically, each maintains a separate bedroom for the other in their respective homes to this day. But when Siegfried eventually moved into his own abode in 1996, the duo's personal relationship had already been rocky for a while. At this time, their on-again-off-again cycle apparently went off-again, even though their working partnership continued.

As with any marriage, it's nigh-impossible for an outsider to guess at the nature and frequency of sexual activity, or if it even exists—and whether both parties involved are being faithful to each other. The duo would often dine out together, but usually ended up meeting different friends and leaving separately. The Vegas betting line was that Siegfried and Roy weren't an actual couple anymore.

It's interesting to note that, of the two, Siegfried had the bigger reputation for promiscuity. The staff joke was that he'd screw a doorknob if he thought it might respond. And the really intriguing staff rumor about his rampant ways is that Siegfried has a child out there somewhere! (Maybe more than one.) Be that as it may, and notwithstanding speculation about intercourse with doorknobs, Siegfried himself has let one rather big cat out of the bag—he admits he's slept with women. Which makes the "baby Siegfried" (or "Siegfrieda") rumor possible, but still unconfirmed.

It should be noted that female fans—who always reacted to the lads like they were rock stars—often made it screamingly clear that they'd love to graduate to groupie status...and get a peek at what's under those trademark codpieces the duo wear onstage. Whether it's beamed at women or men, Siegfried and Roy exude a fierce sexual power.

Has Roy slept with women? Absolutely. Does this mean he and Siegfried are bisexual? Not necessarily. Insiders say beefcakes, not cupcakes, trigger their sexual appetites. Their rare physical couplings with women are simply a way for the power-hungry Germans to exert control. Roy's been described by observers as an octopus with many tentacles, manipulating and demanding extreme perfection from everyone, himself included.

His relationship with Lynette illustrates how he treats associates, especially women. Even though she was the lead female in the show, Roy would berate her, loudly and often, for mistakes and mishaps that couldn't possibly have been her fault. Or he'd stop talking to her for weeks on end, and persuade Siegfried to snub her as well. But like a wounded animal, Lynette would absorb the abuse, then purr contentedly when Roy finally decided to treat her nicely again.

After Lynette and Jimmy became a couple, she stunned him with a startling confession that proved Roy's diabolical skill as a manipulator: she and her leather-clad, tiger-taming boss had slept together. Only once, Lynette claimed—but who really knows? Because what Lynette didn't admit to Jimmy was even more startling: she'd fallen in love with Roy. And that love has never died. Since Roy's mauling, she's been in seventh heaven, say insiders, because now she can dedicate her life to nurturing the Tiger King.

Lynette truly ended up a winner. In her new role as Roy's protector and caregiver, she now challenges even the mighty Bernie Yuman, battling him for control over the duo's business affairs. Yuman, naturally enough, abhors Lynette and considers her an obstacle. But he realizes that his word is no longer the final word.

Despite Roy's debilitating injuries, his hunger for control has never flagged. Even before his mauling, he'd scheme endlessly behind Siegfried's back with Bernie Yuman. Whenever Siegfried would discover one of their little plots, he'd explode and start screaming. But Bernie, whose temper is legendary, would fight right back—and win—while Roy stood innocently by.

Roy needed to be in charge of even the tiniest details. And his manipulations could become extremely petty. One typical example was the production of their yearly Siegfried and Roy calendar, which featured twelve photos of the duo for each month. While at the Mirage, Roy controlled the production, and more often than not, his face filled more

space than Siegfried's. He got away with it because he wouldn't
show his partner the calendar until it was printed. Roy used
the same tactics in their advertising and merchandising
campaigns, always choosing photos based on how good he
looked. Siegfried would get annoyed and then forget all about
it until the next time. Roy's mental domination of his partner
rarely ceased, and he always kept a wary eye out for employees
who might challenge his hegemony.

And that's why Roy had never really liked Lynette's
lover, Jimmy Lavery. He kept Jimmy around because he
trusted his work skills and discretion. But in the end, power-
player Roy came to view the tough Georgian cracker as
someone who'd always stand up to him—especially when it
came to Lynette. And so, shortly before Montecore the tiger
changed all their lives forever, Roy ordered Lynette to dump
Jimmy for good. Lynette, as always, obeyed. The locks on her
house were changed, and just like that, Jimmy was out of
the picture.

For one brief, shining moment, Roy and Lynette were
just where they'd always wanted to be. And then, Montecore
struck....

Suddenly, it seemed, the fairytale had ended. Two
dirt-poor lads had struggled up out of Germany's post-war
ruins, winning fame and fortune riding the backs of fantastical
white tigers...until the dream dissolved into a nightmare on
a blood-spattered stage.

But Siegfried and Roy still believe in magic. Things
have changed, unquestionably, but are all the surprises
really behind them? In a rare interview just before New
Year's, 2008, Roy was asked to comment on the duo's
rumored return to show business. Smiling like a conjurer
who's still got a trick or two up his sleeve, Roy hinted broadly:

"A good magician never lets the cat out of the bag. Act
surprised when you hear about it."

It shouldn't have been a surprise then when a month
later, in early February 2008, Siegfried and Roy suddenly
announced that they'd once again appear on stage. They had
agreed to perform for one night only, in February 2009, at the
annual MGM Power of Love charity bash for the new Lou

Ruvo Brain Institute being built in Las Vegas.

The duo were inspired to take what might be their first step on the comeback trail by old friend and Vegas gossip guru Robin Leach, who talked them into supporting the brain institute with a mind-blowing reprise of the glory days.

In keeping with their mysterious ways, the duo has refused to confirm whether or not there will be animals in the show. But with a year to prepare, and knowing the whole world will be watching, you can bet your last buck these master showmen won't disappoint their millions of fans.

The return of Siegfried and Roy?

Reality...or illusion?

As any good magician will tell you, the audience should always be the last to know.

ACKNOWLEDGMENTS

First and foremost I would like to thank the friends who have come forward and supported me every step of the way. This book is for you.

For Tim and Jay: great friends, better people.

For my loving family—thank you, I wouldn't be here without you.

Thank you to Phoenix Books and the wonderful Miss Henrietta Tiefenthaler—without your encouragement and efforts, this book would not exist.

Last, but certainly not least, for my dogs.

—Jimmy Lavery

I would like to dedicate this book to my family, my wonderful wife Wendy who has stuck by me through all of the trials and tribulations that we have gone through in our thirty years of marriage. When we got married, the headline read "This Marriage Is Bound To Have Its Ups and Downs." We sure have, but we stuck together, and I love her more today than I did when we got married. She is my light, my strength and my reason for living. For this she has my unwavering love and respect. I love you with all my heart forever and ever and sixteen billion years.

To my son Louis, who I love more than anything. It's been a tough road to hoe and we haven't always seen eye to eye, but somehow we have gotten past the woods and can now see the light of day and a new beginning. I am extremely proud of you and your dedication.

To my grandson Gianni, you are the light of my life and your Papa only wants to see you grow up a wonderful man. Live your life with happiness and prosperity, knowing that hard work and being righteous is the only way to move forward in this world.

To the staff of Phoenix Books, you all have been stellar. And to Henrietta, your excellent writing and dedication have brought it all together—thanks for all your hard work!

—Jim Mydlach

There are a few people I would like to dedicate this work to: my parents Wendy and Jim, my grandmother Fran and grandfather Arnold O' Connell.

Thank you for sticking by me and letting me grow up the way I have, through the good and bad, always welcoming me with open arms when you didn't have to. You are truly my best friends. To Grandpa Arnie, you can rest now, but I miss you.

Gianni Louis Mydlach, the most beautiful little boy a dad could ever want! There is not a day that goes by that a tear doesn't run down my face with the joy and love you bring to me. I Love You "G," you are Daddy's Boy.

Alan, my dear friend, thank you...we did it.

To Mr. Roy, I wish that I could have that hour with you that I fought so hard for, to let you know I never gave up on our friendship. I hope you are well and able to spend a long healthy life with some good people and your animals.

To the wonderful people at Phoenix Books, my heartfelt thanks.

Henrietta, quite the writer and now a friend. Thank you for everything you have done in writing this book.

Last but not least, I want to thank all of you who stood by me through it all in your own special ways.

—Louis Mydlach

To Phoenix Books and Michael Viner who adopted the project at the very beginning and gave me the challenge of writing it. To you I am always grateful.

Mike Walker who took my words, and with his extraordinary talent, transformed them into the book that this now is. Thank you for all your sacrifices along the way.

Alina Poniewaz, without whom the book would never have been finished. I don't know what I would do without you.

Sonia, who designed the book and its cover with unparalleled talent. Thank you for all your help and patience over the years.

Thank you to my family for all your support and encouragement every step of the way.

—Henrietta Tiefenthaler

BIBLIOGRAPHY

Abowitz, Richard. "Robin Leach Inspires Siegfried and Roy." The Moveable Buffet. *Los Angeles Times*, February 12, 2008.

Amter, Charlie. "No Comeback for Siegfried & Roy?" *E! Online*, July 27, 2004.

Amter, Charlie. "Siegfried & Roy Shooter Captured." *E! Online*, November 3, 2004.

Associated Press. "The New Frontier is History." November 13, 2007. http://www.lasvegasnow.com/Global/story.asp?s=6780876/.

The Animals Voice. http://www.animalsvoice.com/PAGES/writes/editorial/news/invest/siegfried_exotics1.html/.

Babula, Joelle. "Roy Awaits Surgery to Restore His Skull." *Las Vegas Review-Journal*, October 16, 2003.

Barr, Jeff. *1001 Golf Holes You Must Play Before You Die*. London: Quintet Publishing Limited, 2005.

BBC News, "Jackson Sued For Unpaid Vet Bills." January 7, 2006.

BBC News, "Roy Horn Describes Tiger Mauling." September 16, 2004.

Berger, Phil. "Notebook; Effects Are Lavish For a Big-Time Bout." *The New York Times*, December 6, 1989.

Big Cat Rescue. http://bigcathaven.org/white_tigers.htm/.

Blackmon, Robert, Reginald Fitz, and Michael Glynn. "Roy: 'My Life is Over.'" *The National Enquirer*, August 9, 2004, 30-31.

Blackmon, Robert, Alan Butterfield, and Michael Glynn. "Roy Suicide Try." *The National Enquirer*, November 15, 2004, 34-35.

Blackmon, Robert, Reginald Fitz, and Michael Glynn. "Roy's Last Chance to Walk Again." *The National Enquirer*, August 30, 2004, 11.

CEO Exchange. "Biography: Stephen A. Wynn." http://www.pbs.org/wttw/ceoexchange/episodes/ceo_swynn.html/.

Circuses.com. "Peta's Letter to Office of Inspector General." http://www.circuses.com/siegfriedroy-letter.asp/.

Circuses.com. http://www.circuses.com/siegfriedroy-about.asp/.

Clarke, Norm. *Vegas Confidential: Norm Clarke! Sin City's Ace Insider 1,000 Naked Truths*. Nevada: Stephens Press, 2004

Collins, Glen. "A Dream Born of Liberace and Magic." *The New York Times*, September 21, 1989.

Derr, Mark, and Erica Goode. "A Combustible Combination: Exotic Cats in Private Hands." *The New York Times*, October 7, 2003.

Egusquiza, Rick and Michael Glynn. "Marked For Death: Roy Targetted By Gunman." *The National Enquirer*, October 25, 2004, 24-25.

Fischbacher, Siegfried, Roy Horn, and Annette Tapert. *Siegfried and Roy: Mastering the Impossible*. New York: William Morrow and Company, Inc., 1992.

Fleeman, Michael and Tom Gliatto. "The Circle of Life." *People*, September 27, 2004, 68-73.

Fox, William L. *In the Desert of Desire: Las Vegas and the Culture of Spectacle*. Reno: University of Nevada Press, 2005.

Freiss, Steve. "The truth about Siegfried and Roy: the duo have never denied their past romantic relationship. So why is the media ignoring it?" *The Advocate*, November 11, 2003.

George, Danielle. "Roy Horn Walks Without Help." *All Headline News*, September 12, 2005.

Gill, A.A. *Vanity Fair*, October 2003.

The Globe, "Security Guard's Lawsuit Charges...Siegfried Abused Roy!" October 31, 2005, 69.

Glynn, Michael. "Roy Gives Up on Rehab After Devastating News." *The National Enquirer*, September 13, 2004, 10.

Glynn, Michael. "Tragic Roy Has Secret Stem Cell Surgery to Walk Again." *The National Enquirer,* July 11, 2005, 8-9.

Goldman, Adam. "Producer: Feds Won't Get Tiger Attack Tape." *Oakland Tribune*, August 26, 2004.

Green, Michael S. and Eugene P. Moehring. *Las Vegas: A Centennial History*. Reno: University of Nevada Press, 2005.

Grossberg, Josh. "Roy Relocated; Condition Improving." *E! Online*, October 31, 2003.

Grossberg, Josh. "Roy Talks!" *E! Online*, March 10, 2004.

Grossberg, Josh. "Roy Horn Rehabbing in Denver." *E! Online*, August 13, 2004.

Haberman, Lia. "Roy 'Miraculous' After Big Cat Attack." *E! Online*, October 7, 2003.

Haberman, Lia. "Siegfried & Roy Go On, Sort Of." *E! Online*, October 9, 2003.

Haberman, Lia. "Roy Back on His Feet." *E! Online*, March 2, 2004.

Haberman, Lia. "Siegfried & Roy Video Mystery." *E! Online*, August 25, 2004.

Hall, Sarah. "Siegfried & Roy Tiger Sprung." *E! Online*, October 14, 2003.

Hall, Sarah. "Doctor: Part of Roy's Skull Removed." *E! Online*, October 17, 2003.

Hall, Sarah. "A Christmas Miracle for Roy?" *E! Online*, December 1, 2003.

Hall, Sarah. "Siegfried & Roy Under Fire." *E! Online*, October 5, 2004.

Haynes, Brian. "Former Raider Tied to Shooting." *Las Vegas Review-Journal*, October 7, 2004.

Heffernan, Virginia. "Television Review: For a Vegas Cat Pack, Life is a Cabaret." *The New York Times*, August 31, 2004.

Iverem, Esther. "Trail of 2 Lost Tigers Ends in the Bronx." *The New York Times*, June 5, 1987.

Koch, Ed. *Las Vegas Sun*. www.lasvegassun.com/sunbin/stories/text/2003/oct/07/515711618.html/.

Maclean, Charles. "The Ultimate Illusion." 1991.

Las Vegas Review-Journal. NORM. March 7, 2004.

Las Vegas Review-Journal. NORM. July 23, 2005.

Las Vegas Review-Journal. NORM. September 8, 2005.

Las Vegas Review-Journal. NORM. September 14, 2005.

Las Vegas Review-Journal. NORM. August 24, 2007.

Lewis, Eric C. *A Choice of Miracles: Fifty Years of Magic.* Magical Publications, 1980.

Marquez, Miguel. "Roy of Siegfried and Roy critical after mauling." *CNN.com.* October 4, 2003. http://cnn.com/2003/SHOBIZ/10/04/roy.attacked/.

Montgomery, Sy. *Man-Eating Tigers of Sundarbans.* New York: Houghton Mifflin Company, 2001.

Nash, Alanna. "Siegfried and Roy: Stage Fright." *Reader's Digest,* April 2004.

National Enquirer, Celebrity News. November 11, 2003.

National Enquirer, Celebrity News. February 20, 2004.

National Enquirer, Celebrity News. July 7, 2005.

New York Post. Page Six. July 20, 2004.

The New York Times. "Tiger Mauls Illusionist On the Stage." October 5, 2003.

The New York Times. "Leading Casinos Settle Strike." June 16, 1984.

Navarro, Mireya, and Laura M. Holson. "Onstage Attack Casts Pall Over Las Vegas Strip." *The New York Times,* October 6, 2003.

Pearlman, Cindy. "Like Cats and Dogs." *The Chicago Sun-Times,* October 17, 1999.

PETA. http://www.peta.org/.

Pyron, Darden Asbury. *Liberace: An American Boy.* Chicago: University of Chicago Press, 2000.

Rosenthal, Frank. http://www.frankrosenthal.com/.

Ryan, Joel. "Siegfried & Roy's Roy Still Critical." *E! Online,* October 6, 2003.

Ryan, Joel. "Siegfried & Roy & Baby (Cub)." *E! Online,* December 30, 1997.

Seal, Ulysses S. *Tigers of the World.* Edited by Ronald L. Tilson. New Jersey: Noyes Publications, 1987.

Severo, Richard. "Günther Gebel-Williams, Circus Animal Trainer, Dies at 66." *The New York Times*, July 20, 2001.

Shanken, Marvin R. *Cigar Aficionado.* M. Shaken Communications, Incorporated, 1997.

Siegfried and Roy: Masters of the Impossible. http://www.siegfriedandroy.com/.

Siegfried and Roy, The Mirage Program Book. Feld Entertainment.

Siegfried and Roy, "Beyond Belief" Frontier Program Book.

Silverman, Stephen M. "Arrest in Siegfried & Roy Drive-By." *People Magazine*, November 3, 2004.

Smith, John L. *Running Scared: The Life and Treacherous Times of Las Vegas Casino King Steve Wynn.* New York: Thunder's Mouth Press, 2001.

Strauss, Neil. "Even in Magic Acts, Tigers and Bullets Can Be Lethal." *The New York Times*, October 8, 2003.

Sunquist, Fiona and Mel Sunquist. *Wild Cats of the World.* University of Chicago Press, 2002.

Thorleifson, Alex and Scott Thorson. *Behind the Candelabra: My Life with Liberace.* Dutton, 1998.

Tiger Territory. http://www.lairweb.org.nz/tiger/.

Tyrnauer, Matt. "Married with Tigers." *Vanity Fair*, August 1999, 170-181.

Van Gelder, Lawrence. Arts Briefing. *The New York Times*, March 11, 2004.

Weatherford, Mike. "Siegfried Says Roy's Doing Well." *Las Vegas Review-Journal*, December 2, 2003.

Weatherford, Mike. "Claimant Seeks Horn Meeting." *Las Vegas Review-Journal*, November 10, 2005.

Weatherford, Mike. "Former Guard Sues Siegfried." *Las Vegas Review-Journal*, October 12, 2005.